THE

Published in 2013 by Nick Mead

Printed by Berforts Information Press Ltd. Eynsham, Oxford.

In memory of Hepzibah

Contents

Section One

Values in different routes into primary teacher education with reference to Personal, Social, Health & Economic Education & Citizenship

Will the introduction of teaching standards in professional values and practice put the heart back into primary teacher education? First published in the *Journal of Pastoral Care in Education* (2003) 21(1) pp.37-42 (Taylor & Francis).

The provision for PSHE/C† in the school-based elements of primary initial teacher education. First published in the *Journal of Pastoral Care in Education* (2004) 22(2) pp.19-26 (Taylor & Francis).

How effectively does the Graduate Teacher Programme contribute to the development of trainee teachers' professional values? First published in the *Journal of Education for Teaching* (2007) 33(3) pp.309-321 (Taylor & Francis).

Should relationships education be at the heart of Personal, Social, Health and Economics Education, and, if so, what would be the implications for pre-service teacher education? Unpublished paper given at the Teacher Education Advancement Network (TEAN) annual conference, Aston University, Birmingham May 2012.

Section Two

Values in secondary teacher education with a focus on Religious Education and the spiritual and moral

Mentoring Religious Education teaching in secondary schools. First published in Leicester, M, Modgil, C, and Modgil, S.(Eds) (2000) *Education, Culture and Values* Vol V Spiritual and Religious Education, pp.197-203 (London: Falmer).

The significance of values in the professional development of beginning secondary Religious Education teachers. Unpublished paper given at Birmingham University School of Education graduate seminar series November 2003.

Section Three

Enhancing values in primary teacher education through developing the relationship between Religious Education and Personal, Social, Health & Economic Education & Citizenship

Section Four

Values in secondary teacher education through Citizenship Education and Every Child Matters

Introduction

There is an emphasis in the Coalition's White Paper *The Importance of Teaching* (2010) on the qualities of leadership for teaching; however, little is said about how the values underpinning leadership in the classroom are formed. Self-belief is not enough, as classrooms are diverse, complex and value-laden places. The papers in this volume pose important questions about the opportunities given to trainee teachers to formulate and test out value judgements which impact on every aspect of their practice. Kroll has argued that research into the personal beliefs of student teachers shows the robustness of unrecognised beliefs based on early experiences which impact on assumptions about and expectations of pupils. She believes that:

> even when student teachers express professional values that reflect a democratic, humane and equality oriented perspective, without examining how these values might be manifest in teaching, 'they may not connect their stated values with their actions in the classroom' (Kroll 2012, p.79).

It is intended in the chapters which follow to argue for the explicit addressing of the interrelationship between personal and professional values in order to avoid the disconnect between thought and action of which Kroll speaks. The focus is on process rather than prescription and the progression of the analysis leads to a conclusion that teacher educators need to address the interrelationship between personal and professional values through a values-based critical pedagogy. A final consideration is given to how *School Direct*, as a future school-based model for teacher education in England, may offer potential for the development of such a pedagogy.

School Direct is an important backdrop to the significance of the debate about values education for trainee teachers in this collection. It is therefore necessary, at this point, to define the main features of this school-based route in to teaching:

> School Direct is the new way of training teachers which puts schools at the heart of the process. With School Direct, schools can request training places directly; select the accredited provider of teacher training they want to work with; agree the content and focus of the training programme depending on their needs and negotiate directly with the provider on how the money for training should be divided. Most importantly they can choose the candidate they want – the candidate their school needs, with expectation that the trainee will be employed by the school or wider partnership of schools (National College for Training & Leadership (NCTL) 2013, p.1).

What needs to be highlighted from this definition and borne in mind as this volume progresses are the implications for trainee values education of the development of bespoke training for the needs of a particular school. This will be returned to in the conclusion to this introduction.

Methodologically, the studies in this collection have been conducted by a teacher educator aiming to develop practice through research and are therefore small-scale and consequently have limited reliability. The data represent qualitative and quantitative findings from mainly trainee teachers and some experienced teachers over a fifteen year period. Such data are valuable in that they reflect the impact of significant changes in teacher education, from the implementation of the 9/92 teaching standards through to the development of school-based and flexible routes into teaching. Jerome, writing in 2005, helpfully contextualised some of the early work in this collection within the teaching standards debate:

> The first two standards frameworks 1992-97, 1998-2002 were criticised for paying lip service to reflection and values whilst focusing on a narrow model of *effective* teaching (Reynolds 1999). And, although the most recent version of the standards has returned some aspects of values education (Mead 2003), I believe that agenda is still focused on a rather narrow and depoliticised view of teaching as a largely technical exercise (Jerome 2005, p.6).

The focus of much of the data in this collection has been on the impact of these different sets of teaching standards on the values-laden areas of Religious Education (RE), Personal, Social, Health and Economics education (PSHEe), Citizenship Education and Every Child Matters (ECM). For primary trainees in England these are required elements of the training, some of which will appear in the professional studies strand. In secondary training in England all elements except Religious Education, which is taught by specialists, are required or desired and all should appear in the professional studies strand of the training. Evidence suggests (Office for Standards in Education (Ofsted) 2006; MacDonald 2009; Ofsted 2013; RE All Party Parliamentary Group (APPG) Report 2013) that, nationally, justice is not always done to these areas in training for non-specialists and the case is made in this collection for generalising a much stronger values education from the specific areas researched. After a brief rationale and synopsis of each paper there is analysis and discussion of how teacher educators and researchers have drawn on the data.

The coherence of the collected papers is derived from the first three chapters which, between them, explore the nature of trainee teachers' values education on the three main routes into primary teaching: Bachelor of Education (B.Ed), Post-Graduate Certificate in Education (PGCE) and The Graduate Teacher Programme (GTP). In the light of the introduction of teaching standards in professional values and practice in September 2002, chapter one compares two sets of data from B.Ed. and PGCE primary courses, in order to examine the existing opportunities for values education within the university-based elements of teacher education in one institution. The findings highlighted a qualitative difference in the process of personal and professional development experienced by the two groups of students. Implications of the findings for university training partnerships, university tutors and professional studies programmes were then considered. The conclusion reached at the time of the writing of the paper is that the introduction of teaching standards in professional values and practice may be the next landmark in the process v competence debate about teacher education, and may provide the opportunity to put human development back into the heart of teacher education. A more pressing matter now is the time that might be given to trainee teachers' values education in the new *School Direct* training model. The chapter clearly highlights the longer period of personal as well as professional development offered by the B.Ed. model.

Drawing on chapter one which was published in 2003, Harrison, in her critique of the assessment of teaching standards in professional values and practice, argues for 'developing professionalism' rather than compliance with competencies. Her argument is exemplified in her analysis of a trainee's confusion about the relationship between personal and school values:

> Not only is the trainee experiencing uncertainty about how this school handles values but there is also an indication that there may be a desire to be told which values to give support to (see also Mead 2003) (Harrison 2007, p.335).

The importance of the relationship between teachers' personal development and their effective professional practice is taken up by Rinehart, drawing on chapter one:

> Professional development for teachers, focusing on standards, practices, outcomes and testing, lacks a commitment to people. Education is not about indoctrination of standards, rather it is about the development of people, including teachers (Mead 2003). More effort devoted to the task of personal reflection and synthesis of style could actually promote the desired increase of standards. Therefore teachers' personal development, structured in a personal manner, should receive as much attention as students' development (Rinehart 2004 pp.1-2).

Likewise Bainjath draws upon the chapter in an exploration of the professional development of South African teachers post-apartheid:

> The data analysis revealed that teachers were struggling to adopt change and found that the promotion of human values was values education generally and that teachers were at different levels in their ability to promote values education in their classrooms (Bainjath 2008, p.xv).

In her thesis Bainjath develops the argument that theories of values development are largely concerned with children and do not apply to adults; therefore a theory which explains how adults form or change their values is required. In relation to this Bainjah concludes that there is an increasing need for an understanding of values education to be built into both the initial and in-service training of teachers.

Chapter two, first published in 2004, examines PSHEe/Citizenship opportunities provided for B.Ed and PGCE primary trainee teachers in their school-based training during the first two years of the non-statutory framework. The study identifies some improvement in opportunities to teach PSHE/Citizenship and observe different teaching methods; however, there is no significant improvement in opportunities to engage with staff in a values-based discussion about the aims and purposes of the subject. Of particular significance are the data which demonstrate that less than 50% of trainees have the opportunity to discuss and evaluate the contribution of PSHE/Ct. to multi-cultural awareness and 69% have no contact with Sex and Relationships Education (SRE).

Over recent years the data in chapter two have been used effectively by a range of scholars to flag the paucity of school experience in PSHEe/Citizenship, to encourage trainees to become more proactive in improving their own placement experience and to strengthen the case for improved school-based mentoring in PSHE/Citizenship (Evans and Evans 2007;

Evans, Midgley & Rigby 2009; Brown, Busfield, O'Shea and Sibthorpe 2011; Cooper, H 2011). Evans and Evans, drawing on the data in chapter two, argue that trainees receiving feedback after observations would seem to be the greatest need and would provide the much needed values-forum within the school experience:

> It is possible that trainees' and new teachers' lack of confidence may be overcome, not through training *per se*, but through increased opportunity to be observed and receive feedback on their delivery of PSHEe, both as a separate subject and within main subject teaching. Supportive of Mead's (2004) findings for primary Education, this need for experience and feedback on PSHE delivery was evident in respondents' comments (Evans and Evans 2007, p.48).

Byrne *et al* (2012) have drawn on chapter two in order to strengthen the relationship between values-based health education in the university and reflective portfolio work on school placement. On a broader scale, an evaluation of the teacher development programme standards by European teacher candidates from Turkey, Germany and Denmark has used the data in chapter two to support teachers' values education and the development of teachers' personal characteristics as an important fact in determining teachers' skills (Yelken 2009).

The third chapter, first published in 2007, looks at the Graduate Teacher Programme (GTP), an expanding employment route into teaching which, as such, needs to be scrutinised for the opportunities provided for education in professional values. In the light of Ofsted reports which suggest that GTP trainees often bring particularly well-developed professional values to their training, the purpose of this small-scale study was to gain insights into the nature and implementation of the values of a GTP primary cohort in the first phase of their training. The findings identified that GTP trainees do have well-established values, and high expectations about implementing them, but they experience varying degrees of coherence between these values and their implementation in teaching, learning and classroom management. However, there is sufficient evidence to suggest that the highly individualised nature of the GTP does potentially lend itself to a coherent relationship between professional values and practice. In order for that potential to be realised, the study made three recommendations for teacher educators: enable trainees to integrate well developed professional values into their individual training plans at induction, give particular attention to the reflective and dialogical skills of mentors, and integrate central training into the reflective process of trainees' values education. It is interesting that the last of these three recommendations emerges in particular in the PSHE/Ct. work undertaken in the central training.

Pitfield and Morrison (2009) and Smith and Hodson (2010) saw the relevance of the data in chapter three for the quality of mentoring on increasingly flexible school-based initial teacher education routes and in terms of securing the relationship between theory and practice in pressured contexts. Pitfield and Morrison emphasise how crucial it is that mentoring goes beyond a competency-based approach to understanding the values and motivations of career-switchers in particular:

> The needs analysis on flexible PGCE courses has to do more than simply focus on gaps in knowledge, on what the trainee doesn't know and cannot yet do. It should

be a rigorous process for identifying the existing skills and experiences which this group (mature entrants to teaching) brought to the courses from their previous careers as well as 'recognizing well-developed, well- informed and secure beliefs and values which will underpin all that is new to learn about teaching' (Mead 2007, p.316) (Pitfield and Morrison 2009p.25).

The authors found that mentors on flexible routes were adapting their practice in order to develop more dialogical and values-based mentoring:

> Gloria (a mentor) is echoing a point made by Mead that the needs analysis should inform an ongoing dialogue with the mentee and that mentors should allocate time to engage with student-teachers' reflective practice (Mead 2007) (Pitfield and Morrison 2009 p.25).

The authors argue that dialogical and values-based mentoring is fundamental to engaging trainees in 'a complex set of understandings' in order to overcome the inclination to separate theory and practice in school-based training because of pressure of time. Pitfield and Morrison therefore conclude that flexible PGCE routes are beginning to demonstrate, and definitely need, what is a values-based dialogical type of mentoring, as argued for in chapter three of this collection:

> There is a need for the kind of dialogue that takes place as part of the mentoring process which shows the 'readiness of mentors to go beyond restrictive outcomes-driven mentoring' (Mead 2007p.319) and to take a more holistic view of teaching and learning than a competencies-based approach' (Pitfield and Morrison 2009, p.29).

What is encouraging about this research is the identification of a much more organic and fluid learning process for trainees which has the potential to bind the personal and professional dimensions of becoming a teacher, thereby giving the individual trainee much more agency in their professional development. The importance of this sense of agency is also a key feature of the research undertaken by Smith and Hodson, drawing on the data in chapter three. These researchers want to understand what GTP trainees mean when they say they want to get away from theory. Their findings tell us that they do value theory but experienced in a much more organic context and in relation to the interpretation of what Eraut (2004) has called 'non-codified personal knowledge' acquired on the job. Smith and Hodson draw on the data in chapter three of this collection to argue how mentors need to provide the formal spaces in which they can support trainees in mobilising their existing values and experiences in order to make the connections between theory and practice and so move learning forward in situated contexts (2010, p.265).

The organic relationship between teachers' values and their practice which gives them agency in their work concerns Easterbrook and Stephenson, who draw on chapter three to analyse what happens to novice teachers who do not feel confident in their professional values and abandon good practice early on:

> Graduating from a teacher preparation programme armed with the latest techniques in instruction, younger, less experienced teachers often find themselves in situations in which their values and skills vary or are insufficient to meet the demands of the

job (Mead 2007). When this happens they turn to their more seasoned colleagues for support. A major contributor to the enculturation of student-teachers is the cooperating teacher. Student-teachers' decision-making skills develop through the filter of the cooperating teacher whose belief-systems have developed over the years. In addition, the less precisely a cooperating teacher explains practices to a student-teacher the more likely the student-teacher is to develop inaccuracies and myth-based practices (Easterbrook and Stephenson 2009, p.462).

A particular danger in trainees imbibing myth-based practices is in the area of classroom management when trainees' attitudes and beliefs about student autonomy and the nature of the pupil-teacher relationship are neglected in favour of the mentor's 'quick fix'. Martin and Yin (2009) have drawn on the data in chapter three to argue that any teacher education work in behaviour management must take into account teacher characteristics related to classroom control.

This absence of a strong sense of professionalism rooted in critically examined beliefs and values is discussed in Ostapenko-Denton's comparison between Further Education (FE) lecturers and the GTP trainees in chapter three of this collection:

> What is meant by the term professional? It could be argued that those who seek to acquire this skill must surely have some idea of what it is. This is not borne out by empirical sources and discussion with trainee FE lecturers on the construction of a professional identity which led to the identification of a lack of the same. In direct comparison, when trainee teachers who were training under the graduate teacher programme (GTP) discussed the same topic, their responses showed more of a tendency towards despondency regarding assessment of their professional values focusing on what they are not able to achieve, or do not understand, rather than on the positive aspects of their practice. Nonetheless, there was a much clearer understanding of what professional identity as a teacher actually means when compared to their counterpart in FE (Mead 2007) (Ostapenko-Denton 2012, p.6).

We conclude that the data and findings in chapter three are highly relevant to the future development of teachers' professional identity in *School Direct* training contexts. Kroll draws on chapter three to argue how, in managing teacher education in challenging schools in particular, learning to teach for equity and social justice will only occur if time is allowed for 'the explicit addressing of possible issues that might impact how pupils are supported and how fairly they are treated is highlighted' (Kroll 2012, p.79). Research which has drawn on chapter three clearly demonstrates that the quality of the mentoring will need to ensure that beliefs, values and practice are organically united to provide a strong sense of professional identity which, in turn, provides the sense of agency needed to develop effective teaching and learning. It is worth noting here that a feature of Japanese teachers' professional development is that personal values-based development is nurtured collegially; hence, sharing good practice is naturally collegial (Howe 2005, 2008).

The fourth and final chapter in section one is an unpublished conference paper (2012) which makes the case for enhancing values education in primary, and indeed secondary teacher education, by placing relationships education at the heart of PSHEe. The preceding papers demonstrate that where PSHEe is given due attention, then trainees are encouraged to examine the interrelationship of personal and professional values which, as we have argued, increases teacher agency in their general classroom practice. Chapter four argues that if relationships education were to be at the heart of PSHEe, by its very nature this would require trainees to examine personal and professional values, in order to develop their understanding of key issues for pupils and in the development of appropriate pedagogical skills needed to address these issues. There is no doubt that such a values education for all trainees would inform a more holistic understanding of the needs of their pupils which would, in turn, benefit their professional judgements about classroom practice generally.

The variable experiences of values education across the three primary routes discussed in section one demonstrates both the complexity and fragility of this aspect of teacher education. In particular, the qualitatively richer experience of university-based values education experienced by trainee teachers on a B.Ed route compared with those on PGCE and GTP routes has implications in the current policy climate which seeks to reduce the amount of time spent by trainees within the university (*The Importance of Teaching*, the Schools White Paper 2010). The organisation of the collected papers in the sections which follow these foundation studies is intended to reflect a rigorous investigation into the implications of an uncertain values education for trainee teachers and their intellectual engagement with particular values-laden areas. These areas are secondary Religious Education (RE) and the Spiritual, Moral, Social and Cultural (SMSC); the relationship between primary Religious Education and PSHE/Citizenship; secondary school Citizenship Education and Every Child Matters (ECM). As such, they represent the author's own teaching and research areas as a teacher educator.

Chapter five, published in 2000 and the first paper in section two, is concerned with secondary Religious Education teaching and examines the relationship between the trainee's values-base for wanting to teach Religious Education and the role of the school-based mentor in enabling trainees to fulfil their motivations. The data analysis looks at how effectively school-based mentors understand trainees' beliefs and values about their subject and help them to realise these in their classroom practice. The paper aims to identify the key principles of effective mentoring in a values-laden subject area. This approach is much more fully developed in work undertaken by Sikes and Etherington (2004) using ethnographic and life history methodologies in their study of Religious Education teachers. These researchers position the data in chapter five at a more pragmatic level:

> Even the studies that have looked at practising and student Religious Education teachers (eg Mead 1996) have tended to be concerned chiefly with pragmatic considerations of, for instance, the nature and content of Religious Education initial teacher education and the relationship between pedagogy and aims. These are, of course pertinent areas for research, yet, it is critical we know about the person the teacher is (Sikes and Everington 2004, pp.22-23).

Sikes and Everington claim that the life history methodology, in exploring the interface between the public perception of Religious Education teachers and individual trainee teachers' actual experience, will contribute to recruitment and retention in a shortage subject. However, the analysis in chapter five is intended to examine, at the micro level, how trainees' values are perceived and addressed in the placement school context, thereby ensuring personal development and thus retention. This interface between personal beliefs and values and the public role of the Religious Education teacher is taken up by McCreery (2005) with a focus on primary trainees. McCreery cites chapter five but draws a distinction between the mentoring needs of primary and secondary trainees in terms of self-identity as a specialist and the security provided by well-developed schemes of work. However, the methodology of addressing trainees' personal beliefs and values about the content and aims, and public perceptions of the subject with their training needs is very similar to chapter five. McCreery's conclusion echoes much that has been said about addressing the relationship between personal and professional values in initial teacher education:

> It is essential to know what trainee teachers bring to their teaching. The biography of the student is seen to be important as they need to make explicit their own values and assumptions so that they can be discussed and, perhaps, challenged (McCreery 2005, p.266).

What this conclusion highlights is how important it is to recognise that trainees' experiences working in values-laden curriculum areas such as Religious Education provide insights into the relationship between personal and professional values which ought to be generalisable for the benefit of all trainees. Sikes and Everington (2004) and Baumfield (2007) make this point strongly:

> Trainee Religious Education teachers are a neglected group in the body of research aimed at trying to understand the means whereby beginning teachers negotiate the gap between social expectations of their professional role and their subjective experience (Baumfield 2007, p.206).

This generalisability principle has become increasingly important in university -based research as teacher educators in university faculties have been compelled through the Research Excellence Framework (REF) to produce research that has a maximum impact. Chapter six in section two is an example of generalising about the significance of values in the professional development of beginning teachers from six case studies of Religious Education teachers. McCreery argues that the life history or case study approach avoids compartmentalisation of aspects of individual's lives and reveals how multiple identities influence teaching practice:

> We can identify the relationship between individual, historical and social circumstances and how individuals construct self-identity with values intact (McCreery 2005, p.26).

Chapter six, an unpublished seminar paper (2003), argues that these multiple factors generating complex interactions between sets of personal and professional values are not easily assessed by the prevailing evidence-based approaches current in initial teacher education. As with most of the qualitative data in this collection, the author's intention is to go beyond what might be observable in the classroom to try and understand the part played by values in learning to teach. It needs to be said that the generalisability principle has its flaws and chapter six is imperfect in being neither one thing nor the other. However, it did provide the prototype for chapter seven, which was published in 2006 as a much more focused study of ethnic minority trainee teachers' sets of values interacting with the training process. This study is more informed by the life history approach of Sikes and Everington (2004) than chapter five; however, it is still the intention, as in chapter five, to be pragmatic about the implications of the findings for recruitment and mentoring. There is a more developed cultural, historical, social and religious analysis of the multiple sets of values influencing Black African trainees' progress on a one year PGCE course; these sets of values are categorised as perceptions of education, teacher identity, pedagogy and communication. Baumfield refers to chapter seven in her analysis of the acute position of Religious Education trainees at the interface between individual beliefs and values and the state education system:

> Current and existing research has used narrative methods such as the life history approach to elicit rich accounts of novice teachers' experiences in order to understand what they know and how that knowledge is acquired (eg Mead 2006) (Baumfield 2007, pp.77).

In spite of Baumfield's view that such research 'is of interest beyond the immediate circle of Religious Education educators' (2007, p.77), there are limitations, especially when the data are published in a curriculum subject-specific journal. Sikes and Everington have made a point of publishing in more generic teacher education journals and this does enhance the generalisability principle. Having said this, there has been some African use of chapter seven which relates to historical analysis of black African teachers encountering similar conflicting sets of values in England in the 1950s (Limond 2008). Writing in such a journal as *African Identities* Limond is able to highlight the continuing impact of cultural and social values on teacher identity:

> Contemporary evidence suggests that teachers and student teachers from similarly 'exotic' backgrounds still encounter as much, if not more, bewilderment and hostility from the majority ethnic population in English schools as did V and W (Mead 2006) (Limond 2008, p.40).

V and W are two African teachers sent on a UNESCO-backed programme to live and work in a small rural English market town with the intention of dispelling pupils' monocultural prejudices. Limond believes the project was a failure because the African identities of the two teachers were not allowed to emerge. This was not the case for Student S in chapter seven whose mentor encouraged him to teach about the Rwandan genocide which allowed his Rwandan identity to emerge and which gave him confidence to be his African self in his pastoral relationships and in his communications with parents.

Much of the analysis of different sets of values explored in chapter six informed the work in chapter seven. Rutaisire (2012) draws more on chapter three but applies the African principles identified in chapter seven. His study looks at how initial training in Africa has failed to take into account the sets of values discussed in chapter three and seven. He argues that initial training may provide the superficial characteristics of a successful professional training in its technical application; however, it does not identify the needs and conditions for teacher engagement with pupils which has more to do with teacher professional identity:

> Research evidence (Mead 2007) suggests that policy and practice of teacher education improvement of the knowledge base and the personal development of new teachers have sometimes been seen in opposition rather than complementary. This was because the view of knowledge was disembodied, emphasizing its acquisition and assessment. Yet building and using such a knowledge repertoire

occurs along with the marshalling of other sorts of knowledge and experience by the students as they are constructing their identities of themselves as teachers. Thus understanding teacher professional identity is a very complex process (Rutaisire 2012, p.59).

Rutaisire's conclusion sums up the key argument in section two, which is the need for teacher educators to create opportunities in university and school to make the interaction between complex and often conflicting sets of values explicit, avoiding what Rutaisire calls disembodied knowledge.

The intention to generalise from the experience of specific groups such as Religious Education teachers is a fundamental approach taken in this collection. The aim in chapter eight, first published in 1997/8, was to generalise the findings in chapter five as applied to the spiritual and moral as a dimension of all curriculum subjects. Within the university context the data have provided a way in to the spiritual, moral social and cultural (SMSC) within the professional studies programme. The chapter applied the mentoring principles found in chapter five which are essentially focused on mentors enabling trainees to implement their personal beliefs and values about their professional role within their classroom practice. This is very much a practice-based paper which trainees, and often those with a feel for this area, have found helpful in opening up the values discussion in seminars and in mentor sessions.

The final chapter in section two, published in 1999, is an essay review of a diatribe against anything other than a transmission role for teachers in values education. The publication under review is produced by the Campaign for Real Education and represents the kind of instrumental view of education which is prevalent amongst policy-makers and which this collection is striving to counteract. What Flew and Naylor (1996) condemn as the 'value-free disease' in education is challenged by much of the data in this collection which suggest that, given the opportunities in teacher development, there is a thirst in the profession to engage in a values debate which goes beyond a false dichotomy between values transference and values clarification.

Section three of this collection looks at the implications of the relationship between RE and PSHEe/Citizenship in the primary curriculum for the values education of trainee teachers. The introduction in 2000 of Citizenship as part of PSHEe in primary schools posed a challenge as to how RE should be taught, and raised important questions about trainees' confidence in handling a range of values and world views in the classroom. Chapters eleven and twelve have contributed to debates around these key questions (see Keast 1999; Osler and Starkey 2000; Brett 2005; Eke, Lee and Clough 2005; Halstead and Pike 2007). Chapter ten, first published in 1999, takes a positive view that the introduction of Citizenship will actually improve the affective and evaluative aspects of RE teaching and learning. The premise of the argument here is well articulated by Keast (1999), subject officer for Religious Education at the time of the paper:

> The complementarity I want to focus on really involves the question of values, because I think this is one of the key areas in which the three elements – Citizenship, PSHE and RE – all have an enormous stake (Keast 1999, p.41).

Keast goes on to make the important point that the argument for the complementarity between Citizenship and Religious Education in chapter ten 'identifies some skills and attitudes, not just on the part of youngsters, but on the part of teachers, which will resonate very much with RE' (1999, p.41). Underlying this positive perception is the hope that the complementarity of the subject areas will increase the need for trainees to develop pedagogic skills which will only emerge confidently with a more explicit values education dimension to initial training.

Chapter eleven, first published in 2000, takes up this issue by researching skills common to Religious Education and PSHEe/Citizenship with a cohort of primary trainees. The paper examines the relationship between their values education sessions and the development of their pedagogical understandings. The qualitative data enables there to be a drilling down to the pedagogic processes trainees need to acquire in order to go beyond Flew and Naylor's simplistic polarisation of values transference and values clarification critiqued in chapter nine. Chapter eleven argues that the foundation for acquiring such pedagogic skills is a both a personal and professional development in understanding the significance of and the interaction between different sets of values in the learning context. The chapter concludes that the complementarity between Religious Education and PSHEe/Citizenship provides a strengthening of this understanding for all primary trainees.

Chapter twelve, published in 2001, takes the relationship between Religious Education and Citizenship out into primary schools and researches experienced teachers' understandings of the relationship. The identification of the resultant professional development needs of these teachers confirms the importance of meeting the initial training needs in this area addressed in chapter eleven. What is of particular significance in the findings of this study is the need to develop practising teachers' awareness of how their personal development as citizens interacts with their own exemplification of a common skills set across Religious Education, PSHEe and Citizenship. The conclusion reached is that professional development opportunities are needed in developing staff skills in reflective dialogue. At the end of this chapter is a staff self-assessment exercise which contains such questions as 'what does being a citizen mean to me?' Such questions nurture commitment to professional values in inclusive classroom practices and should therefore be discussed in pre-service as well as post qualification professional education. Increased opportunities for this to happen are likely if, as all the chapters in this section argue, a common skills set across ReligiousEducation, PSHEe and Citizenship is seen to have the potential to strengthen a generalisable values education. Evidence of this happening is found in the response of certain citizenship organisations to chapter twelve.

From the perspective of those organisations promoting Citizenship, such as CitiZED (Citizenship within higher education teacher education) and ACT (the Association of Citizenship Teachers) the data in chapter twelve provided a strong case for supporting the training and subject knowledge needs of teacher educators who are not citizenship specialists:

> Can CitiZED be preparing accessible user-friendly preparation packs of
> introductory materials for these stakeholders? They are key players – either in their
> role as facilitators of cross-subject seminar/training sessions or as mediating the
> thinking of their own trainees in relation to Citizenship through planning issues. We

need subject leaders like Mead (2001), writing from an RE perspective, to conclude that the identification of a common skills base across RE and PSHE/Citizenship should not be seen as a threat to the former but rather an opportunity to enhance the quality of teaching in both areas without detracting from their distinctive contributions.(Brett 2005, p.16).

It is in this way that Brett envisages the development of a 'meaningful values-based learning for *all* trainees' with the potential for a 'depth of analysis which is related to the wider aims of education' (2005, p.16). Brett's position is very much in keeping with the generalisability principle advocated in this introduction which supports a more holistic values education for trainee teachers generated from Religious Education, PSHEe and Citizenship.

Turning now to Citizenship Education, the extent to which trainee teachers will be challenged to critically examine personal and professional values will depend, of course, on the model of Citizenship Education presented to them by their teacher educators. Recent debates about the statutory introduction of Citizenship Education in Key Stages 3 and 4 in 2002 (see for example Leighton 2004; Westheimer & Kahne 2004; Faulks 2006) have been concerned with a prevailing compliance rather than critical model of citizenship for young people. As Wetheimer and Kahne state, 'fostering honesty and good neighbourliness and so on are not *inherently* about democracy '(2004, p.244). The papers which make up section four present a much more justice-oriented concept of citizenship than is perhaps reflected in section three of this collection, and, as such, pose a new challenge to values education in teacher education, relevant to both secondary and primary trainees. In chapter thirteen on the student-led Iraq war protest (published 2004), the communitarian model may be upheld by a number of teachers in the case study school in response to the protest but is not the prevailing response of the senior management team who wish to allow a much more critical concept of citizenship to emerge. Emerging in the academic responses to this chapter are debates about a compliance and a deficit model of citizenship education versus a dynamic concept of student agency which challenges teachers' assumptions:

> There is evidence to support the truth of positive outcomes of the anti-war civic actions, particularly for some young people's sense of agency in the public sphere (Mead 2004b) and the sense of the need for a broader accountability from governing elites (Banaji 2008, p.552).

For Bowman (2012), the study is a 'familiar illustration, abiding even after a decade of the alienation between young people and conventional politics' (2012, p.38). Like Banaji, Bowman recognises that in the case of this particular school, the senior management team play an important part in negating the discrediting of young people's activism as disruptive and thus offer an example of addressing:

> The disconnection between prescribed paths to engagement and adulthood and later treatment by those who prescribed these normative pathways (Bowman 2012, p.38).

As such the case study has offered a model for trainee teachers within professional studies programmes and has informed the work of tutors in leading a critical analysis of trainees values and assumptions underpinning their concepts of citizenship.

The evolution of chapter thirteen into a more developed analysis of the nature of young people's participation in Citizenship Education found in chapter fourteen was aided by the inclusion of a developed version of the former in the Childhoods 2005 conference held at Oslo University. Of particular importance here was the focus of that conference on youth in emerging and transforming societies. This theme was powerfully explored through representations of young people's agency in very fluid political and social contexts, sometimes by the presence of the young people themselves, sharing their experience with educationists in conference sessions. Many trainee teachers and teacher educators hearing those young people would have had their values and assumptions about youth agency challenged. Chapter fourteen, first published in 2010, is an attempt to bring this challenge to the English context by critically examining how conflicting concepts of participation in citizenship education have diminished youth agency.

If the compliance and deficit models of citizenship education which have already been referred to are to be addressed in pedagogy, trainee teachers will need to have a good grasp of how the perceptions of different stakeholders have influenced citizenship since the Crick Report (1998). Of particular concern are the perceptions of academics who believe that political knowledge should be the core business of Citizenship Education, at the expense of other kinds of political engagement by young people. Secondly, trainee teachers should be aware of the perceptions of Ofsted inspectors who judge the quality of Citizenship Education in relation to a school's need for compliance in learning. Thirdly, trainee teachers need to critique superficial understandings of inclusion which reinforce participation as compliance. Chapter fourteen argues that without this kind of values education teachers will miss many opportunities in which pupil agency can be expressed through often messy and complex, but essentially moral, decision-making democratic processes such as those explored in chapter thirteen. Jerome (2012a, 2012b) has drawn on chapter fourteen to expand on these issues in his extensive and scholarly critical evaluation of what he calls the 'citizenship experiment' in England. Drawing on chapter fourteen, as well as his own extensive ethnographic data, Jerome concludes:

> The significant observation seems to be that, whatever the nature of the deficit to be remedied, citizenship may be used to address perceived social problems in the school. This in turn reflects a broader dimension in New Labour's citizenship policy, relating to what has been called the 'responsibilisation' or 'remoralisation' agenda. It also indicates one significant reason why we might expect citizenship to vary between schools (Jerome 2012, p.140).

If trainee teachers are to recognise youth agency they will need to experience themselves a critical pedagogy within their own learning which will challenge their values and the assumptions of a deficit model for young people. Such a critical pedagogy can inform learning within and outside the classroom. Within the classroom Biddulph (2012) has drawn on chapter fourteen to apply such a critical pedagogy to the moral and political arena of sexualities within Citizenship Education:

> Mead (2010) raises the question about how participation within citizenship is to be achieved and I agree with his view of the limitations of the 'liberal project of citizenship', where arguably tolerance is not enough. To be tolerant could imply that

some concession is being made; it is a position of distance, of being a bystander which can be questioned from a moral point of view (Biddulph 2012, p.109).

Biddulph goes on to capture very well the alternative critical pedagogy which will challenge pupils' values and assumptions:

> The challenge is to provide the debate about the plurality of sexuality in an inclusive and sensitive way that pushes students to really interrogate their values and understanding. I genuinely think this would make a fairer and more understanding world (Biddulph 2012, pp.109-10).

Trainee teachers will struggle to achieve this kind of pedagogy if they have not experienced anything like it themselves in their pre-service education. Biddulph is right about the link between such 'interrogation' of values and youth agency in relation to social justice – the 'fairer world'. This same link is fundamental to trainee teachers' going beyond the liberal tolerance of communitarianism which encourages a deficit view of the needs of young people to a dynamic understanding of how their interrogated values can impact on social justice in education.

It has already been stated that a critical pedagogy can also inform citizenship learning outside the classroom for teachers and pupils. It is only a critical pedagogy in teacher education that can give future classroom practitioners a handle on how the civil and the civic have become separated in the evolution of Citizenship Education in England since the Crick Report (1998).That report identified three equal aspects of the subject: the moral, the community and political literacy. Crick acknowledged that the first two played a significant part but the subject was made distinctive from community service and volunteerism by the inclusion of political literacy. In reality the introduction of a statutory citizenship in 2002 for key stages three and four, containing narrow assessment requirements conducive to Ofsted methodology, has led to a classroom-based and exam approach to the subject. The result is a severance of civic knowledge and civil action which puts the emphasis on classroom engagement as action rather than youth agency.

It is clearly evident that debates about citizenship education are prompting fundamental values-based questions about the nature and purpose of learning which trainee teachers ought to engage with. The separation of the civic and the civil is symptomatic of a highly measured inputs-outputs curriculum. Chapter fifteen is an unpublished conference paper (2011),which seeks to look at the relationship between civil experience outside the classroom and formal learning in the classroom and highlight some of the teacher education implications. As such it has provided, along with chapters thirteen and fourteen, case study material for a critical approach to citizenship education in professional studies seminars for trainee teachers. The data stimulate inquiry about the nature of learning in relation to the efficacy of youth agency. In the discussion following the delivery of the data at the CitiZED Conference 2011 there was concern about the paper's heavy reliance on what some may describe as Biesta's 'anything goes' definition of civic learning (2008). However, Peterson (2011) has highlighted how the nature of the relationship between civic knowledge and civil activity continues to remain unresolved in citizenship teaching. Chapter fifteen, whilst recognising these tensions, seeks a way forward for teachers to do justice to youth agency, which is significantly unrecognised in the measurement of school success by Ofsted, as demonstrated in chapter fourteen. Examples in chapters thirteen and fifteen of reconciling the civic and the civil require teachers to employ a critical pedagogy which is inquiry-led and pupil-led, providing opportunities for pupils to make the connections between political decisions and personal experience. As already stated, this will not happen unless trainee teachers experience this first-hand for themselves in some form of values education in pre-service training.

Chapter sixteen is a published review (2012) of Peterson's text cited above which might act as a theoretical companion piece to chapters fourteen and fifteen. Just as pupils need to connect civic knowledge and civil experience, trainee teachers need to draw on practitioner texts such as Peterson's in order to articulate their beliefs and values. The key question for discussion is whether or not civic republicanism offers a more dynamic model of citizenship than communitarianism. Civic republicanism is a reaction against the individualism and atomisation of liberal communitarianism; however, it contains a tension between an intrinsic approach to citizenship based on dispositions and an instrumental, principle-based approach. As chapter fourteen has explored, the latter approach currently prevails in an outputs-based education ethos and this has led to the separation of civic activity from civic engagement. Chapter fifteen is an attempt to explore a middle course between these two approaches which has pedagogical implications for trainee teachers. In addition, the contractual view of the relationship between rights and responsibilities in civic republicanism can lead to the perception that all participation is a good thing. As argued in chapter fourteen, this perception needs to be challenged if the public sphere is not to be neutralised. Value-judgements on these matters will only come about in pre-service teacher education if the questions raised by Peterson are explored alongside case study material such as in chapters thirteen, fourteen and fifteen. Not having opportunities to explore these value judgements will surely impact on trainees' pedagogical understanding, not just in Citizenship Education, but in their wider work.

It is fitting to conclude this final section with chapter seventeen because it demonstrates the impact of civic republican policy-making on trainee teachers' values. The Blairite social justice policy Every Child Matters (ECM) (2004) was an example of instrumental civic republicanism which assumed, on the basis of the social contract, a non-critical compliance from a state children's workforce. However, the separation of dispositions from principles, characteristic of instrumental civic republicanism, had significant implications for the professional autonomy of those who made up the children's workforce, not least teachers and trainee teachers. Chapter seventeen examines this loss of autonomy, particularly in the absence of a critical process of integrating personal and professional values about social justice which surely we want to be at the heart of the education of citizens as teachers.

Chapter seventeen, which was first published in 2011, has been widely consulted and there is encouraging evidence of teacher educators using the data to inform a critical pedagogy which has issues of social justice at its heart. For example, in his online discussion with PGCE Maths trainees at Durham University, Peter Gray argues that, in the light of chapter seventeen, trainees need to critically own policies through their own values-based judgements:

> In reading this [chapter seventeen] it is worth considering that ECM is a living document in the sense that it has no power except in our apprehension and

implementation of it, and that it behoves us to think very carefully about how we can bring ECM to life for the benefit of our learners, of our colleagues and ourselves (Gray 2011, p.1).

Similar critical reflection by trainees on social justice values underpinning health and well-being aspects of ECM has been built into the health promotion component of pre-service training at Southampton University (Byrne *et al* 2012).The researchers draw on chapter seventeen to analyse the connections they wanted trainees to make between knowledge, skills and personal and professional values about health education:

> This approach considers that curricula should not be overly prescriptive but should allow students to have some autonomy so that they can develop not only their knowledge base but also their own skills, attitudes and values towards health issues in order to become effective health promoters (Mead 2011) (Byrne *et al* 2012, p.528).

The researchers go on to define in what sense autonomy in the training process contributes to effective health educators:

> Furthermore the changes encompassed opportunities for the pre-service teachers to reflect on personal values and attitudes towards their own health and that of others, with the intention that they would continue to promote health throughout their careers. (Byrne *et al* 2012, p.528).

Byrne *et al* conclude their rationale by citing one of the key arguments in chapter seventeen which lies at the heart of a critical pedagogy for social justice in teacher education:

> However, merely meeting and evidencing particular competencies is regarded as a technical/functionalist approach to teacher education (Pollard 2005). Furthermore, Mead (2011, p.19) argues that a technical/instrumental approach to pre-service teacher education without the opportunity to reflect upon and develop professional values "can potentially weaken the intrinsic relationship between teachers' values, ownership of professional knowledge and pupil well-being". From our perspective this approach will not result in pre-service teachers that are effective health promoters wherever in the world they may be training to teach (Byrne *et al* 2012, pp.528-9).

That Byrne *et al* can generalise outwards from the close analysis of the relationship between teachers' beliefs and their professional practice found in chapter seventeen represents the culmination of the work in this volume. Chapter seventeen puts the challenges and limitations of values education in initial teacher education, explored in earlier chapters, on a footing which makes teaching a moral and political act. As such, teacher education cannot be conducted other than through a critical pedagogy. It follows that the issue of time for reflection on values in pre-service training, often raised in previous chapters, remains important, but less so than the nature of reflection itself and how trainees collaborate in the process. The type of reflection and collaboration required is glimpsed throughout this collection and, importantly for *School Direct,* there is evidence of its development on school-based training routes as discussed in chapter four.

It is possible to consider, then, that the limited success of values education in conventional university routes has been about lack of trainee autonomy and a more descriptive rather than critical approach to reflection and collaboration. Each of these factors is more about approach than just time. Greater trainee autonomy allows for the integration of personal and professional values: marrying those deeply held motivations with classroom practice. In seminars, mentoring sessions and written assignments, this would be characterised by participatory appropriation: how trainees themselves 'change and develop through being part of the activity and with regard to the activity' (Kroll 2012, p.51) Reflection is not the reductive and often descriptive 'reflective practice' which Schon's (1983) theories have often become: what happened and what I did, followed by smart targets linked to judgements about what was "good" or "unworkable" (Wright & Bottery 1997). By contrast a critical pedagogy driven by social justice requires the development of the moral authority of the trainee in investigating what is best for their students' learning and development. As Kroll argues, teacher educators need to frame reflection within constructivist guided participation, beginning with a fundamental question:

> "How can I provoke constructive conversations about social justice and equity in teaching with my students? What questions, activities and projects help my students take an inquiry stance towards these issues?" (Kroll 2012, p.43).

It follows that reflection constructed from a values-laden question changes the dynamics of trainee collaboration within seminars, as Kroll goes on to identify from her case study group of trainees:

> Overall, during the second semester, the students helped one another clarify their questions and then understand the data they had collected, throwing new light on data interpretation as they shared the data with one another. Collaboration around these inquiry questions was essential to their individual development as teachers. It was a true contrast to earlier years, where students had collaborated, but not necessarily towards greater understanding of their own teaching practice. In earlier instances they provided moral support and specific suggestions (based on their own experiences) that did not necessarily match the issues the student presented. Inquiry and collaboration allowed them to better understand and to problematize the situation before attempting solutions (Kroll 2012, pp.107-8).

To conclude from the above analysis in the light of *School Direct*, research is needed into how the new flagship training schools (Teaching Schools) which position themselves on the sharp end of social justice, might achieve a values-based critical pedagogy and thus an explicit values education for their trainees. Reflection and collaboration have the potential to be qualitatively different if you are caught up in an investigation into learning with professionals who are investing their intellectual and emotional energy in bringing about access and equity for all their pupils. This qualitative difference has been a particular strength of *Teach First*, an expanding school-based route into teaching, recruiting bright graduates straight into challenging schools. In their most recent inspection of *Teach First*, Ofsted considered trainees' personal characteristics, self-motivation, critical reflection and commitment to access and equity to be outstanding. They note how depth of understanding of key issues is achieved through critical reflection, arising from a highly collaborative framework within *Teach First* schools focused on addressing disadvantage (Ofsted 2011).

References

Advisory Group on Citizenship (1998) *Education for citizenship and the teaching of democracy in schools, The Crick Report* (London, QCA).

APPG (2013) *The Truth Unmasked,* all party parliamentary group report on Religious Education (London Religious Education Council).

Bainjath, I (2008) *Changing Times, Changing Values: an Alchemy of Values Education,* doctoral dissertation, University of Kwazulu-Natal, downloaded 5/4/13 at researchspace.ukzn.ac.za/xmlail/handle/10413/1138.

Banaji, S (2008) 'The trouble with civic: a snapshot of young people's civic and political engagements in twenty-first century democracies', *Journal of Youth Studies,* 11(5) pp.543-560.

Baumfield, V (2007) 'Becoming a teacher of RE in a world of religious diversity', *Journal of Beliefs and Values,* 28(1) pp.77-81.

Bowman, B (2012) *Young People's Politics, Engagement and Antipolitics: a thematic review of the literature,* Master in Research dissertation, University of Bath, downloaded on 18/5/13 at people.bath.ac.uk/bd203/docs/Diss_BenjaminBowman_0912.pdf

Biddulph, M (2012) 'Sexualities and citizenship education', in Arthur, J & Cremin, H (2012) (eds) *Debates in Citizenship Education* (London, Routledge) chap.9, pp.100-114.

Biesta, G (2008) 'A school for citizens: civic learning and democratic action in the learning democracy', in Lingard, B, Nixon, J, & Ranson, S (Eds) *Transforming Learning in Schools and Communities* (London, Routledge) pp.170-183.

Brett, P (2005) 'Strategies for embedding citizenship within and across initial teacher education programmes', paper given at the CitiZED seminar: *More than a one-off lecture: citizenship within and across PGCE and other ITE programmes* LSE, London.

Brown, J, Busfield R, O'Shea, A, & Sibthorpe, J (2011) 'School ethos and personal, social, health education', *Pastoral Care in Education,* 29(2) pp.117-131.

Byrne, J, Speller, V, Dewhirst, S, Roderick, P, Almond, P Grace, M & Memon, A (2012) 'Health promotion in pre-service teacher education: effects of a pilot inter-professional curriculum change', *Health Education,* 112(6) pp.525-542.

DCSF (2004) *Every Child Matters: Change for Children in Schools* (London, DCSF).

DFE (2009) *Independent Review of the Proposal to make Personal, Social, Health and Economic Education (PSHEe) Statutory* The Macdonald Report (London, DFE).

DFE (2010) *The Importance of Teaching: the Schools White Paper* (London, DFE).

Easterbrook, S & Stephenson, B (2009) 'Veteran teachers' use of recommended practices in deaf education', *American Annals of the Deaf*, 153(5) pp.461-473.

Eke, R Lee, J & Clough, N (2005) 'Whole class interactive teaching and learning in religious education: transcripts from four primary classrooms', *British Journal of Religious Education*, 27(2) pp.159-172.

Eraut, M (2004) 'Informal learning in the workplace' *Studies in Continuing Education*, 26(2) pp.247-73.

Evans, C & Evans, B (2007) 'More than just worksheets? A study of the confidence of newly qualified teachers of English in teaching personal, social and health education in secondary schools', *Pastoral Care in Education*, 25(4) pp.42-50.

Faulks, K (2006) 'Education for citizenship in England's secondary schools: a critique of current principles and practice', *Journal of Education Policy*, 21(1) pp.59-74.

Flew, A & Naylor, F (1996) *Spiritual Development and All that Jazz*, paper 25 (York, The Campaign for Real Education).

Gray, P (2011) 'Nick Mead: the impact of Every Child matters on trainee secondary teachers' understanding of professional knowledge', Durham University PGCE online google group downloaded 5/513 at http://groups.google.com/forum/?hl=en&fromgroups#/durham2011/XK-wL3AVE.

Halstead, M & Pike, M (2007) *Citizenship and Moral Education: Values in Action* (London, Routledge).

Harrison, J (2007) 'The assessment of ITT standard one professional values and practice: measuring performance or what?' *Journal of Education for Teaching*, 33(3) pp.323-340.

Howe, E (2005) 'Japan's teacher acculturation: critical analysis through comparative ethnographic narrative', *Journal of education for Teaching*, 31(2) pp.121-131.

Howe, E (2008) 'Teacher induction across the Pacific: a comparative study of Canada and Japan', *Journal of education for Teaching*, 34(4) pp.333-346.

Jerome, L (2005) 'Critical citizenship experiences? Working with trainee teachers to facilitate active citizenship in schools', paper given at the International Convention on Education for

Teaching, 50th World assembly, Pretoria, S.A. 12-15th July, downloaded 1/6/13 icet.org/download.aspx?file=YearbookFiles/2005/Paper%20 Jerome.

Jerome, L (2012a) 'Service learning and active citizenship education in England', *Education, Citizenship and Social Justice,* 7(1) pp.59-70.

Jerome, L (2012b) *England's Citizenship Experiment* (London, Bloomsbury).

Keast, J (1999) *Excellence in Religious Education,* Culham St. Gabriel Centenary Conference, downloaded 10/4/13 at www. Culham.ac.uk/sg/content/files/CentenaryConferenceReport.pdf.

Kroll, L (2012) *Self-study and Inquiry into Practice* (London, Routledge).

Leighton, R (2004) 'The nature of citizenship education provision: an initial study', *Curriculum Journal,* 15(2) pp.167-181.

Limond, D (2008) 'Strangers and Sojourners: who were miss v and miss w?' *African Identities,* 6(1) pp.29-43.

Martin, N & Yin, Z (2009) 'Teacher characteristics and classroom management styles: implications for professional development', *Contemporary Issues in Education,* Louisiana Education Research association (LERA) 3(1) pp.34-41.

McCreery, E (2005) 'Preparing primary teachers to teaching religious education', *British Journal of Religious Education,* 27(3) pp.265-277.

Mead, N (1996) 'Mentoring religious education teaching in secondary schools', Unpublished research paper (Oxford, The Farmington Institute).

Mead, N (2003) 'Will the introduction of professional values put the heart back into primary teacher education?' *Pastoral Care in Education,* 21(1) pp.37-42.

Mead, N (2004b) 'The provision for personal, social, health education (PSHE) and citizenship in school-based elements of primary initial teacher education', *Pastoral Care in Education,* 22(2) pp.19-26.

Mead, N (2004b) 'The management and impact of a student-led Iraq war protest in a fresh start school', *Pastoral Care in Education* 22(4) pp.6-12.

Mead, N (2006) 'The experience of black African religious education trainee teachers training in England', *British Journal of Religious Education,* 28(2) pp.173-184.

Mead, N (2007) 'How effectively does the graduate teacher programme contribute to the development of trainee teachers' professional values?' *Journal of Education for Teaching,* 33(3) pp.309-322.

Mead, N (2010) 'Conflicting concepts of participation in secondary school citizenship', *Pastoral Care in Education,* 28(1) pp.45-57.

Mead, N (2011) 'The impact of *Every Child Matters* on trainee secondary teachers' understanding of professional knowledge', *Pastoral Care in Education,* 29(1) pp.7-24.

Midgley, A, Rigby, P, Warham, L, & Woolnough, P (2009) *Teaching English, Developing as a Reflecting Secondary Teacher* (London, Sage).

Mills, K & Kilburn, V (2011) 'Personal and social development', in Cooper, H (ed) *Professional studies in primary education* (London, Sage), chap.9, pp.135-148.

NCTL (2013) *School Direct: Quick Start Guide for Schools 2014/15* (London, NCTL).

Ofsted (2006) *Towards Consensus? Citizenship in Secondary Schools* (London, Ofsted).

Osler, A & Starkey, H (2000) 'Education for democratic citizenship: a review of research, policy and practice 1995-2005,' *Research Papers in Education,* 21(4) pp.433-466.

Ostapenko-Denton, A (2011) 'A hermeneutic investigation into perceptions of professionalism and professionality amongst FE and HE lecturers in an FE college', *Seeker, Journal of scholarly activities and research*, Truro & Penwith College, 1(1) pp.5-12.

Peterson, A (2011) *Civic Republicanism and Civic Education* (Basingstoke, Palgrave Macmillan).

Pitfield, M & Morrison, L (2009) 'Teachers' experiences of mentoring on a flexible initial teacher education programme: implications for partnership development', *Journal of Education for Teaching,* 35 (1) pp.19-32.

Reynolds, M (1999) 'Standards of professional practice: the TTA and initial teacher training', *British Journal of Educational Studies,* 47(3) pp.247-260.

Rinehart, F (2004) 'Professional development on a personal level', unpublished paper for M.Ed, Ashland University USA, downloaded on 10/3/13 at personal.ashland.edu/~dkommer/Irq papers Fall o4/Rinehart Final,pdf.

Rutaisire, J (2012) *An Investigation into Teachers' Experiences of In-service Training and Professional Development in Rwanda,* Ed. D. dissertation University of Sussex, downloaded on 9/4/13 at sro.sussex.ac.uk/39343/.

Schon, D (1983) *The Reflective Practitioner* (New York, Basic Books).

Sikes, P & Etherington, J (2004) ' 'RE teachers do get drunk you know': becoming a religious education teacher in the twenty-first century', *Teachers and Teaching: Theory and Practice,* 10(1) pp.21-33.

Smith, K & Hodson, E (2010) 'Theorising practice in initial teacher education', *Journal of Education for Teaching,* 36(3) pp.259-275.

Teach First (2011) *Ofsted Report: summary of the findings,* downloaded on 11/5/13 at wwwteachfirst.org.uk/web/FILES/Teach First Ofsted Report Summary FINAL26132_1375,pdf.

Westheimer, J & Kahne, J (2004) 'What kind of citizen? The politics of educating for democracy', *American Education Research Journal,* 41(2) pp.237-269.

Wright, N & Bottery, M (1997) 'Perceptions of professionalism by the mentors of student teachers', *Journal of Education for Teaching,* 23(3) pp.235-252.

Yelken, Y (2009) 'An evaluation of the teacher development programme standards by European teacher candidates from Turkey, Germany and Denmark', *Educational Sciences: theory and practice,* 9(4) pp.2077-2094.

Section One

Values in different routes into primary teacher education with reference to Personal, Social, Health & Economic Education & Citizenship

Will the introduction of teaching standards in professional values and practice put the heart back into primary teacher education? First published in the *Journal of Pastoral Care in Education* (2003) 21(1) pp.37-42 (Taylor & Francis).

The provision for PSHE/Ct in the school-based elements of primary initial teacher education. First published in the *Journal of Pastoral Care in Education* (2004) 22(2) pp.19-26 (Taylor & Francis).

How effectively does the Graduate Teacher Programme contribute to the development of trainee teachers' professional values? First published in the *Journal of Education for Teaching* (2007) 33(3) pp.309-321 (Taylor & Francis).

Should relationships education be at the heart of Personal, Social, Health and Economic Education and, if so, what would be the implications for pre-service teacher education? Unpublished paper given at the Teacher Education Advancement Network (TEAN) annual conference, Aston University, Birmingham May 2012.

Will the Introduction of Teaching Standards in Professional Values and Practice Put the Heart Back into Primary Teacher Education?

NICK MEAD, *Senior Lecturer, Oxford Brookes University*

In the light of the introduction of teaching standards in professional values and practice in September 2002, this study compares two sets of data from B.Ed. and PGCE primary courses, in order to examine the existing opportunities for values education within teacher education in one institution. The findings highlight a qualitative difference in the process of personal and professional development experienced by the two groups of students. Implications of the findings for university training partnerships, university tutors and professional studies programmes are then considered. The conclusion reached is that the introduction of teaching standards in professional values and practice may be the next landmark in the process vs. competence debate about teacher education, and may provide the opportunity to put human development back into the heart of teacher education.

Introduction

Previous research undertaken (Mead, 2000) has highlighted the impact of a personal, social, health education and citizenship (PSHE/CT) elective course on the personal and professional values of a group of twenty-two fourth year bachelor of education (B.Ed.) students. This elective has run throughout the fourth year of the course, combining taught sessions with school-based research so that theory and practice are interrelated.

Since that research was undertaken, the Teacher Training Agency (TTA) has introduced the £6,000 bursary for trainee teachers following the post-graduate one-year route. As a result, statistics indicate that the undergraduate route, such as the B.Ed., is contracting rapidly and the post-graduate certificate in education (PGCE) is becoming the mainstream route into teaching. Although institutions may be giving the professional studies element of the PGCE course a PSHE/CT focus, there is obviously not the time available to undertake an extensive process of reflective thinking and research such as the B.Ed. elective students undertook. It is evident, therefore, that any comparative study of the B.Ed. and PGCE experience of values education is not a like for like comparison. However, what this study attempts to do is to make a comparison of how students' understanding of the relationship between personal and professional values develops on each course. Such a comparison is valid because institutions need to identify and sustain quality student experience within changing modes of training. The comparison is also pertinent to the government's introduction of new initial teacher training standards in September 2002, the first of which is standards in professional values and practice.

It seems that the Teacher Training Agency (2002) outcome statements for professional values and practice, exemplified in the standards handbook of the Teacher Training Agency (2001), describe a set of skills which can only be fully achieved through a *process* of personal as well as professional preparation. The handbook states that students will be expected to demonstrate that they can:

'*articulate* their *own* considered professional values' (st.1.1, p. 6). '*Recognize and challenge* discrimination, prejudice and stereotyping' (st. 1.1, p. 6). '*Respond constructively and sensitively to personal issues* raised by pupils' (st.1.2, p. 7). '*Model and promote the values that underpin the purposes of education, such as respect for the truth and for the opinion of others*' (st.1.3, p. 8).

Each of these, but the last in particular, poses a fundamental philosophical challenge to the competence-based model of teacher training, which has prevailed since general teaching competences were first set out in Department for Education and Skills (DFES) Circular 9/92.

Background

The comparison between the two sets of students in this study needs to be set in the context of the *process vs competence* debate about teacher education. The language of the new standards for professional values and practice is still that of competence-based training, for example, 'uphold by demonstrating' (TTA, 2002: 6); yet, if we apply this to trainees modelling the values that underpin the purposes of education such as 'respect for the truth', we do shift the focus of education (including teacher education) from skills to philosophical principles. In fact, as Carr (2000) argues, the very existence of professional values assumes that there is such a thing as objective truth:

> if there is really no such thing as objective truth to be had, even in principle, then education as anything more than equipping people with useful practical skills is simply sophistry and delusion. As a result there can be no objective rational basis for regarding teaching as a matter of principled obedience to more general professional imperatives. (p. 119)

Pring (1994) develops Carr's fundamental premise that if we introduce professional values into teacher training, then we go beyond professional competence:

> teachers are committed to those values and relationships which belong to the very special transaction which goes on between teacher and learner. The moral formation which is required for this very special transaction reflects a combination of personal and professional development and skills. (p. 184)

The moral formation is clearly described as a process involving caring for the curriculum because of its worth and not its utility, a concern for evidence and reasoned argument, a respect for alternative viewpoints, a search for understanding and the ability to use theory to interpret experience. Pring concludes that such values, 'are precious, hard to come by and are easily lost' (p. 184).

A significant feature of a process of moral formation is the personal commitment made by the individual. This is particularly highlighted in early professional development literature which acknowledges that the personal/professional dynamic has to be the starting point for continuing professional development:

> no matter how persuasive particular aspects of a shared social or occupational culture may be, or how well individuals are socialised into it, the attitudes and actions of each teacher are rooted in his/her own ways of perceiving the world. (Nias, 1989: 156)

Tann recognized back in 1993, a year after the first set of teaching standards were introduced, that what Nias is addressing must be part of initial training. Students do come to their training with personal theories about education and what Tann found was that: 'students experienced great difficulty in making personal–public links because, "we don't know the words"' (1993: 68). Tann goes on to conclude:

> this appears to be something that needs to be addressed early on in a course to provide students with language with which they can share their personal experience and learn from others' public experiences. Without this prerequisite reflection can hardly begin. (1993: 68)

The *process* of human development described here does not have to be incompatible with the acquisition of professional standards, but it is what gives those standards meaning to the individual student. This may be the difference between teacher training and teacher education, as argued by Fish (1996):

> the competence-based model of teacher training reflects certainty of knowledge, understanding and skills, based on measuring the observable. The competence-based model to date is a training exercise rather than an educational enterprise and narrows its concerns to the acquisition of basic skills as opposed to developing understanding; refining practical and theoretical knowledge and engaging in scholarly activity. (p. 47)

Most significantly, for values education, Fish goes on to argue that such a model may present knowledge 'as absolute', 'render amoral the deeply moral', and 'pretend the possibility of objectivity in the face of certain subjectivity' (p. 47).

The comparative research data which follows has been set in the context of the *process vs competence* debate, because it is hoped that good practice in existing teacher education might be identified, and used, to inform discussions about the introduction of teaching standards in professional values and practice.

Methodology

Previous data collection from two cohorts of fourth year B.Ed. students undertaking an elective in PSHE/CT involved a course evaluation sheet to the twenty members of the first cohort and a reflective piece of writing in response to the following: 'trainee teachers need to think and talk about their values before entering the classroom, if they are not to pass on their own values uncritically'. The second cohort of seventeen trainees was asked to reflect on the kind of professional development they would like a Citizenship co-ordinator to provide which would develop teacher self-concept. The responses were analysed, categories of response identified and from these key findings were extrapolated.

By contrast, the limited opportunities to collect data from postgraduate students speaks for itself and it was, at the conclusion to a whole cohort lecture on PSHE/CT near the end of the course, that the students were asked for a written response to the question: 'what opportunities have I had on the primary PGCE course to think and talk about my values as a teacher?'. With one answer of varying lengths from 140 students, a grounded theory method was used, allowing dominant themes to emerge from a broad attempt to categorize the answers. The intention was to compare these dominant themes with the existing B.Ed. findings, which might highlight qualitative differences in the development of personal and professional values during initial training.

Summary of Findings

The data suggests that the PGCE students had a good understanding of the importance of values in teaching on entry to the course, but they did not necessarily feel that they had experienced a process of personal and professional development in relation to those values during their training. By contrast, the B.Ed. students seemed to progress from seeking initial assurance to becoming more confident about handling values in university discussions and in their teaching.

Findings from the PGCE Data

As the literature has borne out, students do bring personal theories about the educational process to their training and postgraduates have a strong awareness of the importance of teachers' values. Students found a frustrating mismatch between the importance of values in the classroom and the lack of time to address values in their training. They are able to articulate the relationship between values and teaching which they felt they had not fully experienced:

> I feel we should be given more opportunity to discuss our values as teachers, but more importantly, we would like to feel that they are listened to. This would help us to develop our own confidence, self-esteem and moral and spiritual values in preparation for imparting them to our class. (student A)

As graduates, these trainees are also expecting to engage in debate: 'lots of time hearing what the government theorists and educationalists think our values should be but not really any time to think about and discuss our own' (student B).

What also comes across is a description of what the students themselves perceive to be a process of personal and professional development which they did not feel they had actually experienced. Many

thought that the professional studies programme offered some opportunities for reflecting on values, but amongst those responses, a distinction was made between discussing general values and reflecting on the interrelationship between personal and professional values:

> opportunities have arisen to discuss our feelings but not our values. (student C)

> It tended to be values in general rather than my own values. My own values have been discussed more with friends on the course. (student D)

Of particular significance is an awareness of a need to work through the relationship between personal and professional values. Given the opportunity, however brief, to reflect on this, clearly poses a philosophical dilemma for one student: 'if these are your "teacher values", then surely they are the same as your personal values. If not, then you are teaching to values that you don't (fully) believe' (student E). Another student puts student E's dilemma in context:

> on this course there have been few specific opportunities to discuss my own values. Any discussion has been informal with friends. It seems that personal values have come second to the values of the school. On school experience I have found myself following the teaching values of the class teacher, even when I have not agreed with them. (student F)

As writers such as Tann have argued, students are seeking to develop a language which can enable them to express confidently the relationship between the personal and the professional. One student felt that she was not confident in her values because she felt that they had been questioned without the opportunity for discussion. This suggests that students are aware that they need to go through a *process* of ongoing dialogue with each other and their tutors, which enables them to personally modify and shape the relationship between their personal and professional values. Without such a process, those students who either believe that their values are identical to everyone else's, or who are afraid to articulate their values in case they may be 'deemed as inappropriate' (student G), will not be given the opportunity to mature as professionals. An awareness of the importance of this process is expressed more explicitly by students H and I:

> those with strongly held values tend to express them frequently in university sessions, however, these are rarely challenged by the less confident and therefore I'm unsure as to whether their values have been shaped. (student H)

> Both personal and educational values have not been adequately covered, leaving many opportu-

nities for teachers to enter the profession with prejudice. (student I)

Almost instinctively, these PGCE students are describing a values education experience which on entry to the course they might have assumed to be a pre-requisite for professional life in the classroom. Some rightly point out that expectations in this area are raised by the requirement to fill in a personal statement on their Graduate Teacher Training Registry (GTTR) form, expressing why they want to teach. Others who have had interviews for teaching posts rightly point out that some interviews are largely about professional values. In many ways these findings confirm the *process vs competence* tension in teacher training and this is particularly well summed up by student J:

> a PGCE should not be a recipe – we all need to think about moral and spiritual growth. This is something that cannot be taught, but it could be encouraged. I believe that we should continually re-evaluate our own values as our experience widens. (student J)

Findings from the B.Ed. Data

Although a very different experience as a discrete PSHE/CT optional course, the B.Ed. data describes a qualitative difference in one aspect of the training which the PGCE students might have been expecting on entry to their course.

The data indicates students experiencing an initial uncertainty about how schools handle values and a desire to be told which values to espouse:

> there is currently too little research literature written by too narrow a range of authors to provide a theoretical assurance to our beliefs. We are still lacking an accepted criteria of what society's values are and until both of these missing aspects are improved and available the citizenship course will only help us understand an individual's values and be of no broader benefit than that. (student O)

This raises the challenging question about whether schools transmit values, clarify values or provide a framework of core values within which children can securely reflect on and evaluate the range of values encountered in a pluralistic society, and modify their own values in the process. Although initially seeking the kind of assurance expressed by student O, the course evaluations indicate students progressing from recognizing the limitations of approaches one and two to a growing confidence in handling approach three. This is expressed in their assessment of their own experience of the third approach on the course:

> this course gives depth to teachers which may otherwise be missing in their training. So much

time is spent on acquiring and imparting know-ledge. A greater understanding of Citizenship and related values enables teachers to be more well-rounded and hopefully better teachers. (student E)

Another student takes this further and makes the connection between the confidence gained through her own experience of the third approach on the course and the significant recognition that the class-room is not a value-free zone:

> it would have been extremely helpful to have been given time to have had citizenship lectures much earlier in the course as it is something which should be an integral part of your time in school. I have certainly benefited (and I hope my pupils have) from re-assessing and re-evaluating my own values and the values I aspire to demonstrate in the classroom. (student L)

A fourth student links the processes of re-assessing and re-evaluating with a pluralistic values-laden classroom:

> the elective has helped me to understand and realise the importance of being aware of different values amongst staff, pupils and parents and how one might deal with them. We are not always aware of how these different values are influencing the children who encounter us. (student P)

The data suggests that the students' understanding of how teachers handle values has been gained through their own experience of the approach of the course, which is secure, formative and inclusive, and avoids either extreme of values transmission or values clarification.

Secondly, students recognized the value of developing skills in philosophical inquiry and moral reasoning. Student evaluations of the course aims emphasized positive 'opportunities for thoughtful reflection on values in the classroom; their evaluations of learning outcomes from the course highlighted how, 'during the course we have developed skills in reflective discussion, moral reasoning and philo-sophical inquiry'; the strengths of the course were identified as, 'opportunities for discussion and time to reflect', 'an expression of much that is unspoken', and 'ways into the teaching of values which develops these as part of the professional and personal development of the teacher'. Students written reflec-tions on the course highlighted how they had deepened their reflective skills and how this had increased their awareness of the need for skills in open dialogue:

> the elective has given me the opportunity to think about and reflect on my own beliefs. I think I now have a greater awareness of my influence (or potential influence) on the children in my care.

Teachers who are not made explicitly aware of the need to have an 'open mind' when it comes to teaching children may find that they are not giving due care or attention to children's spiritual, moral, social and cultural care and education. (student Q)

Thirdly, the *process* of self-understanding which the B.Ed. students feel the course has led them through is linked, in turn, to their confidence in the pedagogic skills required in the teaching of PSHE/CT:

> children will ask questions about values. It is essential that trainee teachers feel ready to be able to deal with these situations in a classroom and throughout the school. No one can be an effective model of values if the term is not understood thoroughly or the teachers do not have a clear picture of their own values. If one is unsure of values that stand in the classroom and school then the children will be unsure. (student T)

This confidence seems to be derived from the process of making students' implicit values explicit and allowing them to be shaped by dialogue with others, as part of a process in achieving moral and spiritual autonomy:

> surely every teacher training course should include values education in order that the implicit might become explicit and children can benefit from confident teachers with clarified understandings. (student U)

Spiritual and moral autonomy begins to emerge as students are invited to reflect on and evaluate their morals and values and to consider whether they are appropriate for the classroom:

> the course allows for reflection but also gives alternative views and suggestions about the values you hold. (student V)

The outcome of this process is related by one trainee directly to classroom ethos:

> sharing opinions and looking at what others have said about values helps to give us confidence and new ideas for creating the kind of classroom ethos that we would like. (student W)

To conclude, the B.Ed. data seems to describe a *process* in which students are educated in values. By this, I mean that they undergo a process of formation, such as described by Pring, which provides them with both the skills and understanding needed to handle the relationship between personal and professional values. In turn, the B.Ed. students are able to articulate how such formation is the basis for effective PSHE/CT pedagogy.

Comparative Findings and their Implications for Teacher Educators

The first comparative finding is that an intellectual understanding of the role of the teacher in values education is best gained through a *process* of personal and professional development, such as experienced by the B.Ed. elective students. These students participated in and evaluated approaches to values education and, as a result, gained confidence in a role in which personal and professional values sit comfortably together. The PGCE data indicates how much those students wanted and expected to engage in a similar developmental process and how much they wanted to acquire that intellectual understanding about how schools and teachers handle values. What they felt they experienced, by contrast, was some discussion about general values, rather than the specific relationship between personal and professional values. The student who talks about following the values of her class teacher, 'even when I have not agreed with them', has not had the opportunity to work this through, nor has the student who talks about 'imparting values to pupils'.

The second comparative finding is that both groups of students identify dialogue as the medium through which the process of values formation should take place. The difference between the two groups is that the process of personal and professional development experienced by the B.Ed. students enables them to develop new skills in philosophical inquiry and moral reflection, which are the tools of dialogue in values education. In addition, as the B.Ed. elective has interwoven theory and practice, B.Ed. students make the connection between the acquisition of these skills and effective PSHE/CT pedagogy, which ensures the open mind, the recognition of prejudice and the sensitive response to personal issues raised by pupils. PGCE students expressed a good understanding of how dialogue 'shapes' values and the need for this to happen if teachers are not to be prejudiced. However, unlike the B.Ed. students, they tended to express a lack of confidence about articulating the relationship between personal and professional values, with more questions raised than answered. When students claim that they do not need to discuss and review their values because they are the same as everyone else's, or they are afraid to discuss them in case they are inappropriate, it becomes apparent that there is much work to be done in providing PGCE students with the tools of values education, which will equip them for the pluralistic classroom.

The third comparative finding is that the development of self-understanding experienced by the B.Ed. students is linked by them to effective PSHE/CT pedagogy. They express self-understanding as 'making implicit values explicit' and becoming 'a confident teacher' with 'clarified understandings' who can be 'an effective model of values' and 'create the kind of classroom ethos they would like'. By contrast PGCE students do not make such a link, but student A quoted earlier is hinting at it when she speaks of her own need to develop, 'confidence, self-esteem and moral and spiritual values' in preparation for teaching. These comparative findings raise interesting questions in the context of the *process vs competence* debate about teacher education. For example, should training institutions mirror the permeation of values across the curriculum which the PSHE and citizenship frameworks are promoting in school? How do training institutions do this when they are subject to the more corporate and income-driven values of a large university?

A way forward here might be through tutors and mentors discussing and auditing how professional values and practice permeate the training partnership. Very few PGCE students identified school placements as providing explicit opportunities for values education. Although often overwhelmed by the amount of content to get through, university subject tutors might now feel free to discuss and audit the opportunities within their own programmes of study for explicit values education. Dare we revive opportunities to contextualize our subject within the wider purposes of education and offer personal and professional philosophical perspectives on this? Some tutors may feel the need to develop pedagogic skills in their own subject, which enable students to regularly examine, evaluate and modify the relationship between personal and professional values in that subject. Can we give time to discussing whether the Professional Studies Programme is where we try to cover everything else other than the curriculum, or is it a values-focused course which brings the same set of reflective questions and methodology to each whole school issue, thereby giving students a set of transferable reflective skills?

Conclusion

If the introduction of teaching standards in professional values and practice is not to be merely another set of competences to be ticked off, we will perhaps have the chance to revive that belief, so well expressed by Bottery (1992):

> that teachers are first and foremost human beings with whose development the school should be as concerned as it is with that of the pupils. Teachers are viewed as important because they are part of the purpose of education, the development of people. (p. 175)

References

BOTTERY, M. (1992) *The Ethics of Educational Management.* London: Cassell.

CARR, D. (2000) *Professionalism and Ethics in Teaching.* London: Routledge.

FISH, D. (1996) 'Values, Competency-Based Training and Teacher Education', in C. Selmes and W. Robb (eds), *Values in Teacher Education*, 2, pp. 44–50, Aberdeen: National Association of Values in Education.

MEAD, N. (2000) 'Researching Skills Common to Religious Education and Citizenship', in S. Clipson-Boyles (ed.), *Putting Research into Practice in Primary Teaching and Learning.* London: Fulton.

NIAS, J. (1989) 'Teaching and the Self', in M. Holly and C. McLaughlin (eds), *Perspectives on Teachers' Professional Development.* London: Falmer.

PRING, R. (1994) 'The Year 2000', in M. Wilkins and D. Sankey (eds), *Collaboration and Transition in Initial Teacher Training.* London: Kogan Page.

TANN, S. (1993) 'Eliciting Student Teachers' Personal Theories', in J. Calderhead and P. Gates (eds), *Conceptualising Reflection in Teacher Development.* London: Falmer.

TEACHER TRAINING AGENCY (TTA) (2001) *Handbook To Accompany Standards for the Award of Qualified Teacher Status and Requirements for the Provision of Initial Teacher Training* (consultation document). London: TTA.

TEACHER TRAINING AGENCY (TTA) (2002) *Qualifying to Teach, Professional Standards for Qualified Teacher Status and Requirements for Initial Teacher Training.* London: TTA.

Correspondence
Oxford Brookes University
Westminster Institute of Education
Harcourt Hill
Oxford, OX2 9AT
Tel: 01865 488294
E-mail: nmead@brookes.ac.uk

The Provision for Personal, Social, Health Education (PSHE) and Citizenship in School-based Elements of Primary Initial Teacher Education

NICK MEAD, *Oxford Brookes University, Oxford, UK*

This small-scale research study looks at the PSHE/Citizenship framework and the opportunities for student teachers to understand and experience within school the relationship between values, personal and social development and learning. A questionnaire was given to two sets of student teachers on their final school-based placements. The research suggests that there needs to be greater recognition of the centrality of multi-cultural awareness and understanding within the political literacy section of the PSHE/Citizenship framework. This is the counterpart to a previous study of the opportunities for values education within the university-based elements of Primary Initial Teacher Education (Mead, 2003).

Keywords: Initial teacher training; primary; personal, social and health education; citizenship; inclusion.

Introduction

The focus of this study is the significance of Standard 2.2 in the 2002 Professional Standards for Qualified Teacher Status which states that student teachers should be able to 'demonstrate that they know and understand the Values, Aims and Purposes of the National Curriculum' (Teacher Training Agency (TTA) (2002), p. 27) and are 'familiar with the Programmes of Study for Personal, Social and Health Education and Citizenship' (PSHE/Ct., ibid.). The guidance for assessing this standard makes a fundamental link between the values underpinning the curriculum which are focused on the principles of inclusion, and the explicit expression of those values through PSHE/Ct.:

> When judging trainees' knowledge, assessors may wish to consider, for example, is the trainee familiar with the contribution of PSHE/Ct. to the Values, Aims and Purposes and General Teaching requirements of the National Curriculum? (TTA, p. 27)

This link has implications for the values education of student teachers, something lacking in the university-based elements of PGCE courses, as I have previously argued (Mead, 2003). Little acknowledgement is made of the *process of change* professionals may undergo during and after training, which enables them to espouse values which give coherence to everything they do. In this study I am interested in examining the implications of this for the school-based element of teacher education.

Background

It would seem that the TTA guidance expects school-based mentors to be able to articulate the links between curriculum values, personal and social development and effective learning, and assess their student's understanding of this, 'although trainees may not teach PSHE/Ct.' (p. 26). It is difficult to see how this understanding can be assessed simply on the evidence of the student's overall planning, teaching and management. Reynolds (2001) argues that planning is a skill and does not reflect a *process* of change in personal perception, which the concept of inclusion may require:

> Inclusion demands a particular evaluative standpoint: that we value others equally. Inclusion also demands that we act on those values. The role of values is crucial here. Subscription to central values of inclusion, such as respect for the humanity of others, acceptance of difference and belief in equality, is essential. This is so because typically values direct our everyday decisions and professional practice. (p. 468)

It follows that providing for inclusion demands a disposition on the part of the teacher to promote the good for each pupil. Such a disposition, as Reynolds argues, is located in the teacher's concern for social justice as a citizen. Whether that disposition has been arrived at, and how, will have to be the concern of the school mentor, as well as looking for evidence for inclusion in planned differentiation and classroom provision.

A key part of this process must be the way in which discussion about, observation of, and the teaching of PSHE/Ct. will enable students to make implicit values explicit and particularly through the key elements of the PSHE/Ct. Framework (DFES/QCA, 1999) which embrace inclusion, citizenship with multiculturalism central to political literacy, and sex and relationships education (SRE).

Just as Reynolds has argued that a teacher's exemplification of inclusion is informed by their own values of social justice as a citizen, so I have argued elsewhere (Mead, 2000, 2001) that the discrete teaching of Citizenship within the primary PSHE/Ct. framework will ideally lead to student teachers and experienced teachers exploring their own concept of citizenship. Mentors might exemplify the *process* of articulating their own understanding of citizenship, in constructive dialogue with their pupils, and with student teachers. Challenging as it may be, this would ideally happen in those aspects of political literacy introduced into the 2000 PSHE/Ct. framework and which express the inclusive ideal underpinning teaching and learning. Those aspects focus on democratic approaches to 'different kinds of rights and responsibilities' (DFES/QCA, p. 139) 'the consequences of racism' (ibid.) and an 'appreciation of the range of ethnic identities in the United Kingdom' (ibid.).

As Le Roux (2001) argues, the degree to which multicultural education is to be realized will depend on 'the attitudes, knowledge and behaviour of classroom teachers' (p. 18). Robinson and Robinson (2001) have highlighted how, since the Macpherson Report on racism, following the Stephen Lawrence murder inquiry, it is no longer acceptable for student teachers' mentors to refuse to address aspects of multiculturalism. Teacher educators do have a responsibility to engage student teachers in developing appropriate curriculum content and teaching methods, which address racism and difference. In school this might be focused on the relationship between pedagogy and teacher values, both at the level of managing diverse classrooms and teaching about difference in the context of PSHE/Ct.

According to the guidance for assessing Standard 2.2 mentors will need to ensure that students 'know how PSHE/Ct. might reduce health inequalities and promote inclusion, participation and action' (TTA, p. 27). Health Education, as South, Tifford and Walsh (1998) have demonstrated, has suffered from inconsistency of provision in Initial Teacher Education (ITE), with the emphasis, until recently, on information imparting and less on decision-making skills. The introduction of Sex and Relationships Education (SRE) as part of Curriculum 2000 has brought with it a set of guidelines for ITE (Teacher Training Agency, 2000). These embrace both values and skills and assume that student teachers will have the opportunities to practise them in school, with the guidance of a mentor:

Trainee teachers are not exempt from the realities facing all teachers contributing to Sex and Relationships Education and can expect, particularly during their school-based training, to meet similar issues to those outlined in the DFES' Guidance. (TTA, p. 1)

South, Tifford and Walsh (1998) emphasize the need for student teachers to engage with values and understanding, which informs planning and teaching. The TTA guidance identifies the need for mentoring in the selection of appropriate materials and teaching methods, and opportunities to learn from an experienced teacher about how to set boundaries.

If we believe that learning to teach is a '*process* of human development' (Mead, 2003, p. 38) the contribution of teacher education towards an inclusive education will be through student teachers discussing values which inform planning with colleagues, by experiencing PSHE/Ct. which ideally makes inclusive values explicit and, by engaging in critical reflection with a mentor who supports, observes and above all understands the process the student is undergoing. We now turn to the data for evidence of the extent to which this process is developing within the school-based element of teacher education.

Methodology

The main source of data was a questionnaire given to two sets of student teachers on their final school-based placements. Five structured questions were asked about student teachers' opportunities to:

- discuss PSHE/Ct. policy and planning with staff, including the coordinator;
- observe PSHE/Ct. being taught in a variety of ways;
- teach PSHE/Ct. using a variety of methods and skills;
- discuss and evaluate the extent to which PSHE/Ct. contributes to the multi-cultural awareness of pupils;
- observe or teach SRE.

The questionnaire was administered over the 2000–1 and 2002–3 period during which time the Curriculum 2000 PSHE/Ct. framework was published and implemented in a non-statutory form. The 2000–1 group consisted of thirty-one B.Ed. students, all of whom were collecting data for a PSHE/Ct. dissertation. The 2002–3 group consisted of seventy-one PGCE students. In addition, fifty mentor reports from both periods were scrutinized for PSHE/Ct. targets at the interim and summative stages of a final placement.

Summary of Findings

1. The data suggests that, over the two periods of the research, opportunities to discuss the aims and purposes of PSHE/Ct. have not increased commensurate with the opportunities to teach it.

2. In 2002–3, 36 per cent of students were unable to observe PSHE/Ct. being taught, but there is an improvement of 12 per cent on the 2000–1 period of those able to observe more than one method.

3. In 2002–3, 90 per cent of students taught a PSHE/Ct. lesson, but as finding one shows, discussion overall dropped and 17 per cent of the 90 per cent taught without any guidance or planning.

4. In 2002–3, 42 per cent of students discussed and evaluated the contribution of PSHE/Ct. to multi-cultural awareness, an increase of 10 per cent on the previous period. Of these, 73 per cent discussed values as well as planning.

5. A significant 69 per cent of students in 2002–3 had no contact with SRE. However, the quality of the observational opportunities did improve on the previous period.

Findings

1. Opportunities to Discuss the Policy/Planning and Delivery of PSHE/Ct. with Staff Including a Coordinator 2000–1

Totals: Nil: 19%
Documents only: 7%
Discussion: 74%

Opportunities to Discuss the Policy/Planning and Delivery of PSHE/Ct. with Staff Including a Coordinator 2002–3

Totals: Nil. 30%
Documents only: 11%
Discussion: 59%

Over the two periods of the research, lack of time, the absence of a policy, a scheme of work with discrete time and a coordinator were the main reasons for the lack of discussion about the aims and value of PSHE/Ct.:

I tried to discuss the policy with other staff but there was no coordinator or recent policy.

PSHE/Ct. was not being carried out in the school and there was no policy in place.

The same reasons for the lack of discussion exist in 2003 but are multiplied by 15 per cent. Possible reasons for fewer opportunities to discuss might be the demands of the literacy and numeracy hours over this period, in spite of the introduction of the PSHE/Ct. framework in autumn 2000. Another reason is that the 2000–1 sample is made up of B.Ed. students who were all collecting PSHE/Ct. dissertation data and who might have been more insistent about talking to someone.

It is worth considering if the quality of the discussion was any better when there seemed to be more of it. The 2002–3 data shows limited discussion, largely determined by the need to plan and teach a lesson of PSHE/Ct. as a requirement of the final placement:

the school provided opportunities to teach PSHE/Ct. during my time there, although there did not appear to be an established programme, thus I did not discuss planning further than what I could do for each session.

Very brief discussion with class teacher prior to first lesson of teaching it.

There is some evidence in the 2002–3 data of a few opportunities to go beyond simply planning:

Opportunities to discuss were good, the coordinator had produced a very thorough and comprehensive policy which she explained very well.

There were good opportunities to discuss as the policy was being rewritten.

I had the opportunity to meet with the PSHE/Ct. coordinator to discuss the PSHE/Ct. curriculum and the aims.

Good quality discussion includes consideration of the aims and purposes of PSHE/Ct.:

We had a discussion about the importance of PSHE/Ct. lessons and the issues that may arise due to such lessons.

Aims and purposes may also be linked to evaluation of the teaching:

I was able to discuss the policy with my teacher-tutor and mentor and evaluate lessons taught.

Although there appear to be more opportunities to discuss in 2000–1, the quality of the discussion does not seem to be any better than in the 2002–3 period. Discussion for some students constituted 2–3 minutes in the staff room. For some there was no real opportunity to discuss the policy, 'however, we would discuss what had to be taught'. The importance attached to PSHE/Ct. by the mentor, and the enthusiasm and efficiency of the coordinator were factors, which affected the quality of discussion. Some students had been able to talk with the coordinator, attend a staff meeting with a focus on PSHE and follow this up by talking with their teacher-tutor. Others had engaged in fuller discussion through attending INSET based on the revision and implementation of a policy document.

Examples of good practice are evident, but there appears to be no qualitative development of discussion between students and coordinators about the value and purpose of PSHE/Ct. which is commensurate with the increased opportunities to plan and teach it.

2. Opportunities to Observe a Variety of Methods of Teaching PSHE/Citizenship

2000–1

No opportunity: 32%   Opportunity to observe: 68%

2002–3

No opportunity: 36%   Opportunity to observe: 64%

Of 2000–1 students 32 per cent were not able to observe good practice in PSHE/Ct., largely because of the absence of discrete PSHE/Ct. or its unpredictable appearance on the timetable:

> PSHE wasn't explicitly taught within the school and there was no timetabled slot. Therefore I was unable to observe any teaching.

> PSHE was often taken off the timetable to make room for other activities to happen. In seven weeks there was only one opportunity to observe and one opportunity to teach.

Similar reasons are given by 36 per cent of 2002–3 students, some of whom point out that the only PSHE/ Ct. was that taught by the student:

> PSHE was only taught during my lessons and disappeared from the timetable when I was not teaching.

> There wasn't much in place and I had to initiate the teaching and planning of it myself.

As a result, some students felt that they were feeling their way:

> I didn't really get a chance to see it and when I taught it I was really guessing as to the correct way.

> Another student states that, 'the class teacher did not really model PSHE/Ct. teaching for me, as the school didn't really do it in Year 5'. As a result, this student drew on some experience of PSHE/Ct. during her first school experience and, 'the years I have spent "handling" my own son'.

The majority of those able to observe anything across both periods of the research observed one lesson with one method used, e.g. circle time in Year 4. Some students cited as their one observation a PSHE/Ct. element in another subject, for example, 'RE was taught in a variety of creative ways'. The difficulty with this, from a training perspective, is ensuring the student's understanding of how RE might be contributing to the cross-curricular teaching of PSHE/Ct.

There is only a 4 per cent increase in opportunities to observe over the two periods, but is there any improvement in the quality of the observations? This would include observations of a variety of teaching styles and observations in different key stages. Of those who did observe in 2000–1, 24 per cent saw a variety of methods and observed more than one lesson across key stages:

> Role-play, discussion, circle time, written work, all were used as methods when PSHE/Ct. was taught.

> I was able to observe different year groups participating in PSHE/Ct. This was good to see and to note the progression that is made through the separate departments within the school.

> I was given the opportunity to observe three other PSHE lessons at key stages 1 and 2.

Of those who observed PSHE/Ct. teaching in 2002–3, 36 per cent saw a variety of methods and across year groups, an improvement of 12 per cent. Where there was consistent provision, students highlighted the opportunity to observe each teacher using 'their own approach', even within the context of a method like circle time. This is important modelling because it demonstrates the way in which the relationship between the personal and the professional relate in the context of PSHE/Ct.

3. Opportunities to Teach PSHE/Ct. Using a Variety of Methods and Skills

2000–1

No opportunity to teach: 16% Opportunity to teach: 84%

2002–3

No opportunity to teach: 10% Opportunity to teach: 90%

In the 2000–1 period limited opportunities to teach PSHE/Ct. are caused by the absence of discrete time, a scheme of work and a coordinator. Students gave negative responses such as the following:

> There were no opportunities as the school did not teach PSHE explicitly.

> I would have liked to have tried circle time but it wasn't planned into the timetable and I wouldn't have known where to start.

The data suggests that the reasons why PSHE/Ct. might not be taught remain in 2002–3 but time is made for a significant number of students (90 per cent) to teach a lesson. The findings suggest that more students are being provided with the course entitlement to teach at least one PSHE/Ct. lesson, but are not necessarily working from a weekly scheme of work or policy which has been discussed with a coordinator, and they have not necessarily been able to observe experienced teachers model a variety of teaching methods with different age groups.

As opportunities to teach PSHE/Ct. are high over both periods of the research we need to consider if there has been any progress in the quality of the opportunity to teach. This would include support in planning and resourcing and mentoring in pedagogy. Ideally it would include the opportunity to teach a sequence of lessons.

Of those in 2000–1, 46 per cent who had the opportunity to teach PSHE/Ct. actually taught a sequence, based on a scheme of work and using a variety of methods/resources with some mentoring:

I taught a seven week sequence of lessons to the class. This worked well and I was pleased with the results. The children really enjoyed the lessons and became very open and enthusiastic about the subject.

I implemented PSHE, (none to observe) via circle time, conflict resolution, open forums and positive affirmations activities.

I taught six PSHE lessons focusing on drama as a method. I then used reflection through log-books for children to record feelings.

I would use methods such as discussion on a particular topic, for instance set up a story, and discuss what the characters would or should do. I would try to relate to them by sharing my previous experiences and how I felt. This involved group work and individual work.

Of those in 2002–3, 81 per cent who were able to teach PSHE/Ct. actually taught a sequence of lessons and used a variety of methods. The length of time varied from 20 minutes to 1 hour per week. However, although the opportunity to teach was provided, 17 per cent of students were not planning from, and being guided by, a school scheme of work:

Yes I was allowed to use my own ideas and teaching methods in order to teach PSHE.

I was given a free hand to do this and tried several different approaches including drama.

In some cases, such freedom was positively creative:

I employed a variety of different methods and indeed the other teachers used my planning to adapt their own strategies on a number of occasions.

However, for such a challenging area of teaching, it was surprising how some students were left to decide on the lesson content, in one case, 'based on what I thought the children needed to be looking at'. Students

may have had the entitlement to teach PSHE/Ct. but for some classes this was a new experience and students would have needed more mentoring, especially lesson observation feedback:

I used a variety of methods to teach the subject, although time was very restricting (20 minutes per week). Children in the class were not at all used to the teaching methods and sometimes seemed unresponsive, for example, in circle time.

Only three students in the 2002–3 group explicitly refer to their mentor or class teacher observing them teach and giving them feedback. This is supported by the scrutiny of 50 interim and summative mentor reports from both research periods. Overall, only 8 per cent contained explicit targets for developing PSHE/Ct. teaching.

Some students were teaching the PSHE/Ct. framework through other subjects which poses the question, particularly in the case of Science, whether or not values came into it. One student taught healthy eating through Science, but felt that she only really addressed values in a dedicated period of PSHE, which she organized herself, and for which she received less guidance and mentoring.

Finally, we are still left with 10 per cent of students who felt uncomfortable about asking to teach PSHE/Ct. once:

There was not a formal slot timetabled for PSHE. This meant that to teach it I put the teacher under pressure to reorganise the timetable.

4. Opportunities to Discuss and Evaluate the Extent to which the Teaching of PSHE/Citizenship Contributes to the Multi-cultural Awareness of Pupils

2000–1

No opportunity to discuss: 68%   Opportunity to discuss: 32%

2002–3

No opportunity to discuss: 58%   Opportunity to discuss: 42%

Three points emerge across both periods of the research relating to the absence of the opportunity to discuss and evaluate the extent to which PSHE/Ct. contributes to multi-cultural awareness. The first is any opportunity to evaluate the benefits of PSHE/Ct. teaching:

I think the school recognised the importance of PSHE in relation to this but I wasn't guided as such to the benefits of PSHE.

Secondly, students did not necessarily receive mentoring and lesson feedback on 'how to take children forward in their social and cultural development'. Thirdly, and of particular significance, was the assumption made by a number of students that multi-cultural awareness was not relevant to their school:

This didn't happen because there were no multi-cultural children in the school.

The first two points clearly relate to the mentoring of PSHE/Ct. teaching which we have discussed in the previous finding. The third point reflects more the perceptions of the individual student and ought to be addressed in the Professional Studies element of the university-based sessions.

In order to understand how the school contribution to teacher education in multi-cultural awareness might develop, we need to look at the quality of the discussion that went on in schools over the research period. About 50 per cent of those who discussed the subject in the 2000–1 period, actually discussed values more than objectives and outcomes:

I observed my teacher-tutor teaching circle time. I discussed the social and cultural effect of this with her afterwards. Otherwise, there was very little feedback given on my own teaching of PSHE.

There was discussion with the PSHE/Ct. coordinator and the RE coordinator about future planning. The PSHE coordinator was able to give an overall history of pupils' moral, social and cultural development and through which curriculum areas this was achieved.

Yes, I was monitored by my class teacher and we did get into depth about what the children got from the lesson and to check if the objectives were PSHE based. Thankfully they were and we looked at how the social and cultural aspects were developed during the lesson.

The other 50 per cent tended to discuss objectives and outcomes more than values, such as those surrounding multi-cultural awareness:

After each PSHE lesson, as with other lessons, discussion (very brief) was held between myself and the class teacher (also my mentor). These were not discussed in the light of their contribution to the moral, social and cultural development of pupils, only in terms of how fun the activities were!

Two lessons were observed, one by my mentor and one by my class teacher, but the discussion was about the quality of teaching in relation to the learning objectives rather than the social and cultural aspects of PSHE.

Of those who discussed multi-cultural issues in the 2002–3 period, 73 per cent actually talked about the values relating to social and cultural development which PSHE/Ct. might contribute to, rather than just the process of planning and the outcomes, such as pupil enjoyment. This is an improvement on 2000–1 of 23 per cent:

There was not much diversity within the school and my teacher was keen to address this. However, we realised it was going to be a gradual process. The RE programme had also been altered so the children had a greater awareness of other cultures.

This was limited, although when evaluating my lessons with my teacher-tutor, I was able to discuss these social and cultural issues.

This improvement in the quality of discussion is echoed in the mentor reports which show that 75 per cent of PSHE/Ct. targets were related to promoting cultural understanding and are found in the 2002–3 period. However, the 2002–3 responses also highlight the lack of observations and mentor feedback for many, identified in finding 3. Although some students may have been teaching respect and difference and, in the case of one student, the multi-cultural make-up of Britain, overall they received very little guidance with such sensitive issues, and in some cases, encountered 'a staff reluctance to discuss and give opinions'. The remaining 27 per cent of the 2002–3 group tended to discuss objectives and outcomes, confirming the trend in the previous period, although a smaller percentage.

5. *Opportunities to Discuss, Observe or Teach Any Aspects of Sex and Relationships Education*

2000–1

No opportunity: 58%   Opportunity to observe: 0

Opportunity to discuss: 19% Opportunity to teach: 23%

2002–3

No opportunity: 69%   Opportunity to observe: 14%

Opportunity to discuss: 6% Opportunity to teach: 11%

One practical reason given for no contact with SRE relates to the timing of school placements and when in the year a class does SRE; however, some schools have addressed this by enabling students to observe other year groups. Another reason is the perception that SRE does not apply to Key Stage 1, a misperception which ought to be addressed through familiarity with both the PSHE/Ct. framework and the SRE guidelines. A third reason is an assumption made in some schools that students should have nothing to do with this area of the curriculum; for example, one student had to teach ICT while another group had SRE with the class teacher, thereby preventing any observation or teaching opportunities. Another student stated that:

> I was not allowed to cover this with my class. This section of the teaching unit was kept until my placement had finished. It was felt that a student couldn't handle teaching in these areas.

The three reasons for a lack of opportunity can be addressed and certainly more students could observe experienced teachers teaching SRE. If this were possible, we might look at the data to identify what quality of discussion and mentoring a student might expect. In the 2000–1 data this largely consisted of an interview with the Head or PSHE/Ct. coordinator. In the 2002–3 period students had some opportunities to discuss policy when this was under review and included in staff meetings:

> Upper school were discussing the teaching of SRE and I was able to take part in the discussion and hear the approach that they decided to take.

> SRE was undergoing a policy change and so I had the opportunity to contribute to ideas for teaching and approaches.

Students in 2002–3 had more opportunities to observe others, including outside specialists:

> My teacher-tutor taught SRE during my first week using a video, this was the last lesson in the unit.

> Very little observed, one lesson of PSHE where the teacher followed a scheme from a book (read it out and asked questions of class) and watched a sex education video.

> I observed the nurse's visit to year 6 and she told the children that she would be offering drop in sessions and would be available at secondary school in September.

Although fewer students had any contact with SRE in the 2002–3 period, there are signs that the quality of observations and discussions which did occur have the potential to link values with approaches.

Again, although fewer students had the opportunity to teach SRE in 2002–3, we need to analyse the quality of teaching opportunities across both periods in order to highlight good practice. There are those who taught with guidance and mentoring:

> I taught about relationships and friendship through drama and reflection. We talked about setting boundaries in a staff meeting and teachers reflected on their experience.

> Within the Science curriculum I was required to teach a sequence of lessons about healthy living. In the course of this sequence I taught about relationships and had informal chats about setting boundaries with the teacher who held circle time sessions and with the Head who was the PSHE coordinator.

By contrast there were those who were given no guidance on setting boundaries, or who relied on their own judgements:

> In terms of setting boundaries, I felt confident in my own knowledge and understanding but it would have been good to have had some input and ways to further the SRE.

In terms of content, the topics of Sex and Relationships were still not always integrated which would provide the values education experience for students. There were those who taught about relationships in terms of the family and friendship and those who taught Sex Education in a science unit, but not in PSHE.

Conclusion to the Research

The data has been interpreted in the light of the premise that inclusive teaching and learning will be achieved by teachers whose professional training is essentially a process of human development. This is why, first and foremost, time for students and colleagues to discuss and evaluate the explicit aims and values of PSHE/Ct. during a final school placement will be one way in which inclusive values permeate all planning, teaching and learning.

Secondly, students clearly appreciate the opportunity to observe different teachers modelling a variety of methods in PSHE/Ct., which exemplifies how they have adapted methods in the process of integrating personal and professional values. This is the reality of the *process of change* Reynolds talks of and the way in which teachers can espouse inclusive values without coercion.

Thirdly, the process which allows values to inform planning and teaching is only glimpsed through a single opportunity to teach PSHE/Ct. Likewise, being given a free hand to do whatever you like in PSHE/Ct. may be a challenge welcomed by some students, but, as we have seen, may not be a managed process of personal and professional development. If students are to undergo a process of change as they engage with values in the classroom, they will need opportunities to discuss with, be observed by, receive feedback from and evaluate with an experienced mentor who understands this process.

To enhance provision in all partnership schools, the research suggests that there needs to be greater recognition of the centrality of multi-cultural awareness and understanding within the political literacy section of the PSHE/Ct. framework. The best examples of mentoring in this area involve discussing, modelling and evaluating the contribution that PSHE/Ct. can make to children's moral, social and cultural development. Most significantly, the research highlights how this mentoring can lead to a student having a placement interim target such as, 'be imaginative in promoting cultural understanding'.

In conclusion, the suggestion that SRE is outside the final school experience may reflect a more widespread view that mentoring in PSHE/Ct. is about supporting a student in teaching one lesson, but, without a great deal of engagement in their formative experience of handling sensitive and controversial issues. The research findings may reassure mentors about what is appropriate provision for SRE. Opportunities to engage in policy and planning revision are valued by students, so are opportunities to observe experienced teachers or visitors. Students indicate that they would also welcome feedback on their development of new pedagogic skills in SRE, which are at the heart of all values education, such as the setting of boundaries.

References

DFES/QCA (1999) 'Framework for Personal, Social and Health Education and Citizenship Key Stages 1 and 2, in *The National Curriculum Handbook for Primary Teachers in England*, pp. 136–41. London: DFEE/QCA.

LE ROUX, J. (2001) 'Effective Teacher Training for Multi-Cultural Teaching', *Multi-Cultural Teaching*, 19 (2), pp. 18–22.

MEAD, N. (2000) 'Researching Skills Common to Religious Education and Citizenship', in S. Clipson-Boyles (ed.), *Putting Research into Practice in Primary Teaching and Learning*. London: Fulton.

MEAD, N. (2001) 'Identifying Pedagogic Skills Common to Religious Education and Citizenship and the Implications for Continuing Professional Development', *Curriculum*, 22 (2), pp. 43–51.

MEAD, N. (2003) 'Will the Introduction of Teaching Standards in Professional Values and Practice Put the Heart Back into Primary Teacher Education?', *Journal of Pastoral Care in Education*, 21 (1), pp. 37–42.

REYNOLDS, M. (2001) 'Education for Inclusion and the Teacher Training Agency Standards', *Journal of In-Service Education*, 27 (3), pp. 465–76.

ROBINSON, I. and ROBINSON, J. (2001) 'Sometimes It's Hard to Get a Taxi When You are Black: The Implications of the Macpherson Report for Teacher Education', *Journal of In-Service Education*, 27 (2), pp. 303–21.

SOUTH, J., TIFFORD, S. and WALSH, S. (1998) *Health Education in Initial Teacher Training: A Survey of Health Education*. Leeds: Leeds Health Education Unit.

TEACHER TRAINING AGENCY (2000) *Sex and Relationships Education, Issues for ITT Providers*. London: TTA.

TEACHER TRAINING AGENCY (2002) *Qualifying to Teach, Handbook of Guidance*. London: TTA.

Correspondence
Oxford Brookes University
Westminster Institute of Education
Harcourt Hill
Oxford, OX2 9AT
Tel.: 01865 488294
E-mail: nmead@brookes.ac.uk

Journal of Education for Teaching
Vol. 33, No. 3, August 2007, pp. 309–321

Routledge
Taylor & Francis Group

How effectively does the Graduate Teacher Programme contribute to the development of trainee teachers' professional values?

Nick Mead*

Oxford Brookes University, UK

Employment routes into teaching, such as the Graduate Teacher Programme (GTP), are making an increasingly significant contribution to teacher training, but does such training provide opportunities for education in professional values? In the light of Ofsted reports which suggest that GTP trainees often bring particularly well-developed professional values to their training, the purpose of this small-scale study is to gain insights into the nature and implementation of the values of a GTP primary cohort in the first phase of their training. The findings identify that GTP trainees do have well-established values, and high expectations about implementing them, but they experience varying degrees of coherence between these values and their implementation in teaching, learning and classroom management. However, there is sufficient evidence to suggest that the highly individualised nature of the GTP does potentially lend itself to a coherent relationship between professional values and practice. In order for that potential to be realised, the study makes three recommendations for teacher educators: enable trainees to integrate well-developed professional values into their individual training plans at induction, give particular attention to the reflective and dialogical skills of mentors, and integrate central training into the reflective process of trainees' values education.

Background

Employment-based routes into teaching

The Graduate Teacher Programme (GTP) is an employment-based teacher training route. It has been in operation since 1998 and 'has grown in size since then to the point where it is responsible for at least one in ten newly qualified teachers (NQT)' (TDA, 2003, p. 1). Such routes, according to Smithers and Robinson (2006, p. 3), are undoubtedly making an important contribution to the diversification of the

*Westminster Institute of Education, Oxford Brookes University, Harcourt Hill, Oxford OX2 9AT, UK. Email: nmead@brookes.ac.uk

ISSN 0260-7476 (print)/ISSN 1360-0540 (online)/07/030309-13
© 2007 Taylor & Francis
DOI: 10.1080/02607470701450296

intake, bringing a higher proportion of mature entrants, more males, and more recruits from ethnic minorities into primary teaching.

There are now 103 GTP providers in existence. Various models exist, including Higher Education Institute (HEI)-based, Local Authority (LA)-based and school-consortium-based. Well qualified and self-starting graduates are selected to be employees of a specific school or within an LA and are given a training salary of £13,000. A training grant of £4120 is paid to the major training school. A minor school placement of a contrasting kind is also required. Although employed, trainees must remain supernumerary so that high quality training can be guaranteed, for example, undertaking directed research tasks in school and attending centrally organised training sessions. A particular feature of the GTP route is an Initial Needs Assessment undertaken by trainee and mentor prior to commencing the programme. This is intended to identify how previous knowledge and experience can be accredited towards meeting the Qualified Teacher Status (QTS) standards, as well as establishing new targets for the induction period. Second, the trainee has an Individual Training Plan which reflects on a weekly basis how previous knowledge, skills and experience are being built upon and new targets set throughout the period of training.

The recruitment to, and structure of, the GTP route into teaching raises two key questions for trainee teachers' values development. First, to what extent do mature and often very experienced individuals have the opportunity to take forward and implement clarified and well-established personal and professional values in their new role? Second, to what extent can the structure of the GTP programme which is primarily school-based, with a limited number of centrally-based training sessions, provide trainees with the opportunities to articulate their values, discuss them with other professionals and trainees, and develop them through reading and reflection? The purpose of this paper is to address these key questions through a consideration of what current literature has to say about values development within GTP training, followed by an analysis of values data collected from a cohort of primary GTP trainees. It would seem that these are pertinent questions to ask at a time when new QTS standards for September 2007 are to be 'underpinned by the five outcomes of Every Child Matters' (TDA, 2006, p. 3). The importance of Every Child Matters (DFES, 2004) for teachers in England is that it will involve them in a value-laden, multi-agency approach to the well-being of all children, based on health, safety, enjoyment and achievement, making a positive contribution and economic well-being.

Existing graduate teacher programme research data

What comes across most significantly in the GTP Ofsted (Office for Standards in Education, Children's Services and Skills in England and Wales) inspection data is the fact that the GTP route as an employment route into teaching attracts many career switchers who would not otherwise have this opportunity available to enter teaching and, as Mayotte (2003) has identified, they bring with them a strong sense of self and, in relation to that, clearly developed personal and professional values:

Research has shown that many career switchers have developed skill in interactions with people, insight into human nature, and a well-defined sense of self through former work. In the move to teaching, career switchers often bring an articulated sense of mission and agency, a strong sense of commitment. (p. 682)

Mayotte's findings are echoed in the Ofsted GTP report findings covering 2003–2004 and 2004–2005:

GTP trainees are highly committed and determined to be successful teachers. Their main strengths are professionalism, their ability to organise and manage classes, and their commitment to inclusion and raising pupil achievement. (Ofsted, 2005, p. 2; 2006, p. 13)

This overall finding is found particularly well evidenced for primary trainees who treated pupils with respect and consideration and recognised the importance of effective support if pupils were to make good progress. They ensured that questions were directed to all groups of pupils and included reticent pupils in class discussion. Well-developed personal and professional values were particularly evident in the trainees' proactive approach to their own professional development:

Most were keen to be successful teachers who took advice readily and worked hard to move their practice forward. Nearly all had shown themselves to be effective learners who had improved during the course of the year. Their progress was attributable to their motivation and ability to get the most out of their training and experience offered. (Ofsted, 2005, p. 12)

Mayotte identifies how a strong self-understanding with its pertaining relationship between personal and professional values does not always easily translate into classroom practice. Trainees may not recognise how previous personal and professional development can be transferred. The Ofsted findings highlight the high level of personal commitment and professionalism of these GTP trainees which is not always matched by sufficient development in depth of evaluations of the impact of teaching on learning (2005, pp. 2–3). For one third of the sample this may reflect too narrow a focus on behaviour management at the expense of reflecting on teaching (Ofsted, 2005, p. 14; 2006, pp. 2, 3).

Such weaknesses do not reflect a lack of commitment to individual needs, differentiation and inclusion; rather, they might reflect a limitation on the part of the GTP programme to deepen the application of individual's strongly held values to the effectiveness of their teaching. The way in which this should happen is through the matching of the Initial Needs Assessment to the subsequent tailoring of the Individual Training Programme (ITP). Ofsted's findings on this process highlight:

In over half of the GTP's the links between initial needs assessment and the development of training plans are tenuous, and a quarter of the GTP trainees visited did not have an adequate training plan to guide their learning and development. (Ofsted, 2005, para. 17, p. 6; 2006, para. 21, p. 7)

From the trainee perspective, 31% felt that the process for assessing their initial needs in the light of their previous experience was only adequate (TDA, 2005, p. 6). Ofsted identifies the key factor contributing to trainee progress to be the mentor's ability to give time and reflection to articulating good practice:

> Where a mentor fully understands good practice in teaching and is able to articulate clearly how pupils' subject learning can be best supported, the quality of the training is high. Such training is challenging and sets high expectations for the graduate trainee. (Ofsted, 2005, para. 25, p. 8; 2006, pp. 3–4, para. 38, p. 12)

The TDA trainee survey of 2005 (p. 11) suggests that 21% of trainees felt that their mentoring was adequate or poor.

Some of the mismatch between the well-developed values of GTP trainees and their implementation in classroom practice suggested by the Ofsted data may reflect what Ball (1999) and Brookes (2005) consider to be the issue of how employment-based routes into teaching are in danger of making initial teacher education (ITE) 'pedestrian and utilitarian, eliminating emotion and desire from teaching' (Brookes, 2005, p. 49). Foster (2001) raises the question about whether trainees on Graduate Teacher Programmes are guaranteed such opportunities to: 'reflect with other trainee teachers or reflect on their experiences and develop a personal framework and rationale for their professional practice' (p. 15). Furlong (2000), Smith and Reid (2000) and Williams and Soares (2002) all suggest that if trainee teachers are to understand pedagogy and the management of children's learning, they need to be encouraged in a university environment to 'think more deeply about the educational purposes underlying their teaching' (Furlong, 2000, p. 6).

In the light of these issues, the purpose of this small-scale study is to gain deeper insights into the strength and nature of the professional values of a GTP primary cohort and analyse the process of them implementing their values in the first phase of their training. It is hoped that the findings may address aspects of the lack of coherence between these values and their implementation within the employment-based training experience. As a result, the conclusions reached might contribute to a more informed view about whether or not employment routes into teaching are in fact in danger of becoming 'pedestrian and utilitarian' at a time when the implementation of Every Child Matters (DFES, 2004) requires teachers to clarify and reflect on their professional values.

Methodology

The GTP cohort consisted of 22 primary trainees, all of whom had developed previous careers such as area sales team manager and outward bound centre warden. In line with the Training and Development Agency (TDA) priority categories for teacher training, 11 of the 22 places were held by teaching assistants (TAs). Data were collected during the induction period in the July prior to the programme commencing through until the end of the second term.

The methods involved a questionnaire on beliefs and values about teaching completed before the course at the trainee induction meeting. The questionnaire consisted of four questions:

1. What are your beliefs and values about teaching as you prepare to enter the GTP programme?

2. How have these beliefs and values been shaped by previous life and work experiences?
3. Do you have any evidence of these beliefs and values which might contribute to the initial ITP audit?
4. How do you think that you will be able to put into practice your beliefs and values about teaching in the initial weeks of the GTP programme?

Second, there was an analysis of the trainees' and mentors' phase one evaluations, covering the transition from the Initial Needs Assessment in relation to previous experience, the setting up of the Individual Training Programme, and the first three months of training. Key evaluations for our data included a 1–4 rating with qualitative comments on the production of the ITP, mentor support, lesson observation and feedback, and whole school support. Third, data were collected from the trainees' evaluations of the central training sessions provided by the GTP Higher Education Institution (HEI) partners. Evaluation sheets asked trainees to record the extent to which the theory and practice in the sessions had met their needs as GTP trainees. Fourth, a qualitative questionnaire was completed which gave trainees the time and the writing space to elaborate on the single question, 'What opportunities have I had on the primary GTP course to think and talk about my values as a teacher?'

Summary of findings

The findings identify that GTP trainees do have well-established professional values on entry to their training, and have high expectations about implementing these values in their classroom practice. The data suggest that in their first phase of training these trainees experience varying degrees of coherence between their professional values and the implementation of these values in teaching, learning and classroom management. However, there is sufficient evidence to believe that the highly individualised nature of the GTP does potentially lend itself to a coherent relationship between values and practice.

Analysis and discussion of the GTP data

The values of GTP trainees at induction

GTP trainees are highly motivated through strong beliefs and values about teaching. The induction questionnaire asked trainees: 'What are your beliefs and values about teaching as you prepare to enter the GTP programme?' It was possible to break the responses down into three categories: values about developing human potential, values relating to the role of the teacher, and values about pupil entitlement. Strong beliefs about developing human potential were expressed by a number of trainees, particularly focusing on 'providing opportunities for children to realise their potential' through 'different learning styles', and which 'could be celebrated by all involved'.

Beliefs about the role and influence of the teacher and qualities needed could be broken down into three kinds.

First, values were reflected in the general influence and responsibility of the teacher. Trainees expressed how primary teachers play a fundamental role in the development of children and have a 'tremendous influence' on their future education: 'Teachers play an important role in the development of children and I believe that teachers must take responsibility, yet also know that to enjoy the job will help to be a positive influence on the students' (Trainee 7). Being a good role model, teaching by example, and setting high standards and expectations were key values expressed by Trainee 12. Values were also expressed about the demands but also fulfilment of the work: 'Teaching is hard but enjoyable work', and 'A worthwhile career where I can make difference' (Trainee 16). Other qualities were identified which reflected positive values about the challenging nature of teaching: 'Multi-tasking, facing challenges, communication, working within a team, dedication, determination, flexibility, ability to foresee circumstances' (Trainee 3).

Second, values were expressed about how children learn. Significantly, a good deal of emphasis was placed on all aspects of the child's development; for example, Trainee 6 states that 'I've wanted to teach for a long time and I believe in a child-centred approach to the pupil and a team approach to the staff'. For some in the cohort who have been TAs these beliefs reflect their previous experience; for others, it may express that valuing of the intrinsic in education, which they may have found missing from their previous career.

What is impressive across the responses is the commitment to individual learning and the crucial role of the teacher's values in this commitment. Trainee 5 talks about how teaching 'plays a major role in a child's personal, social and intellectual development', and Trainee 11 wishes to 'enable children to fulfil their potential as whole people, both in cognitive and social skills'. Trainee 9 describes teaching the child as 'a whole person requiring a "hands on" holistic approach, academically, socially and emotionally'. Trainee 10 highlights the importance of 'mutual respect, tolerance and understanding', linking these to 'self-esteem and confidence as at the root of all achievement'. This is echoed by Trainee 11, who wishes pupils to 'feel valued and to learn to value themselves'. For Trainee 13, self-respect and self-value will enable the child to 'go on to the next stage of their life prepared and confident, being able to reflect on their achievements and abilities'.

Third, values were expressed about classrooms and classroom ethos. The key values expressed relate to an inclusive, enjoyable, purposeful and well-organised learning environment. Trainee 18 places value on an inclusive ethos in which understanding of individual needs 'involves all parties, parents, colleagues, and specialist help as appropriate, in order for pupils to achieve their potential'. Importantly, trainees clearly relate a positive and stimulating environment to a holistic concept of pupil success. Trainee 6 believes that the more enjoyable and stimulating the teaching environment, 'the more responsive children will be, and consequently, the greater the learning and social output will occur'. Trainee 17 sums up the key values well: 'teaching should be enjoyable and have a purpose. The teacher should respect the child's background and culture and have the interests of the class in mind.'

Finally, the data highlight a third category of beliefs about entitlement of opportunity. These data underpin much of the specific examples above and tend to be appended to it, when mentioned explicitly. For some trainees it reflects a strong belief in a more politicised view of education. For example: 'education should be accessible to all regardless of social status, age, race, sex, etc.'. Trainee 4 talks about 'all children having equal access to the curriculum' and Trainee 8 states that every child 'should be given equal opportunity to develop their full potential'.

The beliefs and values identified have been shaped by previous life and work experiences. For Trainee 8, the positive reinforcement of her values had been shaped by working in a special school. In the case of Trainee 9, extensive work with SEN children 'accentuated the importance of self-esteem and the damaging effects when this is undermined'. Trainee 17 felt that fundamental values were formed by discovering as a TA that 'if the child feels respected they are more responsive'.

Values have also been shaped by employment other than in education. Trainee 18, who had worked as a manger in an airline company, and who had been involved in all staff issues, believed that 'understanding what made an individual tick helped to resolve problems'. She felt that this was a key value in her approach to pupils' learning, and significantly influenced her self-concept as a beginning teacher, as evidenced in her beliefs about an inclusive classroom ethos in which individual needs are addressed.

It is clear, then, that GTP trainees begin their training with well-established beliefs and values about teaching and learning, shaped by formative experiences, often involving working closely with individuals in education and elsewhere. We now need to examine the extent to which these beliefs and values are developed through reflection in action within the school-based training.

The development of the values of GTP trainees in phase one of the programme

GTP trainees expect their beliefs and values to contribute to their Initial Needs Assessment in their schools. When asked in the induction questionnaire if they have evidence of their beliefs and values in practice which might contribute to their initial training needs assessment in their school, Trainee 2 readily refers to work undertaken in two previous posts in primary schools demonstrating enthusiasm, knowledge and reflection. Trainee 4 refers to her work as an employer recruiting staff, and Trainees 6, 15 and 18 refer to being observed working as part of a team within a school context and receiving feedback. Trainee 18 believes that she has good evidence of her values reflected in her work supporting a hearing impaired child, 'communicating with all parties concerned and helping the child to integrate into mainstream effectively'.

The expectation of the GTP responsible for training this cohort is that the Initial Needs Assessment undertaken through discussion between mentor and trainee will help identify the key weekly targets for the first term of the Individual Training Plan.

Clearly, teaching standards which have not been encountered previously may become priorities. For example, highly experienced special needs support staff need to develop skills in managing individual needs within the planned differentiation for a class of 30. However, we know that QTS standards in professional values and practice are intrinsic to all the other teaching standards and are at the heart of the individual teacher's motivation and commitment. It must therefore be disheartening for a trainee to feel that the Initial Needs Assessment has highlighted what they cannot do in a classroom rather than recognising well-developed, well-informed and secure beliefs and values which will underpin all that is new to learn about teaching. The quality of this initial dialogue between trainee and mentor is highlighted by Ofsted (2005), but is more nuanced than suggested and will depend on good understandings of the *process* about to be embarked upon.

When asked how they think they will be able to put into practice their beliefs and values about teaching in the initial weeks of the GTP programme after the Initial Needs Assessment, trainees emphasise observation, interaction, reflection, self-evaluation and discussion as the key features of the process. Trainee 2 believes that it will happen through 'working hard with enthusiasm and using self-evaluation'. Trainee 4 anticipates that it will be through observing how particular teachers address different needs within the classroom. Trainee 18 emphasises how observations need to be followed up through discussion with mentor and class teacher. Trainee 12 highlights the importance of reflecting on the process of establishing appropriate relationships with pupils and learning from positive and negative responses. Some trainees believe that their participation in staff planning and policy-making combined with their own reading will help them to clarify and begin to implement their own values in relation to school ethos.

A tentative conclusion at the stage might be that, if refined procedures could provide a closer link between trainees' existing values, the Initial Needs Assessment and the implementation of values through the Individual Training Plan, the GTP programme does offer a potentially structured and integrated process of values-based reflection in action.

The relationship between values implementation and dialogue between mentor and trainee

When we look at the trainees' end of phase one evaluations, it is not surprising, in the light of their expectations, that interaction with the mentor is fundamental to the process of taking forward their values. GTP trainees feel acutely, and more so than PGCE trainees (Smith & McLay, 2007, pp. 48–49), any lack of dialogue which otherwise might make sense of the process they are experiencing. Trainee 1, for example, feels that 'life is not as structured as some of my GTP colleagues' and 'I have to get on with it myself'. Lack of dialogue may be caused by not being observed and debriefed regularly because the mentor is also teaching or involved in management. Trainees expect feedback to be based on effective communication to which they can respond. So, for example, Trainee 1 would like to have more detailed comments on her observation forms instead of the standards 'just being ticked'. By contrast Trainee 5 states that 'we are regularly doing lesson feedback and I find this extremely important and always wish to have honest feedback from which I can learn to improve my practice'.

An encouraging picture of the development of what Whitehead and Fitzgerald (2006, pp. 39–40) term 'generative' dialogical skills emerges when we asked mentors which particular skills they needed in order to help the trainee analyse the processes of teaching and learning. Seventy-five percent refer to self-reflection, communication, and analysis, all of which are key to the process of developing values within trainees' teaching. Mentor 1 highlights 'clarity of thought as a crucial skill', and Mentor 2 describes 'heated discussion' about assessment for learning. Mentor 3 gives us a fuller picture of his self-reflection which Lopez-Real and Kwan (2005, pp. 18–19) identify as central to professional development through mentoring:

> Discussion of teaching issues was useful for both parties—he was able to identify issues which I also recognised as areas for development for himself, myself or the school as a whole. I had to be diplomatic in giving feedback and willing to analyse my own teaching and compare aspects of it with the trainees' teaching. (Mentor 1)

It is now necessary to focus in on the data collected which ask the GTP trainees about opportunities to discuss with their mentor and other staff the way in which they are implementing their beliefs and values in the classroom in phase one of the training. Trainee 1 attributes his confidence in discussing and implementing his values to 'my good relationship with my mentor'. Trainee 2 describes how she has had numerous opportunities to talk about and discuss values with other adults. At the end of the day she and the class teacher invariably discuss the day's highs and lows in respect to their aims, hopes and expectations of the children. Her weekly mentor meetings always include discussion of teaching from the point of view of values and expectations. She has a fortnightly meeting with the Head where he talks about his values in relation to school issues and the trainee is able to reflect on this and bring in her own opinions in her write up of the session. Finally, she aims to write daily observations and reflect on each day, discussing in her writing what she has seen that she likes or dislikes, helping her to formulate and extend her own opinions on school and teacher values. She concludes:

> I feel that my own values have been shaped by my experiences and conversations over the year and will continue to develop, but all the opportunities I have had have helped immensely when I consider my values in relation to my teaching style and the way that I convey values to the children.

Trainee 3 from a background as a pre-school supervisor and TA, and as a parent of two children has had a good understanding of the importance of values in teaching on entry to the GTP programme. She was clear in her own mind of the importance of personal and social development and its impact on learning: 'I have had opportunities to develop this through discussions with my mentor, minor school placement teacher and TA and also my Head Teacher'.

These trainees have benefited from the day to day building of a relationship with their mentor which is a strength of the GTP programme identified by Foster (2001, p. 8). However, by contrast with these very positive opportunities, some trainees felt that there had been no values discussion or values had not been explicitly addressed in the mentoring process. Trainee 4, who had undertaken training in a values programme as a TA, expresses 'how discussion and reflection on my values as a teacher is not something that I have experienced on a planned and formal basis'. The trainee goes on to say that this is an area which has been touched upon with my mentor and with other teachers on an 'as issues arise' basis; for example, in discussions on how best to help children with behavioural/emotional difficulties become better integrated into the class and this has led to broader conversations about values.

Trainee 5 also describes an implicit and less formal discussion of values with other teachers. As with Trainee 4, opportunities emerge indirectly through discussion of behaviour, however, the trainee feels constrained by the school and class teacher's values:

> The main occasions when I have told people or let people be aware of my values is through behaviour management, and showing that I feel strongly about some acts of misbehaviour more than others. However, this is difficult to only express my values, as it is the school's policy that I must follow. The children may be unaware that they are my own personal values and beliefs.

Another trainee describes how they felt in many instances that they have been forced to deal with situations in a 'textbook' or school policy way rather than 'stamp my own style on proceedings'. What is lacking in these examples which, according to Ofsted (2005, p. 14; 2006, pp. 2, 3), can focus too narrowly on behavioural strategies is the importance and benefit of exploring the relationship between school, class and teacher values as experienced by Trainees 2 and 3 so that trainees can develop a coherence between personal and professional values.

In spite of work-based dangers of mechanistic feedback, leaving values implicit or reducing values analysis to behaviour strategies, the data give us a glimpse of dialogue between GTP trainee and mentor, reflecting a longer-term relationship than the one experienced on a postgraduate programme, and which contributes to values implementation. To what extent this is aided by the GTP centrally taught sessions is something now to be considered.

The contribution of the centrally-based GTP training to the articulation of trainees' values

It is quite significant how GTP trainees talk about their training sessions on a needs assessment basis, rather than as offering objectivity, breadth and depth. For example, 'Picture books are an area that I have never really known how to use for the greatest benefit and the session gave me "advice" relevant to what we are concerned with in school'. Good evaluations of sessions tend to reflect the perceived usefulness of the content: 'I really enjoyed this session and it definitely gave me lots of new ideas and confidence to deliver literacy lessons'. Anxiety tends to arise when the session appears to be inspiring but applicability in the trainees' school is seen as problematic: 'It is always difficult to see how we might introduce ideas within our school'. Sessions are valued if they compensate for a lack of inspiration in school: 'I needed to feel inspired about literacy and this session certainly did that'. These data echo that of Smith and McLay (2007, p. 49) who identified how GTP trainees, unlike PGCE trainees, found it difficult to separate 'training' generally from 'practical experience'.

Taught sessions on inclusion, creativity and differentiation are identified by some trainees as offering opportunities for developing their values:

> These sessions have provided me with an opportunity to discuss beliefs and develop my awareness of other's values. This has given me more confidence in my own beliefs (i.e. I am not the only one believes that). (Trainee 2)

Trainee 8 felt that the Personal, Social, Health Education and Citizenship (PSHE/Ct.) session was the first opportunity that she had had to consider her values as a teacher in the context of a discussion (half way through the course): 'I have often independently thought about these whilst planning, teaching and assessing, but feel that I would benefit from more discussion time relating to this particular area'. A number of trainees in addition to Trainee 8 identified the PSHE/Ct. session as offering a qualitatively different reflective experience from other sessions, making values explicit in a way which 'touched on the whole of our teaching experience'. Some trainees did make the important link between *how* they were taught in the (PSHE/Ct.) training session and the development of their own pedagogy in this subject area. For some the impact of the dialogue in the session reminded them of how important it is to take time to discuss such issues with pupils. One trainee describes how: 'the open structure of the session has enabled me to relate the content to my own experience, making it far more relevant. This in turn modelled a useful way to present ideas to my pupils.'

It would seem that GTP central training, in making values more explicit, has the potential to go beyond merely filling gaps in trainees' school-based experience, and provide trainees with the skills of reflective dialogue with other professionals, skills which enable trainees to give some coherence to the relationship between personal and professional values, between current training and previous experience.

Conclusion

GTP trainees are characterised by well-developed professional values and high expectations about implementing such values, beginning with existing evidence from previous careers. Trainers need to recognise and develop the potentially close relationship between trainees' strong values, their Initial Needs Assessment and construction of their Individual Training Plan, which will lend itself to a coherent values development for trainees not easily achieved on traditional training routes.

However, ultimately, coherent values development will be dependent on the expectations and readiness of mentors to go beyond restrictive outcomes-driven mentoring described by Whitehead and Fitzgerald (2006, p. 39) and engage in 'generative' dialogue with trainees about implementing already well-established professional values within the training plan. Clearly, mentor training, well in advance of the induction period, which involves developing skills of clear thinking, self-analysis and self-evaluation is vital in the employment-route context.

GTP centrally-based taught programmes need to contribute to raising trainees' expectations about engaging in dialogue in school. Underpinned by the rigour of relevant literature and a dialogical pedagogy, the taught programme could offer a distinctive contribution to school-based training by bringing the same set of reflective questions and methodology to each curriculum area and whole school issues, thereby giving trainees a set of transferable reflective skills. Such an approach would counter the needs assessment approach of GTP trainees to taught sessions and give coherence to the relationship between central and school-based training found lacking in many GTP programmes (Ofsted, 2005). Those who lead central training sessions need to be aware that through the modelling of skills of professional inquiry into professional practice, they can raise trainees' expectations of experiencing a *process* of values education as fundamental to their teacher *education*.

There is clearly much to be done to ensure that the 'emotion and desire' of GTP trainees' strongly held values become integral to their employment-based development as teachers. However, this study would seem to suggest that there is sufficient potential in the GTP route to give coherence to the development of teachers' values. This reassures us that employment-based routes into teaching are not contributing to making teacher education either pedestrian or utilitarian in this era of Every Child Matters.

References

Ball, S. J. (1999) Global trends in educational reform and the struggle for the soul of the teacher, paper presented at the *British Educational Research Association Annual Conference*, University of Sussex, Brighton, 2–5 September.

Brookes, W. (2005) The graduate teacher programme in England: mentor training, quality assurance and the findings of inspection, *Journal of In-Service Education*, 31(1), 43–61.

DFES (2004) *Every Child Matters: change for children in schools* (London, DFES).

Foster, R. (2001) The graduate teacher route to QTS—motorway, by-way or by-pass?, paper presented at the *British Educational Research Association Annual Conference*, University of Leeds, 13–15 September.

Furlong, J. (2000) School mentors and university tutors: lessons from the English experiment, *Theory into Practice*, 39(1), 12–20.

Lopez-Real, F. & Kwan, T. (2005) Mentors' perceptions of their own professional development during mentoring, *Journal of Education for Teaching*, 31(1), 15–24.

Mayotte, G. (2003) Stepping stones to success: previously developed career competencies and their benefits to career switchers transitioning to teaching, *Teaching and Teacher Education*, 19, 681–695.

Ofsted, (2005) *An employment-based route into teaching, an overview of the first year of the inspection of designated recommending bodies for the Graduate Teacher Programme 2003/04* (London, Ofsted).

Ofsted, (2006) *An employment-based route into teaching 2004/05, an overview of the second year of the inspection of the designated recommending bodies of the Graduate Teacher Programme* (London, Ofsted).

Smith, K. & McLay, M. (2007) Curates' eggs? Secondary trainee teachers' experience of the Graduate Teacher Programme and the Postgraduate Certificate in Education, *Journal of Education for Teaching*, 33(1), 35–54.

Smith, E. & Reid, D. (2000) Considering the concept of the 'collaborative model' of the Secondary Post Graduate Certificate in Education Course, *Mentoring & Tutoring*, 8(3), 251–259.

Smithers, A. & Robinson, P. (2006) *Teacher training profiles 2006* (Buckingham, Centre for Education & Employment Research).

Training and Development Agency (TDA) (2003) *Graduate Teacher Programme survey 2002* (London, TDA).

Training and Development Agency (TDA) (2005) *Result of the Graduate Teacher Programme survey 2005* (London, TDA).

Training and Development Agency (TDA) (2006) *Standards for Qualified Teacher Status 2007 (draft)* (London, TDA).

Whitehead, J. & Fitzgerald, B. (2006) Professional learning through a generative approach to mentoring: lessons from a training school partnership and their wider implications, *Journal of Education for Teaching*, 32(1), 37–52.

Williams, A. & Soares, A. (2002) Sharing roles and responsibilities in initial teacher training: perceptions of some key players, *Cambridge Journal of Education*, 32(1), 91–107.

Should relationships education be at the heart of Personal, Social, Health and Economics Education and, if so, what would be the implications for pre-service teacher education?

Summary research report

Nick Mead, Oxford Brookes University, UK, 2012

Background

This study argues that relationships education should be at the heart of Personal, Social, Health and Economic Education (PSHEe) in order to provide meaningful contexts for all the themes within the subject and thereby provide much needed coherence. McLaughlin and Alexander (2005) identify the 'increasing fragmentation of the subject as new topics or headlines have been added to the territory' (2005, p.2). They argue that there is a need for a 'more holistic approach, one that brings together fragmented, narrow aspects of the curriculum and school life which have arisen as a result of the competing agendas of school standards, the economic role of the school and meeting the needs of all young people (McLaughlin and Alexander 2005, p.3).

Why might relationships education address this fragmentation? The changing significance of relationships for young people as part of the impact of globalisation is well documented by recent research into adolescent health and well-being:

> Trends across nations suggest that adulthood in the future will require greater social versatility, including abilities to function in relationships that are less scripted by community norms and that bridge multiple social worlds (Larson *et al* 2001, p.31).

These researchers argue that to have, in the 21st Century, only one way of relating to, or gaining mastery of, a social world is to be increasingly handicapped. Arising from such research is a set of arenas for relationships which might usefully embrace the key themes in PSHEe: family, community, peers, romance and sexuality, school and work. Each of these arenas requires skills, such as forming and leaving relationships which are 'less scripted by institutional norms and depend more on personal agency' (Larson *et al* 2002, p.51).

If relationships education were to become central to PSHEe it would provide a significant challenge for teacher education, especially pre-service education. We know this to be the case because of the pedagogical concerns arising from the creation of Sex and Relationships Education (SRE 2000) which was intended to contextualise sex education within loving and meaningful relationships:

> Schools should ensure that pupils receive their sex education in the wider context of relationships education. SRE should develop positive values and a moral framework that will guide their decisions, judgements and behaviour (DFE 2000, pp.19-20).

However, this has represented a huge professional challenge for many teachers, evidenced by relationships education within SRE often being the weaker component of PSHEe, more vulnerable to being squeezed out because of 'staff comfort levels' who view it as 'contentious and problematic' (Formby 2011, p.171). The government's SRE review steering group report (2008) observes that much SRE teaching has failed to address the issues that concern young people by not adopting a stronger focus on relationships. The complexity of the challenge for teachers is evident in the report's recommendation that SRE be more closely integrated into the PSHEe curriculum and should be:

> Inclusive and relevant to all young people, including young people with disabilities, LGBT young people and should take account of young people's ethnic and faith backgrounds' (DCSF 2008, p.9).

The rationale underpinning this study is that the argument for reframing PSHEe around relationships education both provides leverage in the current debate about the place of PSHEe within the 2014 curriculum and addresses the urgent need to have a required focus on PSHEe in all initial teacher training courses, as recommended by the MacDonald Report (2009).

The curriculum expert review panel report (2011b) talks of the importance of PSHEe in relation to the 'constructive interaction between subject knowledge and individual development' (p.58):

> The expert panel takes the view that awareness of a provision for both of these elements is important for effective learning and educational quality (Department for Education 2011b, p.12).

Reference has already been made to the mastery of many social worlds and the development of interpersonal competencies and qualities which cultivate trust, reciprocity and collaboration. It is hoped, then, that a new coherence within the subject framed around relationships education will strengthen its contribution to young people's sense of agency, for example in problem solving and working constructively, both collaboratively and alone. The corollary of this curriculum development would be a requirement for a much more rigorous approach to pre-service education in the subject.

Methodology

The study sets out to test the importance of relationships education and its implications for pre-service training by using the PSHEe curriculum review consultation process for the 2014 curriculum (DFE 2011a). An online search identified a sample of 22 consultation responses for scrutiny. All responses were accessible within the public domain and none of the agencies had indicated to the DFE that they wished to keep any part of their response confidential. A cross-section of responses were selected from local authorities, trade unions/professional associations, religious and humanist organisations and key physical and mental health agencies. Responses to government questions about aims, content and best practice in PSHEe were scrutinised for references to 1) the place of relationships education and 2) its implications for pre-service teacher education. The sample was grouped into types of agencies and references were logged in two columns by the extrapolation of key points from each consultation question, providing both quantitative and qualitative data.

Findings

Relationships education has the potential to provide subject coherence

The findings suggest that 69% of respondents think that relationships education should provide the coherence which is much needed for the PSHEe programmes of study, which are described in their current form as atomised learning experiences. The Sex Education Forum argue that PSHEe 'should be seen as a whole and not a selection of subjects'(2011, p.3). Rotherham Local Authority claim that atomised topics delivered by external agencies on suspended timetable days 'do not allow the opportunity for pupils to address queries, issues, values and attitudes which arise' (2011, p.16). Arguments for best practice in planning put forward by respondents seem to be underpinned by the understanding and values necessary for building positive relationships, rather than too much focus on sex and drugs knowledge for self-protection. The Family Planning Association and Brook state that in their survey of young people over half say that they want contextual understanding achieved through 'coherent and comprehensive programmes of study, rather than more knowledge and one off topics' (2011, p.8). Violence against Women and Girls Advisory Group also argue that pupils want more than one off disjointed lessons or fragmented topics:

> Young people want more than one off lessons in violence against women and girls; they want to develop and build their understanding – they are keen to help and support their friends. It is not enough to deliver sex education in isolation; young people want and need to know about relationships. (Violence against Women and Girls Advisory Group 2011, p.10).

 It is argued that relationships education provides the coherence and interrelatedness of topics and the clarity for individual lesson plans. Rotherham Local Authority argue that this would allow for 'connections to be made between and across topic areas to give learning true meaning'(2011, p.10). For example, there would be more coherence across topics on friendships, family relationships and marriage/civil partnership. A number of agencies such as The British Humanist Association (2011), Accord (2011) and Violence Against Women and Girls Advisory Group (2011) also argue that such coherence facilitates the mapping across topics of key cultural, religious, non-religious and gender factors at the heart of relationship contexts and which can become disembodied in fragmented, one-off topics or drop-down PSHEe days. A strong case is made, then, for coherence and progression which enables pupils to develop outward-facing understandings and values rather than merely acquiring knowledge for self-protection:

> PSHEe is at its best when it is coherent, progressive and integrated and seen as central to the core work of the school (Schools and Students Health Education Unit 2011 p.7).

There are significant pre-service training implications

A number of agencies, such as Rotherham Local Authority highlight the importance of opportunities for the 'exploration of personal attitudes, beliefs and values and those of others which contribute to the development and maintenance of all kinds of positive relationships' (2011, p.5). The Drugs Education Forum states that 'students need sufficient time and the appropriate atmosphere of enquiry' (2011 p.1) and the Sex Education Forum argues that students 'need to develop understanding of how values and feelings influence themselves and others'(2011, p.2). A significant number of agencies, including the Sex Education Forum which draws on survey data from young people (Sex Education Forum 2008, p.5), highlight key relationship areas of concern as family, peers, marriage/civil partnership, domestic violence, sexual bullying and consent, disability, HIV/Aids, self-abuse/harming as well as self-efficacy for the workplace (2011, pp. 12-14). Agencies emphasise the importance of teachers listening to the needs of young people and using local and national data to gain accurate insights which can inform curriculum planning. In terms of teaching approaches, the Family Planning Association and Brook argue for 'a balance between acquisition, exploration and the development of attitudes and skills (2011, P.5) The

National Aids Trust wishes to see the 'building of positive relationships based on open expression and fair power dynamics' (2011, p.5). The British Psychological Society argues for the 'need for teaching that emphasises the importance of meta learning skills; understanding how we learn best, emotional intelligence, interpersonal skills, effective communication and conflict management' (2011, p.3). This latter agency, along with many more, highlight how the views of pupils need to be taken into account.

Agencies, such as the Schools and Students Health Education Unit report that pupils want to be taught by teachers who can focus more on processes rather than knowledge in order to help them contextualise, apply and explore personal and often conflicting values (2011, p.1). In their response the Children and Young People's Mental Health Coalition report that:

> Children and young people told us that interactive lessons offering a
> range of options to get involved with this sensitive subject were essential.
> In particular, videos and any media clips need to be both current and
> relevant. Young people do not want to be 'talked at' nor do they want
> to be given factsheets to read.(Children and Young People's
> Mental Health Coalition 2011, p.3)

This agency goes on to emphasise the importance of open and honest dialogue between staff and pupils and how essential it is to 'foster a climate of trust, cooperation and support and involve the pupils themselves in the process of delivering PSHEe' (2011, p.3). 67%% of pupils, according to one PSHEe Association member survey, value the opportunity to explore real-life scenarios about relationships, which help their attitudes and thinking to develop and change and which contribute to more confident decision-making (2011, p.12). The National Aids Trust in their response, argue for an 'urgent need to develop negotiating skills in relationships in order to build self-esteem, healthy relationships and protection' (2011, p.9).The Association of Directors of Children's Services in their response argue for contexualised learning in which young people 'learn to develop and maintain positive relationships, develop the skills needed in understanding how to deal with risky or negative relationships and how to manage loss (bereavement, separation and divorce(2011, p.5). A faith group, Accord, argues that young people should be helped to deal with the life issues they face both as children and in adulthood' (2011, p.5) and the British Psychological Society (2011) argues that 'the emphasis should be on situating the PSHEe curriculum not only within a national framework but in a way that reflects the situations and locations of specific schools and local contexts' (2011, p.5). Agencies are at pains to point out that if pupils are to progress in this process of contextualised learning they will need to use assessment methods which capture their development as people and not just as academic individuals.

Conclusion

The study identifies a recognition amongst agencies of the centrality of relationships education in PSHEe and its potential to achieve greater subject coherence at a time when the contribution of the subject to pupil self-efficacy needs to be strengthened. The implications of this for pre-service teacher education are significant, but, if addressed, would meet the recommendations of the now-shelved, but still highly relevant, MacDonald Report (2009). In particular, trainee teachers would need to have the opportunity to explore what Mclaughlin and Alexander (2005) call the 'interpersonal complexity which is part of the landscape of the future (2005, p.32). Secondly, they will need to develop skills in coherent planning using constructivist and dialogical pedagogies, building into them assessment methods which do justice to the meaning, value and impact of what has been learnt. Finally, trainee teachers will need to be able to interpret local and national data which can sharpen the relevance of the relational issues informing their curriculum planning.

References

Accord Coalition (2011) accordcoalition.org.uk/wp/2011/PSHE-Response-Form FINAL.d.., accessed 22/2/12.

Association of Directors of children's Services (2011) www.adcs.org. Uk/download/consultation-responses/2011/ADCS response PSHE.pdf, accessed 22/2/12.

British Humanist Association (BHA) (2011) www.humanism.org.uk/_uploads Documents/bha-briefing-2011-review-of-personal-social-health-and-economics-pshe-education-final.pdf, accessed 22/2/12.

British Psychological Society (2011) www.apps.bps.org.uk/_publication files/consultation-responses/Review of PSHE Education-BPS response pdf, accessed 22/2/12.

Children and Young People's Mental Health Coalition (CYMHC) (2011) www.cypmhc.org.uk/resources/download/451, accessed 22/2/12.

Department for Children, Schools and Families (2008) *Government Response to the Report by the Sex and Relationships Education (SRE) Review Steering Group* (London DCSF).

Department for Education (2000) *Sex and Relationships Education, Guidance* (London, DFE).

Department for Education (2011a) *Review of Personal, Social, Health and Economics (PSHE) Education, response form* (London, DFE).

Department for Education (2011b) *The Framework for the National Curriculum, a Report by the Expert Panel of the National Curriculum Review* (London, DFE).

Drug Education Forum (DEF) (2011) www.drugeducationforum.com/index. cfm? Page URL=blog&articleID=8070&ArticleMonth, accessed 22/2/12.

Family Planning Association and Brook (FPAB) (2011) www.fpa.org.uk/ Media/uploads/campaigns and advocacy/advocacy-and-lobbying/fpa-and-brook-response-to-pshe-education-review-nov-2011.pdf,accessed 22/2/12.

Formby, E (2011) ' 'It's better to learn about your health and things that are going to happen to you than learning things that you just do at school': findings from a mapping study of PSHE education in primary schools in England', *Journal of Pastoral Care in Education,* 29(3) pp.161-173.

Larson, R, Wilson, S, Bradford Brown, B, Fusstenberg, F, & Verma, S 'Changes in adolescent interpersonal experiences – are they being prepared for adult relationships in the twenty-first century?', in Larson, R, Bradford Brown, B, & Mortimer, J, (eds) (2002)

Adolescent Preparation for the Future: Perils and Promises, a report of the study group on adolescence in the twenty-first century (Ann Arbor, MI).

Macdonald, A (2009) *Independent Review of the Proposal to Make Personal, Social, Health and Economic (PSHE) Education Statutory* (London, DFE).

McLaughlin, C, & Alexander, E (2005) *Reframing Personal, Social and Emotional Education: Relationships, Agency and Dialogue* (Warwick University, NAPCE).

National Aids Trust (NAT) (2011) www.nat.org.uk/media/.../2011/PSHE Consultation-Response-Form.p…, accessed 23/2/12.

PSHE Association (2011) www.pshe-association.org.uk/news_detail. Aspx?ID=1235, accessed 23/2/12.

Rotherham Local Authority (2011) www.moderngov.rotherham.gov.uk/ mgConvert2 PDF.aspx? ID=44698, accessed 23/2/12.

Schools and Students Health Education Unit (2011) sheu.org.uk/content/page/sheu-response-review-personal-social-health-and-economics-pshe-education, accessed 23/2/12.

Sex Education Forum (2008) Young people's survey on sex and relationships education, www.ncb.org.uk/sef/evidence.

Sex Education Forum (2011) www.ncb.org.uk/media/469189/sef_ Response_pshee_review_nov_2011.pdf, accessed 23/2/12.

Violence Against Women and Girls Advisory Group (2011) www. Endviolenceagainstwomen.org.uk/.../response_dfe_internal_pshe, accessed 23/2/12.

Section Two

Values in secondary teacher education with a focus on Religious Education and the spiritual and moral

Mentoring Religious Education teaching in secondary schools. First published in Leicester, M, Modgil, C, and Modgil, S.(Eds) (2000) *Education, Culture and Values* Vol V Spiritual and Religious Education, pp.197-203 (London: Falmer).

The significance of values in the professional development of beginning secondary Religious Education teachers. Unpublished paper given at Birmingham University School of Education graduate seminar series November 2003.

The experience of black African Religious Education trainee teachers in England. First published in the *British Journal of Religious Education*, (2006) 28(2) pp.173-184 (Taylor & Francis).

Mentoring student-teachers in the spiritual and moral, First published in *World Religions in Education,*(1997/1998) pp.45-49, (London: Shap Working Party on World Religions).

Values transference v Values clarification? Essay review. First published in *Prospero,* (1999) 5(2) pp.85-86 (Triangle Journals).

19 Mentoring Religious Education Teaching in Secondary Schools

NICK MEAD

Introduction

The research in this chapter is prompted by three developments: the emerging role of the mentor in school, the expanding recruitment of Religious Education Postgraduate Certificate of Education (RE PGCE) students from diverse backgrounds, and the government's concern with the standards of initial teacher training (ITT). The research identifies the mentoring needs of RE PGCE students in the light of their academic background and personal, religious and philosophical motivations. It then assesses how effectively these needs are met by mentors, and identifies good practice in RE mentoring. Third, the research examines the influence on RE mentoring of the structure and expectations within the training partnership and identifies areas for improvement. The research findings suggest that, given training which links student needs with good practice in mentoring, mentors can turn a diverse intake of students into competent classroom practitioners. However, the research findings also establish that the extent to which RE mentoring needs are met can be influenced by the structure and expectations within the partnership, and recommendations for improvement are made, which should enhance the role of the mentor. The research concludes that the expanding recruitment of RE PGCE students from diverse backgrounds is justified if mentors engage in a training, as opposed to a supervisory role and become equal, proactive partners in the training process. The research was sponsored by the Farmington Institute, Oxford, who are the copyright holders of the data (see Mead, 1996).

The research design

The type of qualitative research used for the project is defined in Maykut and Morehouse (1994, p. 153) as, 'the emergent design case study approach'. Initially, we specified an awareness of RE mentoring needs in the light of the backgrounds and motivations of students. These needs became specific as data were collected and categorised. We then engaged in the process of discovering how well these needs are met by mentors and the emergent design highlighted certain priorities. Significantly, the data generated other factors pertaining to how the training partnership affected the degree to which mentoring needs are met.

This approach was based around contexts in three training partnerships. One was chosen because it is traditional and well established; another is modern and just established; the third offered contexts in which confessionalism was particularly well-handled. The field work lasted seven weeks, covering the PGCE RE course induction period and initial school experiences. Methods of data collection included Graduate Teacher Training Registry (GTTR) document analysis; participant observation in mentor training and student seminars; questionnaires to two student cohorts; and transcriptions of semi-structured interviews with six PGCE course leaders, fourteen mentors and seven observed mentoring sessions.

What are the mentoring needs of RE PGCE students?

Our data identify three broad needs which reflect the diversity of students entering the RE profession. The first is how subject competence is addressed; the second, how varied student motivations are turned into classroom practice; and the third, how subject aims are understood.

Subject knowledge findings suggest that RE PGCE courses run in traditional academic universities, which have theology/RS departments, tend to attract well-qualified theology/RS students. An example is institution E which has 60 per cent of its PGCE intake with theology/RS degrees and 40 per cent with degrees which have an RS component or none at all. More recent courses in more modern institutions which do not necessarily have a theology/RS department tend to recruit a higher proportion of graduates with either combined RS or non-specialist degrees, such as philosophy, social sciences, combined studies. An example is institution D which has 70 per cent of its intake with combined RS or non-specialist degrees. However, both types of institution demonstrate a widening academic base in their intake, following the Gates Report (1993). For example, although traditional Institution B has 58 per cent with Theology/RS degrees, it has 36 per cent with non-specialist degrees which is comparable to the 31 per cent with non-specialist degrees at modern institution F.

The data suggest that there will be gaps in subject knowledge and this has implications for mentoring. It also raises the question about whether a student, with or without a theology/RS background, has the right intellectual orientations for teaching RE. It is possible, for example, that a philosopher may display more appropriate skills than a theologian. There is a wider issue here about the nature of subject competence in RE with which mentors need to engage.

Data from 52 students in two institutions enabled us to identify three key motivations for wanting to teach RE, out of a possible eight: 23 per cent spoke in terms ranging from 'communicating and encouraging ideas in a stimulating environment', of enjoying the challenge of devising programmes to, 'hold their interest and fire their imagination' Although we might call these general teaching motivations, it is possible to discern within them some of the basic intellectual skills required in RE teaching. Of these students, 21 per cent held convictions about the spiritual, moral and cultural value of RE:

> My academic background is in Philosophy but I am keen to teach RE because I am convinced of its importance throughout every pupil's school life. At its best I think RE should provide children with a

context for moral reasoning, a sense of their own identity within the universe and a basis for understanding their own and other cultures, as well as knowledge of particular religions.   (Student F)

This intellectual base is linked by other students to actually wanting to give pupils the means to change and develop and to share in their spiritual development. Students see the outcome of this intellectual enterprise as relating to the dilemma in our society about the relationship between belief, morality and action: there is mention of the influence of personal ideas and values on behaviour, of 'responding to moral dilemmas which dominate our lives', of 'giving pupils convictions and wisdom to change things', and there is a good deal about teaching respect for culture, law and morality.

Of the sample 17 per cent identified skills in RE which they had valued and wished to pass on to pupils. Mention is made of reflective skills: 'the ability to think effectively', 'to think critically' and to use knowledge to understand and accept the 'sheer variety of human nature and its beliefs'.

RE mentors need to understand these motivations which, for many students, are more significant than subject knowledge. They reveal certain intellectual orientations and skills compatible with understanding and evaluating religious ideas. School experience can focus and deepen these or can threaten them. Mentors need to nurture such motivations and shape them into realistic classroom competences.

We went on to find out to what extent these motivations relate to students' understanding of subject aims. Data from questionnaires conducted in week 2 of the course reveals: 19 per cent confused about subject aims; 44 per cent were able to give a basic definition; 12 per cent believed the subject was confused itself; and 25 per cent were able to give a definition pointing to knowledge, understanding and reflection with some understanding of the principle of learning from as well as about religions.

It is evident that, because they have the right intellectual orientations and skills for the subject, students are well ahead on methodology, but this is yet to be matched to a clear understanding of subject aims and progression. Students in the final group are advanced and tutors will be working fast to ensure all gain similarly clear subject aims before they get too far into the first school placement. Mentors will need to be aware of the students' level of understanding of subject aims and progression at the commencement of the course, how tutors address this, and how they will need to develop it in the mentoring process, enabling students to match their imaginative ideas for classroom practice with sound aims and progression.

How do mentors meet the needs of RE PGCE students?

Having identified the mentoring needs, we proceeded to describe the mentoring process in order to measure the degree of good practice in meeting these needs.

The data overwhelmingly point to the mentor–student relationship as the foundation of good mentoring. In RE the relationship provides the context within which motivations are shared:

> It's about building up trust quickly. It does seem to work. I don't know how but perhaps it's because there is no hidden agenda. We're here to help them pass and I am very honest about my own teaching. (Mentor C)

The honesty mentioned says something about the mentors' need to explain the relationship between their own motivations and what they think they are achieving in the classroom. It is not surprising that effective mentors see their role as more than supervisory and based on mutual respect of motivations. In the process of turning motivations into classroom practice, such mentors are sensitive and supportive, for example in not letting a lack of subject knowledge undermine initial classroom experience. They can also lay the foundations for constructive self-criticism, an essential skill for lone RE teachers, without demoralising the student.

Concerning the mentoring of subject knowledge, mentors seem to be saying two important things: first, there is a certain amount of subject knowledge about six world religions which is needed; second, RE is not the same creature as that which constitutes a so-called specialist qualification:

> Students are often disappointed because it's not the subject they thought it was – often they don't recognize it when they observe because their experience is what they had at university and that is completely different. (Mentor C)

This suggests that an understanding of subject principles may be more important than the amount of subject knowledge.

Effective subject knowledge mentoring seems to be about providing well-motivated students with strategies and resources for acquiring appropriate subject knowledge. Mentor A talks about 'setting targets in subject knowledge research so that they are aware you have to keep working on it and it is part of good practice'. In order to ensure *appropriate* subject knowledge is selected for the lesson, effective subject knowledge mentoring will be done in the context of planning lesson aims and methodology.

As personal motivations figure largely in RE teaching, mentors are anxious to identify the extremes of indifference and confessionalism:

> I've had one or two students in the past about whom I've had that underlying feeling that they simply wanted to extend their university course. (Mentor F)

> One student had this view of what he wanted to do and I said this is not on but he felt it was my view against his. He was confessing his own world view and identifying himself with the subject. (Mentor C)

It seems that both indifference and confessionalism are dealt with effectively by mentors who have worked through, and can account for, the relationship between their own motivations and their classroom practice. This enables the mentor to articulate what the student may be experiencing in the classroom and so facilitate discussion, leading to effective strategies. For example, a female Muslim mentor is very clear in her own mind about avoiding confessionalism, as she explains it to students:

> It is perfectly all right for you to wheel yourself on in the lesson as the personal exhibit, but then wheel yourself out and bring on the teacher. I am a facilitator, a confessional approach wouldn't improve their learning experience. When I offer a Muslim view, it is as acquired knowledge in an educational context. (Mentor D)

Other mentors talk about the need to encourage students to develop an open, enquiring atmosphere in which spirituality, rather than dogma, is valued.

In order to help students develop clarity in subject aims, mentors need to demonstrate the links between the aims of the agreed syllabus, the school's scheme of work and the RE teacher's lesson plans. Mentors who do this well are usually engaged in reviewing their work; for example, modifying the scheme of work in the light of agreed syllabus revision.

To learn from as well as about religions, through knowledge, understanding and reflection, requires the school scheme of work to employ a variety of teaching styles. The mentor has the task of linking subject aims to teaching styles which is crucial in the mentoring process because it is the means by which the subject comes alive and contributes to the spiritual and moral growth of children. An example follows of Mentor C and Student A building up the links between aims and methodology:

Mentor: What is the aim of this Year 8 lesson?
Student: The aim is to teach the significance of the Seder meal to the Jews.
Mentor: Good. What should the activities try and do?
Student: To get across why the meal is important and goes beyond just eating unleavened bread and bitter herbs, its about evoking sympathy and remembrance
Mentor: That's good, exactly how you approach it – so let's think about activities.
Student: We could ask the pupils how they remember things, for example, toys, photos, then we could go on to Remembrance Day.
Mentor: Good. You are beginning with pupils' experience and then moving from individual memories to collective remembrance.
Student: That's the whole point about Pesach which I want pupils to reflect on, that it's shared thankfulness that you are not in that situation now. The pupils could make up their own symbolic ways of remembering things – or the Exodus and then we could introduce the Seder artefacts which would then mean something, and perhaps act out the meal.

As this mentoring session develops it is clear that the student is being encouraged to link aims and method in a way which will engage pupils in the meaning and value of the RE content for others and for themselves.

Confusion about attainment and progression in RE arises because both theology/RS students and non-specialists have derived their intellectual orientations from university courses which do not relate directly to RE at the different key stages. Mentors need to direct students away from their own experience to the actual *process* whereby pupils grasp an understanding of and are able to reflect on religious concepts. Assessment becomes clearer to students when mentors relate clear subject aims to lesson outcomes.

At the heart of mentoring discipline in RE is the mentor's ability to communicate to both pupils and PGCE students what it is that they are trying to achieve in the lesson. Classroom *ethos* is one of the keys to this:

> Where RE does cause a discipline problem is when the children perceive it as you trying to get them to believe something – the barriers go up. It's not a problem if it's about exploration – everyone has a spiritual element. (Mentor E)

Holding the line in discussions, a readiness to be genuine and personal and tenacity in the face of what might become personalised anti-RE hostility were other qualities mentors identified as crucial in mentoring discipline.

In the case of both resources and workload, there is a tendency for some mentors to present the worst-case scenario for students in the belief that this will prepare them for anything. There are sufficient data from other mentors to suggest that, given the limitations of the RE situation, it is possible to be creative in the mentoring of these important areas. Some mentors have sessions on creating your own resources and they encourage students to use all the available sources, such as RE centres, the Schools Library Service, the local faith communities and the university. Mentoring workload is not a baptism of fire into an impossible marking load with no time to prepare, let alone reflect. Effective mentors give students strategies for coping but also ensure that there is sufficient time for planning and reflection in a training context.

We would conclude our description of the mentoring process by saying that what we have judged to be good practice are those skills and strategies which seem to be meeting the mentoring needs of the students which we identified earlier in this chapter. Where mentors are not clear about the students' mentoring needs, and where they are not adequately equipped with the necessary mentoring skills, RE mentoring will be less than effective in contributing to the much-needed expansion of the RE teaching force.

On the basis of this assessment, we would argue for an increase in mentor training which might use as an objective starting point the nine recommendations for good practice identified in our research:

1 Establish a training as opposed to a supervisory relationship with students.

2 Encourage students to read up, but mentor subject knowledge in relation to lesson aims and methodology.

3 Discourage indifference and confessionalism as a result of the mentor having worked through the relationship between their own motivations and classroom practice.

4 Demonstrate how the agreed syllabus, the school's scheme of work and lesson plans relate to each other.

5 Enable students to employ different teaching methods to achieve subject aims.

6 Introduce students to differentiation and assessment through *process* and *outcome*.

7 Encourage good discipline through subject ethos.

8 Encourage students to be creative about resourcing.

9 Ensure students have a balanced school experience of RE pressures and time to plan and reflect.

How the training partnership affects RE mentoring

As mentors are partners, it seems inevitable that the structure and the expectations within the training partnership will affect the quality of mentoring, and therefore the extent to which the needs of RE students will be met. Our data suggest that the partnership has a bearing on the quality of RE mentoring in five areas of concern.

The first area is that of responsibility for subject knowledge. PGCE course leaders are committed to recruiting students who have the right motivations, but they are anxious about subject knowledge in the light of the widening intake, and the Circular 4/98 requirement (DfEE, 1998) that PGCE students have 'knowledge, concepts and skills in their specialist subject at a standard equivalent to degree level'. Course leaders do not see themselves as having either the time or the expertise to provide adequate subject knowledge. In their turn mentors are uncertain about who is responsible for subject knowledge. Mentor I demonstrates the sort of confusion to which this uncertainty gives rise:

> I think it is beyond my job to have to teach them the subject matter before they teach the class. I wouldn't want anyone who has done sociology – it's an entirely different appproach.

The perception here is that, if mentors are expected to deal with subject knowledge as well as methodology, they do not wish to be given a non-specialist. However, it seems that the main task for RE mentors is to turn the motivations and intellectual orientations of the likes of sociologists into classroom competences; mentors will not be confident about taking on this task unless subject knowledge responsibility is clarified by the partnership. Clarification will also reassure those mentors who see neither the university nor the school as providing adequate subject knowledge and who realistically judge subject competence according to whether the student has *appropriate* knowledge for the lesson.

We would recommend that, because the right intellectual orientation and enthusiasm figure more largely in student selection than subject knowledge, subject knowledge should be the responsibility of the students if they wish to implement their motivations. Neither the university nor the school are ultimately responsible but both can support the student through lectures, guided reading and distance learning.

Another difficult area is the matching of theory to practice, especially on serial placements. As a result of such a varied intake of students there is pressure to cover a certain amount of theory before students are too far into their first school experience. This puts pressure on mentors in two ways: theory often gets in the way of dealing directly with experiences; and second, mentors may find it difficult to handle the dual role of the trainees as students and professionals, sometimes treating them as less than colleagues and without due attention to their motivations. Course leaders see some of these tensions in school giving rise to an uneven matching of theory and practice for which they feel they need to compensate. For example, in one-person departments there is often neither the time nor the variety of teaching styles to enable a lot of matching of theory and practice. There is also the need to go beyond the often misleading layer of cynicism about RE within the school culture.

The difficulty of trying to integrate theory and practice across uneven school experiences may be overcome if more theory were to arise out of the students' experience in school. To this end students should be trained by the university to approach their mentor in the right way, asking appropriate questions, in order to draw out the mentor's understanding of the relationship between theory and practice. In their turn, mentors should be trained in how to elicit pertinent questions from students about their classroom experience.

The matching of student and mentor seems particularly important in RE because of the variations in students' academic background, personal motivations and faith commitments. Failure to take account of these factors can lead to inconsistent student performance:

> I have been struck by the way different students get on in different schools. Student J was thought to be outstanding by her first mentor, but went on to a school where she found the mentor totally unwilling to help her, and if she hadn't had the first good experience, she would have struggled. (Course Leader E)

What seems to lie behind such inconsistencies is the fact that RE means different things to different people. Teachers tend to create their own RE in a way that does not happen in other subjects. This means that mentors need to be sensitive to individual students' motivations, but it should not mean that student X can only work with mentor Y: there has to be coherence in RE mentoring across schools if students are to develop a professional approach. A similar balance needs to be struck in the placement of students who are committed to a faith and those in danger of confessionalism.

Matching does enhance RE mentoring but it would be less of a problem for course leaders if mentors became increasingly skilful at mentoring students from diverse backgrounds, giving them opportunities to experiment without being afraid that their own good work in RE would be undermined.

A fourth area of concern is the lack of progression in mentoring in RE within the partnership arrangement:

> Some students have a first placement in a school with discrete RE and then move on to one with something much less. It would be nice if they all built up but it doesn't happen like that at all. When you talk to students they usually have a favourite and tend to polarise their experiences. (Course Leader E)

A more coherent, progressive mentoring might be achieved if positive, diagnostic consultation took place between mentors. This would go beyond the limitations of report writing and give the next mentor a real feel for the professional needs of the student, enabling them to address these, albeit in a very different RE context.

The final area of concern is the effect of the partnership on the confidence of RE mentors. The unevenness of RE in existing partnership schools and the isolation of many lone RE heads of department makes for a reluctance to participate if teaching is to be scrutinised by both the university and other schools:

> I feel apprehensive about the role because you wonder if you are going to deliver what the university wants. (New Mentor C)

Our research suggests that there is a correlation between confidence in professional expertise and a desire to take on RE mentoring. Those who are most confident in their mentoring are usually communicating and sharing their understanding of the subject with other professionals. RE would certainly benefit from mentor training becoming part of professional development in school, facilitated by the professional tutor. This would mean that the large number of fairly isolated RE specialists might then be encouraged to become mentors and, through the training, become more confident practitioners, knowing that what they are doing is valued by the school. School-based mentor training would be supported by HE tutors who are not comfortable with the 'big brother' role but would rather disseminate good mentoring practice.

Conclusion

In identifying the mentoring needs of RE PGCE students and then assessing how well these needs are met, we found that where mentors are clear about the mentoring needs and where they are adequately equipped with the necessary mentoring skills, RE mentoring can succeed in turning a diverse intake of students into competent classroom practitioners. However, we also found that the extent to which the RE mentoring needs are met can be influenced by the structure and expectations within the training partnership.

These findings have led us to make the following recommendations:

- Develop mentor training which identifies the mentoring needs of RE students.
- Develop training materials based on observed principles of good practice.
- Establish that the student is ultimately responsible for his/her subject knowledge.

- Tutors and mentors should devise ways to support students in this.
- Students and mentors should be trained to get the best out of each other so that theory and practice are more integrated.
- Matching students with mentors is important but mentors should become skilful in mentoring students from different backgrounds.
- Coherent, progressive mentoring might be achieved within partnerships if positive, diagnostic consultation took place between mentors.
- Mentor training should become part of professional development within schools.
- Higher education institutes should support school-based mentor training by disseminating good practice, for example, through mentor panels.
- A wider forum might be set up which disseminates good practice across partnerships.

There is concern in the RE world that, having finally persuaded the Technical Training Agency (TTA) to recognise RE as a shortage subject, the increased recruitment from such diverse backgrounds will result in RE initial teacher education being found wanting, according to the criteria of Circular 4/98.

It is our conviction that, in this scenario, the relatively recent role of the mentor can come into its own and develop a professional expertise which will ensure the motivations of a diverse intake of students can be turned into excellent classroom competences.

For this to happen, mentors need to be equal, proactive partners in the training process; after all,

we have moved on from the old PGCE arrangements in which the university provided the programme of study, and then students came into school to practise what they had learnt.

There is sufficient evidence in our research to suggest that many RE mentors are engaging in a training, as opposed to a supervisory, role. However, much more needs to be done to help mentors identify the training needs of the expanding RE intake and provide them with the skills to address these. Not least in RE is the need to give the large number of isolated specialists the confidence to become mentors, for the mutual benefit of the students and themselves.

We conclude that there are strong grounds for being optimistic about the developing pattern of recruitment and mentoring of RE students, and hope that our recommendations can contribute to further developments which will help justify our optimism.

References

Department for Education and Employment (DfEE) (1998) *Teaching: High Status, High Standards*, Circular 4/98. London: DfEE.

Gates, B. (1993) *Time for Religious Education and Teachers to Match: A Digest of Underprovision*. Report prepared for the Religious Education Council of England and Wales. Lancaster: RE-ME Enquiry Service.

Maykut, P. and Morehouse, R. (1994) *Beginning Qualitative Research: A Philosophical and Practical Guide*. London: Falmer Press.

Mead, N. (1996) Mentoring religious education teaching in secondary schools. Unpublished research paper. Oxford: Farmington Institute.

The significance of values in the professional development of beginning secondary Religious Education teachers

Nick Mead, Oxford Brookes University, UK, 2003

Abstract

This paper argues that evidence-based approaches to assessing professional values and practice may not do justice to the complex interactions between sets of values which shape and inform who we are as teachers. Six case studies of beginning teachers attempt to go beyond what might be observable in the classroom to try and understand the part played by values in learning to teach. The paper then reflects on how teacher education and professional development need to create opportunities for making the relationship between values and practice more explicit.

Introduction

Prompted by the introduction of a standard in professional values and practice into the 2002 Standards for the Award of Qualified Teacher Status (QTS), this study seeks to understand how Secondary teachers' professional values develop, from training into the early career years .The reasons for pursuing this study are two-fold: first, to understand the *process* of values formation which lies behind the standard in professional values and practice, and secondly, to identify those features of professional development which support this process.

The study is based on empirical research derived largely from interviews with a student teacher, newly qualified teachers and those in their early career years. All the research subjects were, or are going to be, secondary Religious Education specialists; however, the work of Bergem (1993), Hansen (2001) and Pepin (1999) suggests that the process of professional values formation and development in the early career years might be similar in all subjects.

Background

The contrast between the way in which the Standard in Professional Values and Practice was exemplified in the Teacher Training Agency (TTA) consultation document (2001) and in the final version of *Qualifying to Teach* (TTA 2002) is an important factor in the background to the research. The language of the consultation document describes the beginning teacher actively engaged in a process in which they 'can articulate their own considered professional values' (p.6), and 'can model and promote the values that underpin the purposes of education such as 'respect for the truth' and for the opinions of others' (p.8).

In contrast, although the final document, *Qualifying to Teach,* refers to the need for student teachers to understand the values underpinning the purposes of education, the 'articulating of their own considered professional values' and modelling and promoting 'respect for the truth' disappear. The final document is much more evidence-based, stating that 'high expectations, respect and commitment will be evident in the way a trainee seeks to find out about their pupils and uses that knowledge positively' (p.5). Evidence for a student teacher's understanding of values that underpin the purposes of education will be found in what is observable, such as in planning and pupil teacher relationships. While, of course, values are fundamental to *how* we teach, there is a need to articulate the purposes of education as well. This leads to the impetus behind this study, which is the need to give due consideration to the professional opportunities for beginning teachers to explore and articulate as well as practise their values.

Literature review

Previous research (Mead 2000) into the mentoring of Religious Education (RE) Post Graduate Certificate in Education (PGCE) student teachers identified their motivations on entry to training, and how such motivations might be mentored within their placement schools. A significant relationship between the personal and professional in the mentoring process was identified as a determinant of effective development during training:

> RE mentors need to understand these motivations which, for many students, are more significant than subject knowledge. They reveal certain intellectual orientations and skills compatible with understanding and evaluating religious ideas. School experience can focus and deepen these or can threaten them. Mentors need to nurture such motivations and shape them into realistic classroom competencies (Mead 2000, p.198).

Shaping the personal values of student teachers into classroom competencies seems to be one of the greatest challenges currently facing teacher educators, who have been operating in a competence-based climate for at least a decade. As my study of the values of PGCE primary student teachers (Mead 2003) highlighted, they came to the course with values, 'but did not necessarily feel that they had experienced a *process* of personal and professional development in relation to those values during training' (p.39).

Clearly, there is a difficulty in trying to assess professional values within an evidence-based and competence model of professional education. Inevitably, values shift the focus from skills to philosophical principles. In fact, as Carr argues, the very existence of professional values assumes that there is such a thing as objective truth:

> If there is really no such thing as objective truth to be had, even in principle, then education as anything more than equipping people with useful practical skills is simply sophistry and delusion. As a result there can be no objective rational basis for regarding teaching as a matter of principled obedience to more general professional imperatives (Carr 2000, p.119).

Pring develops Carr's fundamental premise that if we introduce professional values into teacher training, then we go beyond professional competence:

> teachers are committed to those values and relationships which belong to the very special transaction which goes on between teacher and learner. The moral formation which is required for this very special transaction reflects a combination of personal and professional development and skills (Pring 1994, p.184).

The moral formation is clearly described as a process involving caring for the curriculum because of its worth and not its utility, a concern for evidence and reasoned argument, a respect for alternative viewpoints, a search for understanding and the ability to use theory to interpret experience. Pring concludes that such values 'are precious, hard to come by and are easily lost' (p.184).

A significant feature of a process of moral formation is the personal commitment made by the individual. This is particularly highlighted in early professional development literature which acknowledges that the personal/professional dynamic has to be the starting point for continuing professional development:

> No matter how persuasive particular aspects of a shared social or occupational culture may be, or how well individuals are socialised into it, the attitudes and actions of each teacher are rooted in his/her own ways of perceiving the world (Nias 1989, p.156).

Tann recognised back in 1993, a year after the first set of teaching standards were introduced, that what Nias is addressing must be part of initial training. Students do come to their training with personal theories about education and what Tann found was that 'Students experienced great difficulty in making personal-public links because, 'we don't know the words' (Tann 1993, p.68). Tann goes on to conclude:

> This appears to be something that needs to be addressed early on in a course to provide students with language with which they can share their personal experience and learn from others' public experiences. Without this prerequisite reflection can hardly begin (Tann 1993, p.68).

The *process* of human development described here does not have to be incompatible with the acquisition of professional standards, but it is what gives those standards meaning to the individual student. This may be the difference between teacher training and teacher education, as argued by Fish:

> The competence-based model of teacher training reflects certainty of knowledge, understanding and skills, based on measuring the observable. The competence-based model to date is a training exercise rather than an educational enterprise and narrows its concerns to the acquisition of basic skills as opposed to developing understanding; refining practical and theoretical knowledge and engaging in scholarly activity (Fish 1996, p.47).

Most significantly, for Religious Education, Fish goes on to argue that such a model may present knowledge 'as absolute', 'render amoral the deeply moral', and 'pretend the possibility of objectivity in the face of certain subjectivity' (p.47).

To conclude, the research which follows attempts to examine the relationship between what Carr (2003, p.30) calls 'the personhood', or the individual integrity and moral qualities of the teacher, and evidence-based professional values and practice.

Methodology

As the research in this study aims to understand the process of professional values formation, it was felt that a qualitative approach would be most appropriate. The study consists of a small-scale survey of teachers' perceptions using past, present and future subjects from my own PGCE secondary Religious Education course.

Data were collected through the use of semi-structured interviews. Interviewees were selected to represent the period of professional development from training to the early career years. Interviews were undertaken with one student teacher, two newly qualified teachers (NQTs) and three teachers in their second, third and fifth year of teaching respectively.

The interview schedule consisted of six questions:

1. How do you think the following teaching standards in professional values and practice have developed before, during and after (if applicable) your initial training?

- 'have high expectations of pupils; respect for pupils' social, cultural, linguistic, religious and ethnic backgrounds, and commitment to raising their achievement.'

- 'Consistently treat pupils with respect and consideration, and show concern for their development as learners'.

- 'Demonstrate and promote the positive values, attitudes and behaviour that would be expected from pupils' (TTA 2002, p.79).

2. What part have personal values played in the development of your professional values?

3. What part have whole school values played in the development of your professional values?

4. What part have departmental and subject values played in the development of your professional values?

5. Are you aware of tensions which might exist between the values you are trying to exemplify and those held by pupils?

6. Are you aware of tensions which might exist between the values you are trying to exemplify and those held by parents?

Interviews were 40-50 minutes in length and were recorded with the interviewees' permission and then transcribed.

The data have been presented in the form of case studies so as to do justice to the complex interactions of different sets of values over a period of professional development.

Summary of findings

When student teachers, NQTs and teachers in their early careers talk about professional values, they tend to talk about what they believe in, the values in classrooms and espoused by schools, departments, pupils and parents, and those espoused by the community of fellow subject specialists. The research identifies an interdependency of different sets of values held by the individual teacher, which can be categorised as personal, institutional and subject values. The interdependency of these sets of values plays a significant part in the human development of the individual teacher and the shaping of their emerging personhood, not least when sets of values may be in conflict.

Findings

1. Teacher A

Teacher A, five years into his career, is able to reflect on how the early interactions between his personal and emerging professional values caused some challenging and painful moments:

> I think respect and the whole idea that all pupils need to raise their academic achievement across the board was there before, but coming from my background in Northern Ireland, where you don't trust the other side and you don't have such a minority of other religions and cultures, it was not something that had entered my thinking, as I assumed that I would teach there. My coming to England to study threw everything up in the air and I had to very quickly learn a lot at the very start of the PGCE course. I had a lot of soul searching, because, although the principle was there to want all pupils to achieve, I had to widen my understanding and look at it further in (Teacher A).

It is hard to imagine that such 'soul searching' can be supported and nurtured through evidence-based tick boxes in a training profile! Clearly, we could look for evidence in differentiation in planning but such evidence does not do justice to the human development of the individual who, in this case, experienced a fundamental cultural change as a beginning teacher.

And what of post training? Teacher A was fortunate enough to find a school where he felt the whole school values supported his personal development:

> It feels like we are teaching the whole school ethos of respect in this department (Teacher A).

Secondly, the management values of the RE department enabled him to continue to develop personally:

I was able to develop because we were a new department and everything that I did I developed how I wanted, I looked at how I was teaching something, evaluated it and next time tried to improve. By teaching the same lesson you know what works and what doesn't and I could say to my NQT colleague, that didn't work for me, what about trying this instead. Sometimes she will make the same mistake that I did and she may find that what works for me doesn't work for her, but we do talk about how we do things, seeing through schemes of work which we write, and adapting them as necessary if something doesn't work (Teacher A).

Thirdly, Teacher A found that there was sufficient scope within the life of the school to broaden his experience of a diverse range of pupils through involvement in the enrichment programme, particularly residential trips and The Duke of Edinburgh Award scheme.

It is apparent that values inherent in aspects of departmental management and professional development across the school enabled Teacher A to address the cultural change begun in the PGCE year when he left Northern Ireland, and that these values have contributed to effective subject teaching. However, he is aware that the values lying behind the NQT mentoring made a less significant contribution:

My mentor talked through lessons observed and said what she thought was good, what did you mean when you did this, why did you do it that way. I think that sometimes she was overcritical and the things she picked up on, such as a child wearing a coat, I would not see as majorly important (Teacher A).

There is a contrast here between the proactive way in which Teacher A addressed the huge shift in values experienced at the start of his PGCE course, by looking for the opportunities for individual development in the school, and the more evidence-based approach to professional values of the mentor. It is true that both matter but both need to be held together in equal relationship.

2. Teacher B

Teacher B, three years in the profession and about to become Head of Department, talked about how positive values, including respect, listening and empathy had played a major part in her RE teaching since her initial training. She believed such values have to be modelled and also have to be taught in terms of addressing misconceptions. In her current school she also finds that such values are reinforced by whole school values.

However, Teacher B is very much aware of how another whole school value is in direct tension with the positive values she has espoused personally and professionally, namely assessment and target setting. This is perceived as a 'pressure being put on by the school' and linked to this is an anxious expectation that any Ofsted inspector 'would expect a pupil to know which level they are working at and how to get there':

In Key Stage 3 we are now using a sheet for recording levelled assessment three times a year on each of the RE attainment targets. They are each given a level and a target and this is kept in their books. True, this is saying RE is not a doss subject and they are achieving levels which they can compare with other subjects and this does give the subject more status. For me that is not what RE is about at all and the pupils give a lot more than levels of assessment, but that's what we're doing to bring it in line with other subjects (Teacher B).

The tension between sets of values here becomes most explicit when talking with parents about individual pupil's development in RE:

We had a parents' evening last week and I said about how their behaviour had improved in class and how they contributed – all the things which I think are important in RE, and, at the end of it all, all they wanted to know was what level they were on and what would they get at the end of next year at the end of the key stage. A bit sad really, but that is the way it is going. When I am reporting to parents I try to cover every aspect of the subject and the level is only a small part of it. I don't think that's the reason any RE teacher goes in for teaching the subject (Teacher B).

3. Teacher C

Teacher C, reflecting on her professional development from her training into her second year of teaching, does not believe that ticking off of professional values on an evidence-based list does justice to her own development. Although her school has a high profile initiative on behaviour and respect, she believes that the individual development of the teacher is integral to professional values:

You are all at different stages of what your idea of respect is anyway, it's an individual thing. I don't think it's the kind of thing where you can go on a course and say, right I've learnt about respect and treating people equally. I don't think it's like that, I think that it's something which throughout your teaching career you will build upon and will improve all the time, I don't think that you just say I know how to respect people and that's it because you are always going to come across different kids with different backgrounds (Teacher C).

Closely related to this awareness of individual development is a feeling that NQT induction and mentoring tends to be a continuation of evidence-based assessment of values begun in the initial training. Teacher C found that the opportunity to share her values informally in NQT meetings was more beneficial than when the professional tutor talked with NQTs about 'the content of our lessons and what we did in class, rather than these professional values':

I found especially the NQT meetings after school when all the NQTs got together more helpful than the individual ones, because you learn from each other. With your professional tutor it's a teacher you've never seen teach. I found it easier talking with people on my own level who are going to do the same things as you – that was more useful (Teacher C).

Teacher C recalls that it was the Head of Maths who actually observed her teach in the NQT year and whose debriefs made her think about her self-evaluation skills, but she clearly sees a distinction between those skills and the more value-laden dialogue of the NQT forum.

Another forum where personal, professional and subject values can flourish is within the working party structures across the curriculum. Teacher C expresses how RE is valued in her school, which enables her to feel she has something of personal and professional worth to offer colleagues:

> I am the representative for RE on the teaching and learning group which looks at the way subjects use different methods. I like to put across what we do, and it raises your profile in the school, but I think it depends on how the whole school views your subject. Some schools value RE more than others, depending on whether there's a short course up and running or A Level. I think this school's not bad because it has improved this year with good A Level and GCSE results (Teacher C).

Overall, Teacher C highlights how professional development must acknowledge the individual and his or her values. Forums which enable beginning teachers to connect values with practice need to run alongside evidence-based mentoring. However, opportunities to contribute confidently to forums such as cross-curricular working parties can be determined by other sets of values, such as the standing of the subject in the school. It follows that low esteem in a subject area may inhibit confident articulation of the relationship between values and practice. This situation is compounded if the only perceived professional development is evidence-based feedback which is disconnected from values.

4. NQT A

NQT A, a mature entrant, reflected on the relationship between personal and professional values in his previous employment:

> I worked for a Christian publishing company which had a Christian business ethic and this has very much stuck to me and I think these are positive values which I have brought into the educational world (NQT A).

The greatest challenge for NQT A has been the shift from the theoretical compatibility of his Christian values with the standards of professional values and practice and the reality of what those standards actually feel like:

> While a lot of the standards are written down you don't really understand them fully until you have experienced them when you are living out the reality of them. You may say they are good standards but what does that mean in effect, and despite working with two-three schools on the PGCE course you know at the end of the placement you are going to move on. But, as an NQT, you are now in the job for real, you are teaching a full timetable, and I am a Year 7 tutor, and so you learn to fully understand many of the pressures that are placed upon you, making sure that the school runs efficiently, the tutor group runs well, as well as teach RE (NQT A).

Where the tension between personal and professional values has been felt most is in, almost instinctively, wanting to maintain a strong ethical responsibility for the life of the school, while at the same time striving to live out strongly held personal beliefs in the classroom. Success or failure in the latter, in terms of managing positive relationships with pupils, can undermine the former, and consequently, the coherence of the relationship between personal (in this case Christian) and professional values in the work context. Part of the process involves NQT A re-articulating what a professional value such as 'treating pupils with respect and consideration' might actually mean:

What I am learning is that you do need to be firm but also to mix it a little bit as far as trying to win their confidence and respect because you have got to relate to every student and learn that each has a point and to learn not to exclude any pupil from that process. You are now with them for the whole year and they have to work in partnership with you (NQT A).

Perhaps this leap from notional 'good' professional values to living them out would be less painful if, as Teacher B argues, it could be recognised that ticking of standards on a tick list does not do justice to the personal development of the individual teacher. It seems that taking forward an existing interrelationship between personal (Christian) and professional values into a new career has been a major challenge in the process of learning to teach for NQT A, and which has neither been made fully explicit nor addressed as part of the training process.

5. NQT B

NQT B talks about always having had positive values about young people. She talks with personal conviction about 'wanting pupils to see that thinking about values and where they come from is important'. She goes on to talk about valuing her own children, wanting them 'to develop and fulfil their potential, but I have wanted them to be good people as much as anything else.' In addition to these strongly held personal values, this NQT also has deep convictions about her subject:

Coming from a Christian background it would be easy to make the mistake of trying to do things in the light of that. But I want to teach each religion as having its own integrity and its own value and this has influenced how I have thought about my teaching and how I have learnt from my training (NQT B).

These personal and subject motivations led NQT B to give up life as an accountant and go back to college to study for a Theology degree, followed by a PGCE:

I wanted to make a difference and what I see RE doing is giving children the space to think and the freedom to express their thoughts, for the good (NQT B).

However, with so much at stake as a mature entrant to the profession and with such high ideals, the most challenging aspect of the progression from trainee to NQT has been encountering negative pupil attitudes in some classes:

For some children the whole experience of me and RE isn't a positive experience. You get a good week with some classes and then it's dreadful, but I try not to let it influence me and try to be positive, even though I know it will be second best, but I can't work on the basis that I would never come to work if that was the way I felt and O.K. they upset me (NQT B).

NQT B describes this conflict of values being addressed primarily by departmental and school systems:

> I don't like some of them and I try very hard with help to get over that and to use the school systems to do that and the school systems have served me well. I have help from my Head of Department, who, if I am struggling with someone, will take them into their class (NQT B).

But, for NQT B, her personal and subject motivations take her beyond systems to a deeper conviction that the relationships have to be re-negotiated each week:

> You will find, for example, on my lesson plan on a Thursday afternoon that it will say that we are going to do it this way because we are going to try and redeem the relationship once again (NQT B).

This is also why she wishes to avoid threats and holding grudges. Here then is clear evidence of standards of professional values and practice, but for the NQT they are not just being addressed at the level of evidenced action but are at the heart of the identity and integrity of the teacher. How important, then, that professional development should involve talking about our values, as well as how, and if, systems and strategies help us preserve and strengthen them.

6. Student Teacher A

Student A talked about 'the feelings and understanding of how RE teaching should be before I started the PGCE course':

> It's something that has got to come from inside, you can never *really* know what these faith experiences are like and so it's all about developing your own insights into a religion and you've got to encourage that need to find out, that inquisitiveness. The reason it works for me is because I have the need to help and increase learning, to help children learn and feel more complete as people (Student A)

However, Student Teacher A did not find it easy on his first placement to explore these personal convictions within the management ethos of the department:

> There was little discussion about the subject of RE and how it was approached. Discussion tended to be about the general running of department resources, deadlines etc. I found that when I did get philosophical they tended to change the discussion! But there were teachers trying to put a philosophy into practice. Teacher X for example espoused a philosophy and in his room there was a definite ethos and you felt you had to approach the subject with respect. Professional values can be at the level of dress and not as deep as it might be. I came in after months of thinking about how I relate to children and when I came and started it wasn't in depth at all, but chat (Student A).

This was articulated in the first term of the PGCE and is perhaps not well expressed. However, this mismatch between sets of values will not be fully identified in an evidence-based approach to professional values and practice. How might this student teacher be equipped to address the tensions here? As we have already seen, such mismatches or tensions can have a profound effect on the personal and professional development of the individual as they go into their early career years.

We now need reflection on the implications of these case studies for the Teacher Training Agency (TTA), student teachers, higher education tutors, school mentors and professional development tutors.

Conclusion

The main feature of the data is the interdependence of personal, professional and subject values. I suggest that this is how it is, and how it should be, if any teacher is to develop professionally in a meaningful way. In each of the case studies discussion about values reflects the personhood of the teacher as well as practice. Teaching is not merely the skill of acting but is, as Carr says, 'more a matter of being just who we are' (Carr 2003, p.28). Who we are and what we value, as an individual and within our subject, imbue planning, teaching and classroom management with a moral value. If personal, professional and subject values are encouraged to evolve in their interdependency we find teachers who have personal integrity. Carr describes such teachers as:

> Those to whom young people can turn with complete confidence, and on whom they can always rely for unfailing academic and personal help and support (Carr 2003, p.31).

However, the fragile nature of the process of evolving into such a teacher in the early career years becomes more evident when the data highlight the tensions which can exist within the interdependent sets of values. How these tensions are interpreted and managed by the individual and the school must have a significant impact on the development of the beginning teacher.

The TTA claims that all standards are underpinned by professional values, and yet these professional values themselves are to be assessed, as all other standards, by collection of evidence. Clearly, the process of professional development we have been describing requires teacher educators to encourage explicit interaction between values and skills in order to reflect what undoubtedly does happen, what needs to happen and what matters to beginning teachers, as they progress from training to establishing their careers. For example, as Carr says:

> There are obvious dangers in encouraging young teachers to conceive of class discipline more or less exclusively in terms of managerial or organisational skills than of such moral or interrelational virtues or characteristics as care, trust (worthiness) and respect (Carr 2003, p.31).

Teacher educators sharing their awareness of the nature of the process is particularly rewarding, especially when the documentation for teacher education is largely descriptive and functional. If we can understand the process and those factors which encourage it, we will be supporting beginning teachers not just in their professional development, but in their human development.

References

Bergem, T (1993) 'Examining aspects of professional morality,' in *The Journal of Moral Education,* 22(3) pp. 297-312.

Carr, D (2003) *Making Sense of Education* (London: RoutledgeFalmer).

Carr, D (2000) *Professionalism and Ethics in Teaching* (London: Routledge).

Fish, D (1996) 'Values, competency-based training and teacher education', in Selmes, C & Robb, W (Eds.) (1996) *Values in Teacher Education* (Aberdeen: National Association of Values in Education) 2 pp.44-50.

Hansen, D (2001) 'Teaching as a moral activity,' in V Richardson (ed.) *Handbook of Research on Teaching* (Washington D.C., American Education Research Association) pp. 826-857.

Mead, N (2000) 'Mentoring Religious Education in secondary schools', in Leicester, M, Modgil, C & S *Education, Culture and Values, vol. 5, Spiritual and Religious Education,* (London: Falmer) chap.19 pp. 197-203..

Mead, N (2003) 'Will the introduction of teaching standards in professional values and practice put the heart back into primary teacher education?' in *Journal of Pastoral Care in Education* 21(1) pp.37-42.

Nias, J (1989) 'Teaching and the self', in Holly, M & McLoughlin, C (Eds.) *Perspectives on Teachers' Professional Development* (London: Falmer), pt.3, chap.7.

Pepin, B (1999) 'Epistemologies, beliefs and conceptions of mathematics teaching and learning: the theory, and what is manifested in mathematics teachers' work in England, France and Germany', in *TNTEE Publications, 2(1).*

Tann, S (1993) 'Eliciting student teachers' personal theories', in Calderhead, J & Gates, P (Eds.) *Conceptualising Reflection in Teacher Development* (London: Falmer), chap.4.

Pring, R (1994) 'The Year 2000', in Wilkins, M & Sankey, D (Eds.) *Collaboration And Transition in Initial Teacher Training* (London: Kogan Page), chap. 13.

Teacher Training Agency (TTA) (2001) *Handbook to Accompany Standards for the Award of Qualified Teacher Status and Requirements for the Provision of Initial Teacher Training* (consultation document) (London: TTA).

Teacher Training Agency (TTA) (2002) *Qualifying to Teach, Professional standards for Qualified Teacher Status and Requirements for Initial Teacher Training* (London: TTA).

British Journal of Religious Education
Vol. 28, No. 2, March 2006, pp. 173–184

R Routledge

The experience of black African religious education trainee teachers training in England

Nick Mead*

Oxford Brookes University, UK

This study addresses issues surrounding the recruitment and training of black African religious education teachers within the context of the government's intention to make the teaching profession more representative of the wider community. In relation to this there is a strong emphasis in the Teacher Training Agency's *Qualifying to Teach* on selection procedures which promote equality of opportunity and the recognition of individual training needs. The study is informed by the work of Sikes and Everington who have highlighted the place of religion and culture within the personal histories of religious education teachers. Black African members of two successive cohorts of PGCE students are tracked to identify their training needs in relation to their cultural and religious backgrounds. The data identifies four cultural and religious factors which impact on their training to teach religious education in the UK. Finally, as advised by the Carrington Report, recommendations are made for the practice of teacher educators.

Keywords: *Black African; trainee teachers; religious education*

Introduction

Recent research on black trainee teachers training in the UK highlights racism, lack of ease, and the mentor relationship, but little is said about pedagogical assumptions. This may reflect the extent to which previous studies include samples of students who have received their education in the UK, but Jones, Maguire and Watson (1997) do highlight the pedagogic challenges faced by those who have been educated in Africa:

> Nigath thought that 'minority' student teachers who had received their school education in a more traditional environment before coming to Britain could often be at a disadvantage because of the difficulty of developing an understanding of contemporary British

*Westminster Institute of Education, Oxford Brookes University, Harcourt Hill, Oxford, OX2 9AT, UK. Email: nmead@brookes.ac.uk

ISSN 0141-6200 (print)/ISSN 1740-7931 (online)/06/020173–12
© 2006 Christian Education
DOI: 10.1080/01416200500531910

teaching methods, particularly classroom management, on such a short stressful course. Two overseas-educated students, Abedi and Benjamin, complained about the speed of the course, stating that. 'Things went too fast' and 'I need time to adjust'. (p. 140)

Stuart *et al.* (2003) briefly allude to 'culture shock' and make the point that there were those in their survey done on behalf of the Teacher Training Agency (TTA) who 'had recently arrived from countries with very different school cultures and had great problems in adjusting to classrooms where pupils often did not want to learn and where respect for teachers is not given as of right. Some of the Africans interviewed were horrified by the pupils' behaviour' (p. 5). It is clear that the influence of African pedagogy on the personality formation of such trainees, and thus on their identity as teachers, is a key contributory factor to some of the common difficulties experienced in their training. In addition, the paradox for those who come to teach religious education is that Christianity has been a formative influence in shaping African pedagogical assumptions, assumptions which are no longer made in the English common school.

There is much literature on colonial and African pedagogy but I wish to stay close to the experiences of the three trainees who are the case studies for this paper. Their countries of origin and where they were wholly educated are Rwanda, Kenya and Ghana. In the research process I gained insights into their African educational experience which sent me on a quest to understand more from research literature produced within these particular countries. All three trainees talked about religion, culture and pedagogy as one and, as Hedegaard (2003) has argued, their personality formation and self-identity as teachers are a product of their individual community's pedagogic goals.

The history of education in Rwanda is closely bound up with the history of the work of the churches in education. The first Rwandan school was founded by the Catholic White Fathers in 1900. Both the German and Belgian colonial administrations left education largely to the churches. At independence in 1962, 70% of pupils were in Catholic schools and, having been the sole provider until then, the Catholic church became a 'reluctant partner of the state, and ever since the two have existed side by side' (Obura, 2003, p. 112). The result has been an ambivalence which has allowed a prevailing conservative transmission pedagogy to continue, which, in turn, has contributed to perpetuating Hutu and Tutsi divisions with tragic social and moral consequences. How can such an educational background prepare S, my trainee, to deal with controversial issues in religious education in a predominantly white classroom in the south-east of England?

The main strategy to make religious education more inclusive of Kenyan experience following independence (1963) was to introduce liberal Christian life themes, as pioneered in England by Loukes and Goldman in the late 1960s. The constituent elements of the approach were human experience, the biblical experience, explanation, application and response. The findings of the research undertaken by Onsongo at the University of East Africa (Onsongo, 2002), which monitored and evaluated the life themes approach from the time of independence, show that 80% of teachers did not use the approach:

> The majority were found to be following the syllabus and content in the textbook word for word. They made few attempts to discuss the student's day to day experiences in presenting the subject matter. The teacher-centred and Bible-centred approach were found to be dominating most of the teaching. (p. 7)

The actual methods used involved minimal pupil participation: 'Such methods as the lecture method, question and answer, and teacher directed class discussion were the most used. Role play, drama, and pupil demonstrations were the least used' (p. 7).

Another feature of the pedagogy was the way in which lack of resources influenced the pedagogy: 'Even the textbooks were in some cases only for the teacher. Students had to rely on what the teacher had to say and give in the form of notes to be copied' (p. 8). However, the strong apparent focus on the teacher meant that discipline was very good, despite the large class sizes. Teachers did not spend time on control and command and there seemed to be an unspoken respect for the teacher.

Ackers and Hardman (2001) conclude that teachers' conservatism in teaching styles of the kind found in this study results from 'images of teaching which are culturally transmitted and deeply internalised' (p. 257).

Thirdly, and finally, recent Ghanaian research by Sefa Dei (2002) highlights questions about spirituality in the educational system which MA, my third case study, had experienced before coming to train in the UK. Sefa Dei argues that spirituality, as personhood, has been lacking in Ghanaian education because of the imposed linkage between formal religion and spirituality, created by colonial religious institutions assisting in delivering education in Ghana:

> When the sacred is imposed, it does not allow the self to know, learn, and teach from within. When the sacred is imposed through a power relation, the learner cannot recover the sense of community with others. The learner may not easily connect with the subject of study and the self who is teaching. Every learner, educator has a soul—the driving force of human action. The effective educator develops a sensitivity to the ways the body, mind and soul unfold within the learner to create a strong community relationship. (p. 48)

Sefa Dei's definition of spirituality, and the need for it to be developed in an inclusive, indigenous and relevant modern Ghanaian education system, is highly pertinent to current religious education pedagogical thinking in the UK. MA has indicated to me how Attainment Target 2 (learning from religions) in the newly published national framework for religious education (QCA, 2005) is a challenge in her teaching because it involves individual reflection, application and evaluation, within what should be a democratic community of enquiry. This is not what she experienced in her education which was confessional throughout, including her B.Ed. degree, and which consisted of the transmission of Christian beliefs and values. In MA's experience, as in the experience of case studies S and M, there is an implicit link between identity, knowledge, schooling and faith. Recent literature provides insights into difficulties which these trainees encounter in their UK training. The literature also highlights what Horsthemke (2004) considers should be not just Africa's concern, but a global pedagogical debate about the relationship between knowledge transmission, reflection and evaluation in education, which is crucial to the balance between objectivity and indigenous human experience in all cultures.

Religious education is part of this debate (Mead, 2001; Eke, Lee & Clough, 2005), and it is therefore my conviction that in learning how to support black African trainees on my Postgraduate Certificate in Education (PGCE) course, I am enhancing the development of all trainees.

Methodology

Three case studies have been used to identify the training needs of black African trainee teachers who have been wholly educated to university level in their own country, and who have come to the UK to train to teach secondary religious education.

Case study S was aged 36 and the only black African in the 2003–4 cohort. He had been educated in Rwanda and had done a little supply teaching in the south-east of England before beginning the religious education PGCE. Case Study M was aged 28 and had been educated to degree level in Kenya. He had taught a little in a secondary school in Nairobi and had been involved as an outreach worker in a national aids programme. Case study MA was aged 27 and had been wholly educated to B.Ed level in Ghana. She had done a little supply teaching in London before starting the course. Case study M and MA were the only black Africans in the 2004–5 cohort.

The research period was 2003–5, beginning with the tracking of S through the PGCE and into the first term of his Newly Qualified Teacher (NQT) year. Documents and non-participant observations from S's training were used and S was interviewed about his training needs and progress at the end of his first term as a NQT. The recruitment of M and MA enabled the research to be taken forward into the 2004–5 academic year to the point where M deferred and MA progressed to the final phase of the course. Research methods involved individual interviews with M and MA at the end of Term 1 and School Placement 1 about their preconceptions and the training needs arising from the reality of school experience; documents used included all records of the trainees' individual training programmes, including mentor reports and target setting. In addition non-participant observations of teaching over Placement 1 and 2 of the course were used. Records of mentor comments to the tutor were kept as in a research diary.

Summary of the findings

The data has identified the following key areas: the trainees' perceptions of the value and purpose of education, the identity of the teacher, the nature of pedagogy, and the issue of communication. Each area is analysed to show it has a fundamental bearing on the progress of three black African trainees training to teach religious education in the south-east of England. The implications of each area for trainees and teacher educators in universities and schools are raised in each section and recommendations made in the conclusion.

Perceptions of education

There are significant common perceptions of education in the UK which all three trainees refer to frequently. The first and perhaps most powerful is the value of education. S states:

> Behavioural problems are a big challenge for those coming from other countries. In our countries education is a privilege and here it is a right and because of that some kids feel that they are forced to go to school, whereas in Africa they feel privileged because education is a vehicle for development.

M describes how the difference in cultural expectations about education caught him off his guard, presenting him with unexpected challenges, not even fully appreciated in his two-week initial observation period before the course commenced:

> The way we Africans look at education is as a treasure, because in the experience of a lot us it is through education that we have been successful in finding jobs and everyone strives to get a decent education, including myself, my dad and my family.

Sefa Dei (2002) aligns this value of education closely to the values of the Christian faith and argues that this prevents values in education stepping outside formal religious spirituality and engaging more affective pedagogies which explore indigenous and local spiritualities. This is echoed in trainees' responses to a question about the part their faith has played in wanting to become a religious education teacher:

> From a very young age our parents told us that whatever you do, let it be the best, and we definitely knew that God had a place for everybody because the world is big and everyone has a share. I remember in my secondary school there was a motto, 'hard work will make you rich, being lazy will make you a slave'. Along the way this was a motivation and as a Christian you will not receive God's blessing if you are idle. (Trainee S)

M's motivations to become a religious education teacher are closely related to the fact that a Catholic missionary order paid for his entire education and that of his parents:

> We cherish the fact that God provides and this is a religious belief and within our entire system. In Kenya people still go to church on Sunday and do not work. I have found it very difficult to tell my family that I was working on a Sunday in the UK.

This alignment between academic success and Christianity proves to be a major stumbling block for all three trainee religious education teachers, in two ways. First, there is the challenge of teaching a multifaith syllabus in an educational context:

> My normal attitude at home would be Christianity and I would have nothing to do with Muslims. It is a big step to see things from another religious point of view. (Trainee M)

MA from Ghana describes a similar outlook:

> I remember where I lived in Ghana, we had a mosque just two minutes from where I lived and we didn't take much notice of it, and I have really regretted it because I didn't know I would be coming on this course to learn about all these other religions. If I had, I would have taken more notice of them because I had some Muslim friends in the same neighbourhood and I would have taken advantage of that to learn about Islam, but that is not encouraged much in Ghana.

Secondly, there is a genuine bewilderment about the apparent lack of concern for religion within society and education:

> What is surprising is that we had the British and other Europeans colonise us with civilisation and Christianity but when you come to this country you realise that they are not that firmly rooted in Christianity anymore. Churches are being turned into pubs or just neglected. That is not the situation in Ghana where schools are used as churches and having a good moral upbringing is important.

Trainee M talks in a similar vein:

> When we come over here we find a very relaxed attitude towards religion. When we grew up in Kenya the majority of whites were missionaries and we saw them as people who brought God to us. It is therefore quite a shock to come to England and realise that people are very relaxed about religion, and this is not the same because at home we take things for what they are.

The implications of these culturally and religiously determined perceptions of education are significant for Placement 1 of a PGCE and provide black African trainees with their first major hurdle:

> When you go into school and you get responses like 'I don't believe in God' and 'I don't want to know', this is a real challenge. Religion doesn't mean the same thing to others around you, but you have to teach it to everyone. It requires a lot of preparation to do this. (Trainee M)

Trainee M saw this challenge of preparation time compounded by his unfamiliarity with behaviour and attitudes. He argues for clear differentiation in training for such overwhelming needs and this echoes the views expressed by ethnic minority trainees in Jones *et al.* (1997) who said that everything 'went too fast'. Trainee M states that:

> I think partner schools need to have prior warning of these challenges. We are not the same. I am not the same as someone who has grown up here and gone to school in England. There are things which can be assumed and I have seen that. I will get on but I do need as much help as possible in these things. My mentor made assumptions and his attitude too quickly was 'I don't want to know a lot about your planning, it's your class, get on with it'.

Teacher identity

All three trainees emphasise the combination of the Christian faith and the cultural authority of elders as fundamental to the identity of the teacher. All three have great respect for the moral guidance they received from their teachers and attribute their academic and professional success to choices made on their behalf. When MA is asked about what she valued most about her Ghanaian education, she highlights how

> Most of our teachers were there to guide us—whenever you went to them for advice and to carry out choices, they were always willing to support you throughout and I valued this about the system. And the fact that we did as we were told may not be thought of as good, but it does help to a large extent because without that people will fall wayward.

MA believes that the teacher's role as moral guide and authority is derived from the extended family system in African societies. An adult would speak to a child or pupil and they would have to take it without question, 'So I think the same thing affected our way of learning'. As Ackers and Hardman have highlighted (2001), MA also emphasises that the teacher-led pedagogy resulted in few discipline problems: 'the classroom was focused on teaching rather than managing behaviour'.

In religious education teaching in the African context the relationship between faith, culture and teacher identity as moral guardianship is made explicit. How complex it is then to unravel these interconnections in the UK religious education context, as articulated by M, who withdrew from the course at the end of Placement 2. Like MA he also develops the perceptions of the identity of the teacher in Kenya as a guardian, receiving the same respect as a parent and elder:

> Every student has more-or-less the same expectations of the teacher and a teacher could be performing badly but the pupils would not rebel. Here it is different, you have to persuade the students to like you and also manage them and their behaviour, as well as keep them interested and focused.

Even when M was placed in a Catholic school for his second school experience, the relationship between his own Catholic background and his teacher identity was not assumed in the way that he had hoped. His mentor perceptively noted early on that M would not find the ethos and assumptions of a Catholic school in Milton Keynes identical to those in a Catholic school in Nairobi!

One of the striking qualities of all three trainees is their concern for the spiritual and moral well-being of young people, which is fundamental to religious education teaching. As has been identified by Knight (2004) in her research in America, black African qualities of care need to be recognised and developed in teacher education as a significant cultural strength. Their politeness and respect towards pupils is often striking. Undoubtedly, this is based on a religious respect for the uniqueness of the individual, something which gives S a very strong sense of his own worth and his pupils' worth. He has been able to take this forward into his NQT year as part of his modified teacher identity. S demonstrates how we need to develop this quality and blend it with a teacher identity which in religious education in the UK is largely achieved through engaging with pupils' experiences through imaginative pedagogies and interactive modes of communication.

Pedagogy

For all three trainees cultural perceptions of the value and purpose of education and the culturally determined identity of the teacher in turn shape the prevailing pedagogy which they experienced. MA described Ghanaian religious education pedagogy as

> based on the transmission and reproduction of biblical knowledge and the subject was called 'Bible Knowledge'. It was wholly Christian in content, although Islam is the second largest religion in Ghana. Judaism and Islam tended to be taught at university level and very little, if anything was taught about eastern religions.

As identified by Ackers and Hardman (2001) in their videotaping of 204 Rwandan lessons, all three trainees link their experience of limited resources, little differentiation and assessment beyond knowledge to the transmission model of pedagogy and, in turn, the unquestioned authority of the teacher. MA reflects on how learning by rote in Bible Knowledge limited opportunities to develop independent critical thinking:

> Q. Were the independent views of the pupils encouraged. Did the teacher ask your opinion?
>
> A. They would in some instances, but it was more of a formality because at the end of the day the judgement or decision lies with the teacher and they might not always take your views.
>
> Q. What about discussion in RE lessons. Was there very much?
>
> A. I don't remember very much. It was very factually based. We learnt the facts and during exams we reproduced the same facts in our own words. It didn't encourage much thinking.

MA does believe that there was something very stable about the pupil–teacher relationship in her Ghanaian education. This creates a challenge for her as she enters the PGCE course because she has become aware of how, in the UK, teachers' views can be readily challenged by pupils. Her brief experience of supply teaching in London has given her insights into some aspects of instability created by teachers' views being readily challenged by pupils but, on the other hand, she perceives the benefits of open discourse in a multifaith society:

> I have experienced pupils expressing their views. Initially I found this difficult and I gave them what I felt they should know, the knowledge without the discussion. My mentor encouraged me to try discussion and group work on my first placement and it worked.

MA believes that this is essential in a multifaith society and something that she did not experience in her own town where there was little communication between the large Presbyterian community to which she belonged and a large Muslim community with its own mosque.

Significantly, trainee S from Rwanda actually began to develop a more interactive pedagogy on his second school placement when he was encouraged by his mentor to teach about the Rwandan genocide within the topic of suffering and evil. It is interesting to read in Obura's (2003) account of post-genocide Rwandan education, that the main challenge in schools to overcoming future divisions in society is the need to discuss and understand the causes of suffering and evil. As yet, no one is prepared to write a textbook on the genocide. I observed trainee S teaching Year 10 on this subject and I observed him move from a transmission model with maps and information to a discursive model as pupils interjected and asked pertinent questions. As a result, and with the encouragement of his mentor, S introduced focused video viewing which raised political, social and educational issues which were then used in group scenarios involving empathy and opinion, such as a group letter to Kofi Annan and the director of Save the Children Fund. Following this opportunity, it is possible to track in S's mentor's records and my lesson observation sheets how there is an increasing mutual respect between S and his pupils, and a developing balance in his lesson plans between teacher transmission and independent pupil research, discussion and well-formulated pupil opinion.

At the end of Placement 1 MA is able to distinguish between what she describes as 'baby-sitting' as a religious education supply teacher and what she can now do:

> I have a much better knowledge of methodology, for example Cooling's Concept Cracking (1994) than I did when I started supply teaching. I did not do the subject justice then, and in Ghana it is only about imparting knowledge. Things like concept cracking where you relate the concepts to pupils' experience were in doubt before, nor did I consider making it accessible to all as we did not cater for special needs back home.

M acknowledged that he learnt a great deal from his first mentor about how to structure pupil activities, such as the sequencing of religious narrative and the categorising of human activity according to the five Buddhist precepts. M needed to progress towards giving active learning coherence and meaning by contextualising potentially imaginative tasks within the realm of pupil experience. This need was apparent when he wrote an excellent essay on constructivism as applied to religious education by Grimmitt (2000), which demonstrated a good understanding of a pedagogical method new to him, but contrasted with his need to engage with pupil experiences, which might be the basis of their constructions of meaning for an item of religious content.

All three trainees highlight the mentor's ability to affirm their African identity within the pedagogy of religious education. This supportive role of the mentor cannot be underestimated in achieving the integration of teacher identity and pedagogy in a new cultural setting, without denying 'who I am' (Trainee S). Both trainees MA and S seemed to develop confidence about intercultural dialogue as fundamental to pedagogy, and held a belief that they had something unique to offer pupils in the UK. I noticed that this conviction grew as S progressed into his NQT year, and account for it in terms of the ongoing integration of his identity with new pedagogies. For example, at parents' evening, S tells me that he drew on his own Rwandan experience to encourage pupils and parents to strive:

> I gave them some of my experiences. We didn't have all the facilities that the children here have, but even then kids strive to do the best they can, even if there are economic problems. My pupils' parents listened to this and I am not afraid to tell them about my identity, I am very proud of it. It is good for me to come with my culture because there are a few things that you can learn from Africa.

Communication

Issues of language and accent figure in the training of ethnic minority teachers (Osler, 1997, Stuart *et al.*, 2003). In religious education, lack of clarity in explanations and instructions relating to spiritual and moral issues can alienate and undermine a safe and secure learning environment, especially for the more reflective aspects of the subject. M had written and spoken English at the PGCE entry requirement level, and good subject knowledge, but sometimes struggled with precise explanations and instructions. For example, quite often potentially engaging tasks like writing a letter to a friend about the Ash Wednesday school mass were not contextualised within the lives of the pupils, and therefore the personal reflection (Attainment Target 2) was lost in a repetition of the order of the mass already identified in an earlier sequencing exercise. He felt strongly that this aspect of his teaching should have been supported much earlier:

> People need to be aware that there is a big difference between the intellectual ability of an African and some of the cultural challenges that we meet. I would say from my experience that the school needs to be informed that the person coming is from this part of the world, he is qualified well enough for the PGCE but there are cultural issues which you might meet which this person is dealing with as they actually interact with the pupils.

The role of the mentor is key to enabling trainees to develop clarity of explanations and instructions, particularly in religious education where abstract concepts of belief and value have to be contextualised within pupils' experience for meaning and relevance. MA was extremely grateful to her mentor:

> In terms of language, I do realise that sometimes, when I explain things in class, and think that I have explained it well, some students don't seem to get it that much and so my mentor would suggest different ways. There is a lot of work for me to do on this. I know that what I am saying isn't really right and I need to get down to their level or use their language.

MA is hinting here at the complexity of communicating beyond the transmission of knowledge and which is the basis upon which UK religious education pedagogy is built. In religious education there is the deeper level of communication with the beliefs, values and experience of pupils. As Sefa Dei has argued (2002), the dominance of formal religious spirituality in African education and the transmission pedagogic model does not give black African trainees a ready handle on learning from religions in a secular school. It is this level of communication through knowledge of pupils' lives and experiences which MA began to develop before the course in her supply teaching in London, and through regular contact with her aunt's children:

> I lived with my Ghanaian aunt who had two children growing up in this country. They were always challenging their mother in the house which I found very strange. The upbringing here is totally different to that in Ghana.

It was the need to further develop this level of communication which was making it difficult for M to give his thoroughly planned, well-resourced, and to some extent differentiated lessons, the overall coherence and meaning for pupils two-thirds of the way through Placement 2. As a result, he decided to defer from the course in order to develop his communication skills with young people in the classroom in a support role.

Conclusion

The data in this study is limited and the research period is brief, but it does provide a snapshot of training issues which arise for black African trainees during a PGCE religious education course. As such, it is possible to make some recommendations which might form part of teacher educators' staff development, as advised by Carrington et al. (2000). At interview we need to focus on the quality of written and spoken English, but also on the candidate's understanding of young peoples' social, moral, spiritual and cultural experiences and concerns in the UK context, and how these are addressed within the education system. Lack of understanding may be hidden by a very positive cultural feature, which is a concern for the moral and spiritual well-being of young people. Perceptive judgements may enable interviewers to make positive recommendations to help a trainee gain deeper understandings, which might prepare them for training, building on their own positive cultural strengths. At interview we need to clearly separate out the audit of subject knowledge from pedagogical experience and understanding. These candidates are usually well-qualified in all aspects of Christianity, but may have limited experience of exploring religious and moral issues outside a transmission pedagogy, not least intercultural dialogue. Candidates need to have additional pre-course experience of classroom interactions, and during training university tutors need to model dialogical pedagogies in their sessions.

Differentiated training on Placement 1 requires a longer period to build interactions with pupils based on mutual respect, and develop communication skills at the instructional, explanatory and discursive levels, which give meaning and relevance to concepts and tasks because they are expressed within the realm of the pupils' experience. Team teaching may provide opportunities for the mentor to model, modify and recognise the trainee's effective communication whilst interacting with pupils. Differentiated training on Placement 1 and 2 should address the increased preparation time which new pedagogies create for trainees. Trainees often have the intellectual ability to understand a range of methods beyond the transmission model they have been used to. As highly motivated and successful learners in their own cultural contexts, they are good students who research theory well. However, there is a gulf between theory and practice, and the mentor has a significant role to play in helping the trainee translate theory into a sequence of coherent and meaningful pupil activities. The mentor can make a significant difference by encouraging the trainee to authenticate their pedagogy through the incorporation of their cultural values and perceptions into their teaching rationale. This in turn facilitates the emergence of a teacher identity, firmly rooted in culturally appropriate pedagogies and modes of communication, but which does not deny 'who I am'. This last recommendation is at the heart of the life history approach to understanding religious education teachers (Sikes & Everington, 2004) and it reflects work done by Nias (1989) and others on the relationship between teachers' values, identity and what they do well in the classroom. In this sense our workforce in the UK will become more representative of the national and global community if we once again pay attention to the processes of human development which are involved in becoming a teacher, rather than simply training to meet standards or competencies. It is therefore timely that the training needs of black Africans can refocus us on the nature and purpose of teacher education per se.

Notes on contributor

Nick Mead is Principal Lecturer in Education at Westminster Institute of Education, Oxford Brookes University.

References

Ackers, J. & Hardman, F. (2001) Classroom interactions in Kenyan primary schools, *Compare*, 31 (2), 245–52.

Carrington, B., Bonnett, A., Demaine, J., Hall, I., Nayak, N., Short, G. *et al.* (2000) *Ethnicity and the Professional Socialisation of Teachers.* Final report to the Teacher Training Agency (London, TTA).

Cooling, T. (1994) *Concept Cracking: Exploring Christian Beliefs in Schools* (Nottingham, Stapleford Project Books).

Eke, R., Lee, J. & Clough, N. (2005) Whole-class interactive teaching and learning in religious education: transcripts from four primary classrooms, *British Journal of Religious Education*, 27 (2), 159–72.

Grimmitt, M. (Ed.) (2000) *Pedagogies of Religious Education* (Great Wakering, McCrimmons).

Hedegaard, M. (2003) Cultural minority children's learning within culturally sensitive classroom teaching, *Pedagogy, Culture and Society*, 11 (1), 133–51.

Horsthemke, K. (2004) Knowledge, education and the limits of Africanisation, *Journal of Philosophy of Education*, 38 (4), 571–87.

Jones, C., Maguire, M. & Watson B. (1997) The school experience of some minority ethnic students in London Schools during initial teacher training, *Journal of Education for Teaching*, 23 (2), 131–44.

Knight, M. (2004) Sensing the urgency: envisioning a black humanist vision of care in teacher education, *Race, Ethnicity and Education*, 7 (3), 211–27.

Mead, N. (2001) Identifying pedagogic skills common to primary religious education and PSHE/citizenship, *Curriculum*, 22 (2), 43–51.

Nias, J. (1989) *Primary Teachers Talking: a Study of Teaching as Work* (London, Routledge).

Obura, A. (2003) *Never Again, Education Reconstruction in Rwanda* (Paris, International Institute for Educational Planning, UNESCO).

Onsongo, J. (2002) The life approach method in teaching Christian religious education in secondary schools, *The Eastern Africa Journal of Humanities and Sciences*, 1 (1), 1–10.

Osler, A. (1997) *The Education and Careers of Black Teachers* (Buckingham, Open University Press).

Qualifications and Curriculum Authority (QCA) (2005) *Religious Education: a Non-statutory National Framework* (London, QCA).

Sefa Dei, G. (2002) Spirituality in African education: issues, contentions and contestations from a Ghanaian case study, *International Journal of Children's Spirituality*, 7 (1), 38–56.

Sikes, P. & Everington, J. (2004) 'Religious education teachers do get drunk you know': becoming a religious education teacher in the twenty-first century, *Teachers and Teaching: theory and practice*, 10 (1), 21–33.

Stuart, J., Cole, M., with Birrell G. Snow, D. & Wilson, V. (2003) *Minority Ethnic and Overseas Student Teachers in South-East England* (London, TTA).

Teacher Training Agency (TTA) (2003) *Qualifying to Teach, Handbook of Guidance* (London, TTA).

MENTORING STUDENT–TEACHERS IN THE SPIRITUAL AND MORAL

Nick Mead

INTRODUCTION: LESSONS FROM RE

The SCAA conference on moral and spiritual development held in January 1996 agreed that the moral and spiritual should, 'permeate all school activities and subjects in the curriculum,' but found it, 'less clear how this should be tackled'.[1] The conference defined one aspect of spirituality as, 'the sense of identity and self-worth which enables us to value others'.[2] The question is then, what kind of methodology might encourage the permeation of identity and self-worth throughout the life of the school?

Recent research of mine into Religious Education (RE) mentoring[3] may help our understanding of methodology in the moral and spiritual dimension of the curriculum. We are perhaps at a stage in the development of RE Initial Teacher Education (ITE) where we have something to say about how student-teachers generally might be equipped with skills for tackling the moral and spiritual. This also addresses the concern of the SCAA conference about the exclusion of the moral and spiritual from Initial Teacher Training (ITT), the lack of confidence of student-teachers to tackle it, and the need for teachers, 'to be trained in ways to develop the spiritual and moral dimension'.[3]

Recruitment to secondary RE teaching has expanded since the Teacher Training Agency (TTA) recognised RE as a shortage subject. As a result, Post Graduate Certificate of Education (PGCE) courses are recruiting from an ever-widening academic base. Our research suggests that in more modern Higher Education Institutions (HEIs) which have no tradition of Theology or Religious Studies (RS), up to 70% of the intake may have non-Theology/RS degrees. This new breed of RE student-teacher is more likely to be a philosopher or a sociologist that a theologian.

Why are such recruits suited to RE teaching? Our research suggests that they possess appropriate motivations and intellectual orientations for exploring the spiritual and moral.

APPROPRIATE MOTIVATIONS FOR THE SPIRITUAL AND MORAL

Our research identified three key motivations, the first of which is a general teaching motivation based on a, 'desire to communicate and encourage ideas in a stimulating environment'. Second, a recognition of the spiritual, moral and cultural value of RE:

'My academic background is in Philosophy but I am keen to teach RE because I am convinced of its importance throughout every pupil's school life. At its best I think RE should provide children with a context for moral reasoning, a sense of their own identity within the universe and a basis for understanding their own and other cultures, as well as knowledge of particular religions'.

(Student F)

This intellectual base is linked by other students to actually wanting to give pupils the means to change and develop:

'From the RE I have received at GCSE, A Level and degree level, I have realised that pupils must reflect on and be creative with their own experiences, attitudes and emotions in a wide range of topics.'

(Student I)

Part of this is sharing in pupils' spiritual development:

'I have an enthusiasm for children and young people and, in particular, sharing with them religious, social and moral ideas in order to promote their spiritual knowledge and development'.   (Student 9)

Students see the outcome of this intellectual enterprise as relating to the dilemma in our society about the relationship between belief, morality and action: there is mention of the , 'influence of personal ideas and values on behaviour', of, 'responding to moral dilemmas which dominate our lives, of, 'giving pupils convictions and wisdom to change things' and there is a good deal about teaching respect for culture, Law and morality.

The third motivation is that of wanting to pass onone's own positive experience of RE. Students identified skills in RE which are important to them and they wish to develop in pupils. Mention is made of reflective skills: 'The ability to think effectively', 'to think critically,' and 'appreciate and evaluate. 'Importance is attached to effective thinking which enables one to gain an in-depth understanding of human nature:

'It is these skills and this knowledge that I hope to pass on to children through teaching so that they might put to better use their accumulated knowledge, and better relate to others through their understanding and acceptance of the sheer variety of human nature and it's beliefs.'   (Student H)

It is evident that, although a significant percentage of these students have no academic grounding in the spiritual and moral, they do have an intellectual orientation towards exploring questions of identity and self-worth in a social and cultural context. Can such intellectual skills be taught to all PGCE students? Alternatively, should we be looking across the whole PGCE intake for individuals with such skills who might be encouraged to take a lead on the spiritual and moral in their own curriculum area; after all, this may be a model for a way forward in school. Whichever way, subject mentors in schools will need to nurture student-teachers in the spiritual and moral.

MENTORING IN THE SPIRITUAL AND MORAL IN SCHOOL

Prior to the increased school-based element of ITT the role of experienced Heads of Department was to supervise students on teaching practice. Increasingly it will have to be the case that mentors are not just experienced supervisory teachers but skilled trainers.

However mechanistic the TTA's measurement of classroom competences might seem, effective teaching will not be achieved unless mentors begin with students' personal motivations to teach, and through structured classroom experiences, enable them to implement these using effective pedagogic skills.

Understanding the shift from a supervisory to a training role for mentors is particularly helpful in exploring how the spiritual and moral might be approached in ITT. The development of the role of mentor means that the link between students' motivations to teach a subject and the contribution this makes to pupils' identities and self-worth is much closer than under the old PGCE system when there was a demarcation between theory and practice.

1. THE MENTOR/STUDENT RELATIONSHIP

For the moral and spiritual to emerge in any curriculum area during the training process, the student/mentor relationship will have to be more than a supervisory one:

'It's about building up trust quickly. It does seem to work. I don't know how but perhaps it's because there is no hidden agenda. We're here to help them pass and I am very honest about my own teaching.'   (Mentor C)

The honesty mentioned says something about the mentor's need to explain the relationship between their own motivations and what they think they are achieving in the classroom:

Q. 'How far do you go in being personal about what you are trying to do in the classroom?'

A. 'We always discuss that I am trying to get an enthusiastic response to RE and I am very clear about my aims in terms of getting pupils to respect other people. I want the student-teachers to know where I stand with the subject and enjoy being in the classroom with me.   '(Mentor G)

In turn, the mentor will need to respect the motivations of the student:

'I guess I hope I am going to learn from mentoring as well. I prefer to see my role with them as encouraging and facilitating, but also perhaps gaining from their ideas about how to do things.'   (Mentor A)

Perhaps mentors will need to be trained in

how to explore their own set of motivations which led them into teaching, and how the principles of their subject contribute to individual pupil's identity and self-worth; what is clear is that the moral and spiritual will not emerge unless mentor and student are communicating at the level of personal motivations.

2. MENTORING IN APPROPRIATE MOTIVATIONS FOR THE SPIRITUAL AND MORAL

Research into RE mentoring shows RE mentors particularly alert to the extreme forms of student motivations in terms of either indifference or confessionalism:

'I've had one or two students in the past about whom I've had that underlying feeling that they simply wanted to extend their university course'.   (Mentor B)

and the other extreme:

'One student had this view of what he wanted to do and I said this is not on but he felt it was my view against his. He was confessing his own world view and identifying himself with the subject.'   (Mentor C)

It seems that both indifference and confessionalism are dealt with effectively by mentors who have worked through, and can account for, the relationship between their own motivations and their classroom practice. Although confessionalism is not an issue in other subjects, it would be desirable for all PGCE students to develop a balanced understanding of how their approach in the classroom is contributing to the general well-being of their pupils. Other Mentors can take a pedagogic principle from RE, that pupils' identity and self-worth are inextricably linked to the teacher's commitment to each pupil. Both indifference and confessionalism demonstrate how teachers with a lack of, or with inappropriate motivations, can deny the recognition of pupils as individuals in their own right.

3. INTEGRATING THEORY AND PRACTICE IN THE SPIRITUAL AND MORAL

If HEIs contribute to students' understanding of the spiritual and moral across the curriculum, will the students actually identify this way of thinking in school, or will it be a prevailing cynicism that they encounter?RE students sometimes have to get used to a mismatch between theory and a negative perception of their subject in a particular school and this may be true of the spiritual and moral. Students may encounter cynicism amongst teachers about the politicised use of the words 'spiritual' and 'moral'. Even the use of these words can be a block in school to any valuable exploration of identity and self-worth.

It seems that students will need to be trained in how to penetrate what may be a superficial staff room culture and gain an understanding of teachers' perceptions of the moral and spiritual. Students should be given skills in how to approach their mentor in a professional way, asking appropriate questions which enable the mentor to explain the beliefs and values which lie behind their classroom practice. Students may be surprised by what lies behind a cynical exterior!

In their turn, mentors need training which enables them to recognise that the moral and spiritual are not some passing whim of SCAA, which defies definition, but are about pupil identity and self-worth, lying at the heart of sound classroom practice. Mentors would then be able to elicit pertinent questions from students about the reasons for, and value of, certain classroom practices.

4. DISCIPLINE, CLASSROOM ETHOS, AND THE MORAL AND SPIRITUAL

Are there principles in the mentoring of RE discipline which can contribute to an understanding of the development of the moral and spiritual in other subjects?At the heart of mentoring discipline in RE is the mentor's ability to communicate to both pupils and PGCE students what it is they are trying to achieve in the lesson. PGCE students, like pupils, are inducted into the ETHOS of an RE department and it is this which can promote respect and understanding:

'We have our list of RE rules on the wall-because confidential things can be said in this room and respect is needed-we also respect pupil's silence'.   (Mentor E)

Good mentoring encourages an open atmosphere in which all will be listened to and a balanced range of views heard:

'Where RE does cause a discipline problem is when the children perceive it is you trying to get them to believe something- the barriers go up. It's not a problem if it's about exploration-everyone has a spiritual element'. (Mentor E)

The mentor will need to demonstrate how to hold the line in discussion and yet, when appropriate, be ready to be seen to be genuine and personal:

'In my last school we had a lot of British National Party (BNP) people and they would dominate any discussion on racism and intimidate other pupils, so I gained confidence to intervene when necessary'.   (Mentor A)

Mentor F talks about a change to a more conducive atmosphere in a Year 9 lesson:

'Some of the boys started to ask some deep questions and I broke off and was ready to share and some things came out about me and the atmosphere changed. I felt they warmed to me and I would hope to keep that going and they have an idea of what an RE teacher is like-they have got to see you are genuine'. (Mentor F)

The ethos of any lesson says a lot about the moral and spiritual orientations of the teacher. Is there recognition and self-worth given to all?The teacher, whatever the subject, has to hold the line on views and be ready to be genuine and personal, in order to confirm the validity of the enterprise for all in that lesson. There is a skill in RE teaching, in moving between the personal and formal, which gives a spiritual, as well as an intellectual integrity to the work. Here, then, are a number of skills which may play a part in the mentoring process across the curriculum.

CONCLUSION

Many PGCE students from similar academic backgrounds to those entering RE teaching, will have the appropriate motivations and orientations to tackle the moral and spiritual. If we can identify the skills more precisely, we will probably find scientists and mathematicians who will willingly engage with questions about identity and self-worth, and who enjoyed such explorations in RE or PSE at school. A readiness to engage may come about if certain pedagogic skills in the spiritual and moral can be extrapolated from good practice in RE, and are shown to be integral to all teaching.

For subject specialists in secondary schools, this will have to translate into how personal motivations are implemented in classroom practice. Mentors need to have worked this through themselves and be ready to engage with students in exploring beliefs and values about identity and self-worth which undergird their teaching.

Mentors will need to ensure, as part of the training, that students are developing appropriate motivations for the spiritual and moral. This means that they are being encouraged to recognise pupil identity and self-worth as integral to the pedagogic process.

A prevailing school culture of cynicism about the spiritual and moral may mislead student-teachers, but they will have to go deeper to draw out from their mentor the relationship between identity, self-worth and their subject teaching.

Mentors can help students focus on lesson ethos, as an expression of the moral and spiritual, by employing some of the methods used in RE mentoring, in particular the skill of achieving an open, respectful atmosphere, facilitated by the teacher moving between the personal and the formal.   ❐

REFERENCES

1. SCAA Discussion paper No 6:   Education for Adult Life: the spiritual and moral development ofyoung people. SCAA 1996
2. Ibid.
3. Mead N. 'Mentoring Religious Education, Teaching in Secondary Schools.' Farmington Research Project. Warwick University 1996. Copyright: Farmington Institute, Oxford.

REVIEW

Values transference v. values clarification?

NICK MEAD

Spiritual Development and all that Jazz
Antony Flew & Fred Naylor, 1996
The Campaign for Real Education
ISBN 1 872953 24 7, £4.00

> Is it bizarre to demand of pupils in
> primary schools even the most
> embryonic awareness and scrutiny of
> ultimate questions surrounding
> existence? Many professors of
> Philosophy do not expect theses things
> of adults. (Flew & Naylor, 1996, p. 7)

My response to this is 'more's the pity!'
However, Flew & Naylor in their pamphlet
really want to make the point that the concept of
the spiritual as defined by the Office for
Standards in Education (OFSTED) is a nonsense
and an unreasonable expectation to place on
schools and pupils when levels of literacy and
numeracy need significant raising.

Is there a secular understanding of the
spiritual which parents, teachers and pupils
would recognise as a valuable dimension of
education and which is not mere progressive,
child-centred pap, as Flew & Naylor would
believe? The fact is that very young children do
want to address ultimate questions – as every
infant teacher knows – and it is *how* such
questions are addressed which is crucial to the
debate. The intellectual, spiritual and moral
development of young people is at stake.
Professors of philosophy ought to heed this!

Although there has been some concern about
the politicising of words like 'the spiritual' and
'moral' in an educational context, there has been
a readiness on the part of teachers to
acknowledge the Spiritual, Moral, Social and
Cultural (SMSC) as a significant dimension to
their work. It is interesting, too, that ordinands
preparing for work in schools are comfortable
with an educational understanding of the
spiritual which they might complement in a
distinctive way.

It cannot be denied that this pamphlet has a
challenging and provocative tone (the title itself
mocks). However, mockery is all too prevalent
in the text and arguments are not grounded in
evidence of classroom practice. This is
particularly illustrated in the approach taken to
children's moral development:

> The idea that young children should be
> encouraged to make their own decisions
> on whether to smoke, take drugs, steal
> or murder on the grounds that, with
> practice in decision-making, they will
> go on to make better decisions, is
> completely unacceptable in a society
> which seeks to remain civilised. (p. 4)

The thrust of this argument is, as with spiritual
development, directed at what the authors
consider to be the destructiveness of
child-centred approaches; however, in being so
anxious to attack the main protagonists like
Dewey and Rogers, they create a false
dichotomy which does not do justice to much
professional reflection and practice in schools.

The false dichotomy is between what Flew &
Naylor call 'values transference' and 'values
clarification'. Now, there is an important debate
to be had about the role of schools in
transmitting values *to*, and clarifying values *for*,
pupils. Fortunately, we are in an educational
climate in which it is possible to have this debate,
and judging from student teachers' responses to
such debates in their university programmes,
there is a thirst for it.

The educational climate we are in is not one
which has 'lost its way' since the liberal Schools'
Council Humanities Project was introduced in
1967, as Flew & Naylor want us to believe. This
grossly underestimates the complexities faced
by teachers wrestling with materialistic

individualism – married to a heavily content and skills based National Curriculum. The climate is, then, one of seeking ways to combine effective learning and socialisation (the two cannot be separated), which means little dependence on either values transference or values clarification. What Flew & Naylor miss is that in this climate it is possible for teachers to engage in the debate about the moral and spiritual development of children. That is what we are seeing in staff professional development in schools, and in the production of supporting material, with which Flew & Naylor ought to familiarise themselves.

The same false dichotomy between values transference and clarification leads Flew & Naylor to give a misrepresentation of the strides taken over the past 30 years in the development of effective religious education (RE) teaching in schools.

> Progressive child-centred notions have been just as influential in Religious Education as in moral education. A benchmark was the Church of England's Durham report in 1970 . . . given that it involved the replacement of values transference by values clarification it amounted to a major revolution . . . the principal recommendation was that there should no longer be any attempt to press for the acceptance of any particular faith or belief system. (p. 6)

Again, one report or publication seems to be the downfall of the whole moral and spiritual framework according to Flew & Naylor: whereas in reality those RE scholars, like Bob Jackson of Warwick, record the fudge and compromise of RE in the 1960s when values transference did not connect with the reality experienced by young people. It is evident from the development of ethnographic materials in RE which reflect the 'lived reality' of individual faith members within their own communities: also within the wider community. It is evident, too, in the recent clarification of RE learning objectives as 'learning *from* religions' and 'learning *about* religions' that RE is grappling with the interface between values transference and values clarification in an intelligent and creative way. This has given RE a new integrity within education, which is increasingly being recognised by pupils, parents and teachers.

It will be evident by now that Flew & Naylor succeed in stimulating a response, and this of course is the brief of the Campaign for Real Education. Their arguments are extreme, and at times absurd, because they are not founded on evidence in schools. However, in the context of the student teacher seminar, selected passages from this pamphlet help to sharpen the crucial debate taking place in university departments of education about the effectiveness of the school community in integrating learning and socialisation.

[This review highlights the fundamental difficulty of trying to deal adequately with deep questions of faith and values in an inevitably superficial mish-mash school environment. More contributions please on this issue. Ed.]

Section Three

Enhancing values in primary teacher education through developing the relationship between Religious Education and Personal, Social, Health & Economic Education & Citizenship

The challenge of Citizenship to Religious Education. First published in *REsource* (1999) 22(1) pp.12-15 (Professional Council for Religious Education).

Researching skills common to Religious Education and Citizenship. First published in Clipson-Boyles S. (Ed.) (2000) *Putting Research into Practice in Primary Teaching and Learning,* Chapt. 15, pp.165-175 (London: David Fulton).

Identifying pedagogic skills common to primary Religious Education and PSHE/Citizenship and the implications for continuing professional development, First published in *Curriculum* (2001) 22(2) pp.43-51 (Studies in Education).

The Challenge of Citizenship to Religious Education

Nick Mead

After taking the first cohort of BEd students through a PSE/Citizenship Elective at Westminster College, Nick Mead reflects on both the practical and theoretical dimensions of the relationship between Citizenship and Religious Education. He suggests that Citizenship presents a positive challenge to Religious Education, rather than a threat, and that RE teachers should be playing a significant part in the debate about the skills for Citizenship pedagogy which all teachers will need to acquire.

The Debate within Current Teacher Training

Recent INSET and Initial Teacher Training courses at Westminster College, Oxford have sought to make positive links between RE and Citizenship. The two main aims of such courses have been:

1 to enable teachers to become familiar with certain skills and attitudes located in Citizenship and

2 to evaluate how such skills and attitudes might benefit the quality of RE teaching.

A new BEd Elective attracted 50% of its recruits from main course RE trainees; this in itself is an indicator of the natural links perceived between RE and Citizenship. The elective seeks to evaluate and justify the place of Citizenship within the primary curriculum in the light of the three strands of the Crick Report (1998): Social and Moral Responsibility, Community Involvement and Political Literacy. Evaluation and justification seem to arise from the skills and attitudes base of the proposed Citizenship programme. The most challenging aspect of evaluating the place of Citizenship is the need for teachers to look at their understanding of how schools handle values. To reflect on values transmission and values clarification and to begin to make explicit one's own values and the impact of these on pupils has proved to be a new experience for many trainee and serving teachers whose profes-

sional development has revolved around a content-driven curriculum. In the process of such reflection teachers gain confidence through entering into dialogue and this seems to affect both their own and pupils' self-esteem:

> Surely every teacher training course should include values education in order that the implicit might become explicit and children can benefit from confident teachers with clarified understandings. (Trainee Teacher)

> The course has given me the opportunity to think about and reflect on my own beliefs. (Trainee Teacher)

Skills and Attitudes

How can the skills and attitudes of Citizenship offer a positive challenge to the effective learning *about* and *from* religions in RE?

1 Dialogue and spiritual literacy
First of all through the skills of dialogue and spiritual literacy. Political literacy implies skills, values and attitudes needed for good citizenship. Democratic education promotes spiritual, moral and intellectual autonomy; this means that spiritual education is about engaging in dialogue with others who hold different values as part of the process of achieving spiritual autonomy. Emphasis on skills of dialogue within Citizenship therefore challenges RE to rise above what John Hull calls 'religionism' (1992, 2). This challenge takes us right back to the debate about the religion-based nature of the QCA Model Syllabuses and the increasing number of primary schemes of work which are content-bound by religion and allow limited opportunities for those skills of reflection, application and evaluation which are rooted in thematic dialogue across religions.

2 Philosophical inquiry and moral reasoning
Secondly, Citizenship challenges us to look at skills of philosophical inquiry and moral reasoning within RE. The Crick Report states that 'It is a mistake to think of primary school education as pre-citizenship' (2.11). This undoubtedly challenges assumptions about children being pre-religious, sometimes detected in Key Stage 1 teachers saying they wouldn't do such and such with their pupils in RE because they are not yet ready.

The concept of the primary class as the 'community of inquiry' developed by Matthew Lipman (1991) demonstrates the potential for learning from religions within RE. The use of moral and religious narrative out of which pupils identify key issues they wish to discuss seems to provide a way forward in RE which prevents the multi-faith becoming the multi-fact. Yes, children are natural philosophers and Citizenship challenges RE co-ordinators to create within their lessons the ethos of the community of inquiry.

Look at the Citizenship Learning Outcomes for Key Stage 1 in the Crick Report (46) and see how closely they correspond to many of the skills and attitudes in good RE:

- Express a personal opinion.
- Discuss, take turns and respond to others.
- Work with others and gather their opinions.
- Empathise.
- Reflect on issues of social and moral concern presented in different ways.
- Take part in a simple debate and vote.

3 Teachers' skills

Thirdly, Citizenship challenges teachers' skills in self-understanding and self-esteem. The 1996 Values Forum identified teachers' personal qualities as being 'as important as their academic qualities' (SCAA 1996, 17) and yet noted the lack of confidence in the PSE/SMSC values education area. That this need should be addressed is apparent from the responses of trainee teachers to the Citizenship Elective at Westminster:

> A greater understanding of values enables teachers to be more well-rounded. (Trainee Teacher).

Citizenship is challenging RE co-ordinators to know and value themselves in the process of achieving their own spiritual and moral autonomy. We know what the effect can be of poor teacher self-esteem on children's learning and this has a direct bearing on the quality of learning from religions in RE.

4 Pupil self-understanding and self-esteem

Fourthly, Citizenship challenges RE to focus on the quality of pupil self-understanding and self-esteem in the process of learning from religions. As one trainee teacher put it:

> All trainee teachers should have the opportunity to learn about how Values Education improves a child's self-esteem, the importance of this and how it shapes their lives. (Trainee Teacher)

This trainee is an RE specialist who through a Citizenship course has come to recognise the spiritual and moral autonomy of the individual pupil and as a result should be more confident as a future co-ordinator in encouraging her colleagues to develop effective learning from religions.

Therefore, there is a relationship between Citizenship, RE and the good school which RE co-ordinators ought to consider. The effective school movement has tended to focus on productivity and outcomes as the measure of school effectiveness. The skills and values within Citizenship encourage us to consider the good school in terms of respect for persons, truth and justice. RE can make a significant contribution to school effectiveness if it rises to the four challenges presented by Citizenship. RE can contribute to respect for persons, truth and justice if it rises above 'religionism' and encourages children to enter into dialogue across a range of views. It can contribute if it is truly multi-faith and not multi-fact so that there is dialogue in the context of a good balance between learning about and learning from religions. Finally, it can contribute if both teachers' and pupils' self-understanding and self-esteem are integral to the quality of learning about and learning from religions.

The Debate within Current Literature

The positive relationship between Religious Education and Citizenship which we are advocating is supported by an emerging type of literature which provides a distinctive philosophical reflection on the role of Religious, Moral and Spiritual Education in the wider context of Values Education.

The focus of Hobson and Edwards' *Religious Education in a Pluralist Society* is very much in the spirit of the Crick Report's emphasis on philosophical inquiry and moral reasoning as part of the process of Values Education. Skills in democracy in the classroom are echoed in the principles of liberal education outlined as essential in RE:

> Critical rationality, personal transcendence and epistemological coherence … so that students would thus come to decide that some beliefs are better based or more rationally defensible than others, are more consistent both within themselves and with other branches of knowledge, and lead to a more personally meaningful world view. (Hobson and Edwards 1999, 57)

The authors emphasise the way in which pupils can conduct the process of inquiry, reasoning, reflection and evaluation and remain secure within their own faith or non-faith position with the freedom to change their stance if they felt that there was sufficient reason to do so. Here is the essence of learning from religions and the democratic process of listening to others and reaching an informed opinion: skills in Citizenship which the Crick Report identifies as desirable learning outcomes for Key Stage One!

Hobson and Edwards' book is an important contribution to the pedagogic process of what Monica Taylor in *Agenda For Educational Change* calls 'sharing in dialogue from diverse sources' (253). In response to Trevor Cooling's thesis that faith formation is more important than 'promoting reflective understanding of the relationship between belief and knowledge and promoting civic values,' Taylor argues for a:

> ... critical pedagogy, including developing the skills of intercultural discourse, with attention being paid to moral reasoning and the narratives of modern meaning-making. (Shortt and Cooling 1997, 265)

Taylor would argue that it is through such discourse that Cooling's faith formation can find an acceptable and reasonable place which guarantees it receives proper understanding and evaluation.

This articulates something of the aims of the ethnographic approach taken by the Warwick RE Project 'Bridges to Religion' and a process now being advocated by Taylor and others who see such dialogue as being at 'the core of education'. What Taylor is anxious to point out is the significance of skills of *intercultural discourse* for all teachers in the context of Citizenship and Values Education:

> Many teachers are professionally cautious about dealing with the moral, the spiritual and the religious because they have not been adequately inducted into ways of dealing with these forms of thought, and the complex controversial issues with which they deal, in their initial training, nor are they sustained by it in continuing professional development. (Shortt and Cooling 1997, 266)

Taylor's recognition of a neglected area in what have become content-driven teacher training programmes puts the debate about the relationship between effective multi-faith RE and Citizenship at the heart of the development

of new pedagogic skills. It is commendable that the editors, John Shortt and Trevor Cooling, invited Monica Taylor to enter into discourse as an example of good practice in rational inquiry. Both effective RE and effective Citizenship require teachers of any faith background or none to enter into dialogue with each other and critically reflect on their pedagogy and 'the strategies by which they handle the implications of their subject for ultimate, temporal and spiritual questions' (266).

Those of us in RE teacher training who are attempting to cross-fertilise skills in intercultural discourse into Citizenship courses would probably say that the handling of spiritual dialogue is the most challenging of these skills. I am not sure if Andrew Wright's *Spiritual Pedagogy* is the appropriate text to address this challenge. As it is published by the Culham Institute one hoped it would be pitched at the level of professional development which Monica Taylor has identified as so essential for new and serving teachers.

In the first two sections of his book Wright challenges received notions of spirituality which have undoubtedly contributed to teachers' uncertainty about handling this whole area. However, a less erudite style is needed if teachers and trainees are to gain confidence from such a text.[1] I have used parts of the third section of the book which deals with spiritual literacy with trainee teachers and this seems much more accessible. The tone is both inspiring and pragmatic and sits comfortably with seminar and INSET discussions about the nature of learning from religions and similar pedagogic skills required in the teaching of Citizenship. For example, Wright discusses the need for the teacher to balance the nurturing of the child in the spiritual values of the individual school with the development of a 'critical insight' into the spiritual values of others – echoes here of Monica Taylor's *intercultural discourse* but defined at the spiritual level:

> Through the fundamental aims of the school, its spiritual ethos and the celebration of this through collective worship children will be inducted and nurtured within a particular spiritual tradition. Secondly, within the taught curriculum children will have the opportunity to develop a religious literacy in which the spiritual traditions of the school are opened up for critical investigation in the light of alternatives. (Wright 1998, 97)

The pragmatic outcome of this in Wright's argument is the recognition of the need for a school to identify and make explicit its spiritual values so that within a framework which is secure for both teachers and pupils 'spiritual literacy' can be developed through 'inter-cultural discourse'.

What clearly emerges from the current debate about the relationship between multi-faith Religious Education and Values Education is that the development of the former from its predominantly phenomenological approach to the current ethno-graphic trend enables it to make a significant contribution to the introduction of new pedagogic skills for all teachers.

Although rather confessional in tone, Watson and Ashton in *Priorities: Grounds for Fresh Thinking in Education* are making a similar point in their argument against the 'conditioning power of positivism' evident in the content-driven nature of the National Curriculum. They claim that the phenomenological approach in RE encourages attitudes such as indifference:

> ... leaving a gap which is unlikely to remain void – hence the aggression and acquisitiveness so typical of positivist-influenced societies. This can be perceived in the following comments: 'I don't know anything about God. It's got nothing to do with me,' and, 'Why should we have to learn this stuff? If you don't know about it, it doesn't affect you.' (Watson and Ashton 1999)

The argument continues:

> Failure of educators to teach children about religious insights is to risk indoctrinating through omission. Irrespective of personal belief or disbelief, the teachings provide an important and valid area of enquiry to which all pupils are entitled to be introduced ... they inform reflection in ways which are profound, operating at unconscious and subconscious levels in ways which contribute to a gradual development of values. (Watson and Ashton 1999, 199–200)

One may not subscribe to what I detect to be Watson and Ashton's pro-Christian and anti-positivist stance but they are rightly emphasising the important contribution which Religious Education can make to under-standing how all teachers might be skilled in order to achieve spiritual, moral, social and cultural development for all pupils.

It is a good thing that as we are just beginning to

clarify learning from religions we in RE have the opportunity to contribute to a much wider debate which affects the skills of all teachers as they face the challenges of implementing Citizenship. The development of a body of scholarly literature combined with innovative Initial Teacher Training PSE programmes are important contributions to a debate which will be ongoing in teacher training institutions and schools during the preparations for the intro-duction of Citizenship into the curriculum in 2000.

Note

1 In response to a request to produce 'a shorter, more accessible and more specifically teacher-oriented version' of *Spiritual Pedagogy*, Andrew Wright has now written (1999) *Discerning the Spirit: Teaching Spirituality in the Religious Education Classroom* (Abingdon: Culham College Institute).

References

Advisory Group on Citizenship (1998) *Education for Citizenship and the Teaching of Democracy in School* The Crick Report (Qualifications and Curriculum Authority).

Hobson, P and Edwards, J (1999) *Religious Education in a Pluralist Society* (Woburn Press).

Hull, J (1992) 'The Transmission of Religious Prejudice', Editorial, *British Journal of Religious Education* 14:2, 69–72.

Lipman, Matthew (1991) *Thinking in Education* (Cambridge University Press).

School Curriculum and Assessment Authority (1996) *Education for Adult Life, The Spiritual and Moral Development of Young People* (SCAA).

Shortt J and Cooling T (eds) (1997) *Agenda For Educational Change* (Apollos).

Watson, B and Ashton, E (1999) *Priorities: Grounds for Fresh Thinking in Education* (Moorhills).

Wright, A (1998) *Spiritual Pedagogy: A Survey, Critique and Reconstruction of Contemporary Spiritual Education in England and Wales* (Culham College Institute).

Nick Mead is Senior Lecturer in Religious Education at Westminster College, Oxford

Chapter 15

Researching skills common to religious education and citizenship

Nick Mead

This chapter seeks to identify pedagogic skills that are common to religious education and citizenship. The research findings highlight the processes which teachers should be encouraged to engage with if such skills are to be developed in the classroom. The conclusion reached is that attention paid to the development of such skills may begin to address the notion of an, as yet, unfulfilled broad and balanced curriculum which contributes to children's moral and spiritual growth.

Background

Hobson and Edwards (1999) have shown how religious education is being challenged to go beyond an understanding of religions to providing skills of critical reflection and evaluation which will enable children to interpret and make sense of our pluralistic world. This challenge to religious education has coincided with the emergence of a global concern for the moral nature of citizenship. The School Curriculum and Assessment Authority's (SCAA) MORI poll (1996: 20–2) which informed the Crick Report (Advisory Group on Citizenship (AGC) (1998) showed that young people are interested in moral questions but are cynical about political leadership.

The challenge to religious education to become more reflective and evaluative in its approach to beliefs and values and the coincident concern for the moral nature of citizenship brings into sharp relief the nature of the relationship between religious education and citizenship within the primary curriculum. This is not only a philosophical issue but also a practical one, bearing in mind that the Crick Report recommends five per cent of curriculum time for citizenship in an already crowded curriculum.

Concern about teacher and pupil skills within citizenship pedagogy came to the fore in the Crick Report consultation process, following the first draft of the report. Those consulted expressed a need for teachers to have 'The confidence, knowledge and skills to be able to deliver effective Citizenship education' (AGC 1998: 75). In relation to pupils' skills, the point was made that in some cases the culture of a school might need to change to enable pupils to be given opportunities to reflect and critically evaluate. Participants in the consultation exercise wanted further clarification about the relationship between citizenship education and other subject areas and the spiritual, moral, social and cultural. In the light of the development of skills in reflection, application and evaluation in religious education, it would seem logical to look to existing good practice in that subject within a school for exemplification of pupil and teacher skills in citizenship.

The Crick Report has three strands, the first of which may be described as moral development: 'Children learning from the very beginning self-confidence and socially and morally responsible behaviour both in and beyond the classroom, both towards those in authority and towards each other' (AGC 1998: 11, para. 2.11). The report makes the important point that the whole of primary education is not pre-citizenship; children are already forming, through learning and discussion, concepts of fairness, and attitudes to the law, to rules, to decision-making, to authority, to their local environment and social responsibility.

The research of Hughes (1975 cited in Bottery (1990: 63–5)) has demonstrated that children could make sense of what they were asked to do in his 'hiding from the policeman' moral task because they know what it is to hide from somebody – it is part of their experience and they can become involved in it. Piagetian moral tests by contrast can be artificial, abstract and outside the children's experience. Such research benefits the development of skills in religious education and citizenship because it suggests that moral development is a product of social communication and that one of the crucial roles of the teacher is to provide guidance for the child in the structuring and facilitating of communication situations.

Here we can begin to see the mutual benefits to be gained from pursuing a relationship between religious education and citizenship. The concept of the primary classroom as the 'community of inquiry' developed by Matthew Lipman (1991) provides a good model for both curriculum areas. There is a need in religious education to use moral and religious narrative out of which pupils identify key issues they wish to discuss in order to achieve learning *from* religions (QCA 1994: Target 2). The skills of empathy, reflective, application and evaluation associated with Attainment Target 2 in religious education correspond to skills identified in the Crick Report from Key Stage 1 onwards:

- The ability to make a reasoned argument both verbally and in writing
- Ability to consider and appreciate the experience and perspective of others
- Ability to tolerate other viewpoints
- Ability to develop a problem-solving approach
- A critical approach to evidence put before one and ability to look for fresh evidence
- Ability to identify, respond to and influence moral challenges and situations

(QCA 1998: 44)

The social communication facilitated by the model of the 'community of inquiry' not only develops skills common to religious education and citizenship but also key attitudes crucial to positive moral development. The QCA model syllabuses and probably most recently revised local agreed syllabuses refer to the attitudes of commitment to a set of values by which to live one's life; fairness in terms of giving careful consideration to other views; respect for those who hold different beliefs and avoiding ridicule; self-understanding, including a sense of self-worth and value and finally, a positive attitude of enquiry which includes a readiness to change one's point of view. There is much here that is common with the values and dispositions identified in the Crick Report:

- Belief in human dignity and equality.
- Judging and acting by a moral code.
- Courage to defend a point of view.
- The practice of tolerance.
- Willingness to be open to challenging one's opinion and attitudes in the light of discussion and evidence   (AGC 1998: 44)

To conclude our examination of the first strand of the Crick Report we can say that exemplification of good practice in moral development may be already in place within a school's religious education programme. If an audit of skills in moral development show this not to be the case, then let the implementation of citizenship be the catalyst to improve the quality of religious education!

The second strand of the Crick Report is community involvement : 'Children learning about and becoming helpfully involved in the life and concerns of their communities, including learning through community involvement and service to the community' (AGC 1998: para. 2.11b).

One of the key points emerging from the Crick Report consultation process was that teachers need to take into account the local context in which schools would be teaching about citizenship and democracy. The local context is also crucial in the formation of the religious education scheme of work and and it is a legal requirement that the policy document clearly relates the aims of the subject to the local needs. What can be learnt from the distinctively local organisation of religious education which will complement this second strand of citizenship?

The close relationship between religious education and the local community encourages teachers to use visits and visitors which, if done well, help to develop many of the moral and social skills common to religious education and citizenship. The emphasis on learning *from* religions corresponds very much to the Crick use of learning *through* community involvement. The most effective use of religious education visits and visitors involves dialogue between the children and members of the faith communities which encourages empathy, reflection and evaluation and in turn develops positive attitudes of respect, fairness and enquiry. Again, are the pedagogic skills to facilitate open dialogue with community members in place already in religious education? If not then let citizenship be the inspiration to make this happen.

The third strand of the Crick Report is political literacy: 'Children learning how to make themselves effective in public life through knowledge, skills and values. Political literacy is wider than political knowledge alone. It encompasses preparation for conflict resolution and decision-making in relation to the economic and social problems of the day' (AGC 1998: 13, para. 211). Political literacy in democratic education promotes spiritual, moral and intellectual autonomy; this means that spiritual education is about engaging in dialogue with others who hold different values as part of the process of achieving spiritual autonomy. It involves self-understanding in terms of the value of the individual in relation to the community. For religious education, spiritual autonomy and the value of the individual is at the heart of political literacy. It follows that pedagogic skills in facilitating children's spiritual development is at the heart of religious education and citizenship.

Hay and Nye (1998) have been able to identify for teachers the conditions, processes and strategies which facilitate spiritual development; conditions such as religious language, the language of beliefs and the language of fiction, the processes of interiorising, self-identification and the strategies of philosophising, reasoning and moralising. Clearly, creating such conditions involves the skills of learning *from* religions in particular and the skills of citizenship such as the ability to respond to and influence social, moral and political challenges which impinge on the spiritual dignity and autonomy of the individual citizen.

The international trend towards inter-cultural discourse in religious education and concern about the moral dimensions of citizenship have led to an examination of the three strands of the Crick Report in terms of skills common to both curriculum areas. Having identified common skills we now turn to research evidence which suggests ways in which schools might develop them.

Action research

The action research which follows is based on course evaluations from two cohorts passing through a new citizenship final year BEd elective. The ongoing processes by which we evaluate ITT courses is a type of action research which should be made more use of, particularly when such courses are responding to TTA requirements which in turn reflect curriculum innovation affecting the professional development of all primary teachers. In the absence of any substantial research on citizenship in ITT it seemed essential to reflect with the trainees on the training process and extrapolate principles of good training which might inform future INSET for serving teachers. This reflective process was also to take into account that some of the trainees would become religious education or citizenship coordinators and would be able to use these principles of good practice in their planning and staff development.

The research focuses on the processes involved in primary trainee teachers becoming aware of and developing confidence in a set of pedagogic skills common to religious education and citizenship. Data collection involved the following.

- A course evaluation sheet was given to the 20 members of the first cohort. The sections invited reflections on the following:
  1. To what extent have the course aims been met?
  2. What evidence have you of the desirable learning outcomes?
  3. What do you consider to be the strengths of the course?
  4. What do you consider to be the weaknesses of the course?
  5. What suggestions would you make for developing the course?
- A reflective piece of writing was requested in response to the following: 'Trainee teachers need to think and talk about their values before entering the classroom if they are not to pass on their own values uncritically'.
- The second cohort of 17 trainees were asked to reflect on the kind of INSET they would like a citizenship coordinator to provide to develop teacher self-concept.

The responses were analysed and categories of response identified and from these key findings were extrapolated. The evaluation analysis was categorised according to the questions; the reflective piece of writing was categorised according to pedagogic skills and the INSET suggestions fell into categories of approach. Small-scale action research of this kind primarily benefits reflective practice and practical planning within a specific context. It does provide a model of good practice in the context of religious education and citizenship as both areas require pedagogic skills of reflection, application and evaluation.

The findings

Finding 1

The areas of beliefs and values and spiritual and moral development often go unspoken and are areas in which teachers often lack confidence. The data indicates trainees experiencing uncertainty about how schools handle values and a desire to be told which values to espouse:

> There is currently too little research literature written by too narrow a range of authors to provide a theoretical assurance to our beliefs. We are still lacking an accepted criteria of what society's values are and until both of these missing aspects are improved and available the Citizenship course will only help us understand individual's values and be of no broader benefit than that.
>
> (Trainee O)

This raises the challenging question about whether schools are in the business of transmitting values, clarifying values or providing a framework of core values within which children can securely reflect on and evaluate the range of values encountered in a pluralistic society and modify their own values in the process. The course evaluations indicate that although initially seeking the kind of assurance expressed by Trainee O, trainees progress from recognising the limitations of approaches one and two to growing confidence in handling approach three. This is expressed in their assessment of their own experience of the third approach on the course:

> This course gives depth to teachers which may otherwise be missing in their training. So much time is spent on acquiring and imparting knowledge. A greater understanding of Citizenship and related values enables teachers to be more well-rounded and hopefully better teachers.   (Trainee E)

Another trainee takes this further and makes the connection between the confidence gained through her own experience of the third approach on the course and the significant recognition that the classroom is not a value-free zone:

> It would have been extremely helpful to have been given time to have had Citizenship lectures much earlier in the course as it is something which should be an integral part of your time in school. I have certainly benefited (and I hope my pupils have) from re-assessing and re-evaluating my own values and the values I aspire to demonstrate in the classroom.   (Trainee L)

A fourth trainee links the processes of reassessing and re-evaluating with a pluralistic values-laden classroom:

> The elective has helped me to understand and realise the importance of being aware of different values amongst staff, pupils and parents and how one might deal with them. We are not always aware of how these different values are influencing the children who encounter us.   (Trainee A)

It is evident that this first finding is at the heart of the trainees' intellectual understanding of how school should approach beliefs and values and the spiritual and moral. This intellectual understanding has been gained through their own experience on the course of an approach which is secure, formative and inclusive and has none of the polarisation of values clarification and values transmission.

Finding 2

Trainees recognised the value of, but have had limited opportunities to develop skills in philosophical inquiry and moral reasoning. The data highlight two key responses. Firstly, there is real appreciation of the opportunity to activate these dormant skills, albeit at the eleventh hour of the course! Trainee evaluations of the course aims emphasised positive 'opportunities for thoughtful reflection on values in the classroom'; their evaluations of learning outcomes from the course highlighted how, 'during the course we have developed skills in reflective discussion, moral reasoning and philosophical inquiry'; the strengths of the course were identified as 'opportunities for discussion and time to reflect', 'an expression of much that is unspoken', and 'ways into the teaching of values which develops these as part of the professional and personal development of the teacher'. Trainees' written reflections on the course highlighted how they had deepened their reflective skills and how this had increased their awareness of the need for skills in open dialogue:

> The elective has given me the opportunity to think about and reflect on my own beliefs. I think I now have a greater awareness of my influence (or potential influence) on the children in my care. Teachers who are not made explicitly aware of the need to have an 'open mind' when it comes to to teaching children may find that they are not giving due care or attention to children's spiritual, moral, social and cultural care and education.   (Trainee D)

Secondly, trainees expressed some dismay at how such skills have not been integral to a four-year training process. Trainee course evaluations recommended that the personal and social education elective be retained and introduced over years three and four of the four-year course. In trainees' written reflections on the course there is evidence of a recognition that the skills of philosophical inquiry and moral reasoning ought to underpin the intensive and often dominating ITT National Curriculum requirements: 'A broad curriculum is not merely teaching the ten National Curriculum subjects but an integral part of the utmost importance is to nurture the child's own set of values so that they can become better citizens' (Trainee F). These two aspects of Finding 2 do draw our attention to trends in ITT which we have been aware of as we have witnessed the emergence of a national curriculum for teacher training which mirrors something of the content-driven school curriculum. Are the challenges of making sense of our lives in pluralistic societies going to lead to a reconsideration of pedagogic skills?

Finding3

Trainees have become aware during the course that handling beliefs and values and the spiritual and moral requires the teacher to have self-understanding. Course evaluations picked up on the interrelatedness of teacher self-understanding, pupil self-understanding and professional practice within the structure of sessions. Trainees' reflective written comments suggest that developing self-understanding is part of an educational process and there is recognition of the need for differentiation: 'I believe it would be beneficial for other trainee teachers to be *educated* in this area of the curriculum' (Trainee H). 'An awareness needs to be highlighted. This may not be necessary for all but if it makes one person question their values then it is worth it. It is very important and needs to be made explicit' (Trainee K).

Teacher self-understanding is linked to confidence in the pedagogic skills we have identified as common to citizenship and learning *from* religions:

> Children will ask questions about values. It is essential that trainee teachers feel ready to be able to deal with these situations in a classroom and throughout the school. No one can be an effective model of values if the term is not under-stood thoroughly or the teachers do not have a clear picture of their own values. *If one is unsure of values that stand in the classroom and school then the children will be unsure.*   (Trainee T)

This confidence seems to be derived from the process of making teachers' implicit values explicit and allowing them to be shaped by dialogue with others as part of a process in achieving moral and spiritual autonomy: 'Surely every teacher training course should include values education in order that the implicit might become explicit and children can benefit from confident teachers with clarified understandings' (Trainee J).

Spiritual and moral autonomy begins to emerge as teachers are invited to reflect on and evaluate their morals and values and to consider whether they are appropriate for the classroom: 'The course allows for reflection but also gives alternative views and sugges-tions about the values you hold' (Trainee I). The outcome of this process is related by one trainee directly to classroom ethos: 'Sharing opinions and looking at what others have said about values helps to give us confidence and new ideas for creating the kind of class-room ethos that we would like' (Trainee N).

The data supporting Finding 3 suggest that the lack of confidence in the whole citizen-ship area noted by SCAA (1996: 17) does relate to teacher self-understanding. Are we say-ing that if teachers are to be effective in this area they need to be aware of how they are achieving spiritual and moral autonomy as part of becoming full citizens?

Finding 4

Trainees are particularly aware of the relationship between teacher self-understanding and pupil self-understanding in religious education and citizenship. What is significant in the trainees' written reflections is the natural link made between teacher confidence derived from self-understanding and pupil confidence and raised self-esteem: 'I believe that all trainee teachers need to develop an awareness of their own values from an early stage in their training. They should be aware of how these values affect their pupils and their response from their first practice and observation in school' (Trainee C). This awareness of the effect of our values on each other is likely to reflect the experience of dialogue within this elective group and it seems to have sensitised them to the process of achieving spiritual and moral autonomy. Their reflective comments suggest a heightened awareness of the same process of achieving autonomy among their pupils: 'All trainees should have the opportunity to learn about how values education improves a child's self-esteem. They should know the importance of this and how it shapes the children for their later lives' (Trainee G).

Denis Lawrence (1998) has identified the integral link between teacher and pupil self-concept and self-esteem; finding four points to a challenging dimension of this relationship, which is the raising of self-esteem through the teacher and pupil *sharing* the experience of achieving spiritual and moral autonomy.

Implications for teaching

The four findings are helpful in providing ways forward in the development of pedagogic skills common to the areas of religious education and citizenship. Underpinning skills and confidence in these areas is the need for an intellectual understanding of how schools approach beliefs and values and the spiritual and moral. I suggest that such understanding comes from the kind of personal and professional development experienced by my elective students. Little time is given to dialogue between staff focused on how the school handles values. Without a series of such experiences in which teachers gain confidence in the processes of dialogue, the desired pedagogic skills cannot flourish.

Many teachers feel the tension between pupils wrestling with conflicting values and the pressure caused by the need to get on with the next task. Schools may now have a mandate to reconsider the range of pedagogic skills they are using and begin to develop expertise in moral reasoning and philosophical inquiry. If the intellectual understanding has been established it is likely that staff will welcome the kinds of INSET opportunities provided by Jenny Mosley's Circle Time and June Auton's Human Values Foundation. Such INSET opportunities do challenge staff to harness new pedagogic skills and may lead to the reviewing of whole school policies on religious education and citizenship.

Primary religious education specialists may be particularly aware of the part played by their own growth towards spiritual and moral autonomy. The Crick Report puts this clearly in the realm of political literacy as it involves an understanding of the value of the individual in relation to political and economic systems. There may be the opportunity now to develop this dimension in school as a result of the Crick Report and clearly the correlation suggested by the data is that teachers with a sense of their own spiritual and moral growth can effectively assist the same growth in their pupils. Values forums can be highly productive if focused around the aims and values of the school; this is an exercise which governors may wish to participate in as well. The teacher who is aware of their own moral and spiritual growth may be more ready to engage in philosophical and moral reflection with pupils.

Finally, there is the exciting but challenging dynamic in religious education and citizenship pedagogy which is a teacher/pupil shared experience of achieving spiritual and moral autonomy. This may be facilitated by the Matthew Lipman 'community of inquiry' ethos using moral narrative resources such as *You, Me, Us* (Home Office/Citizenship Foundation 1994). However, it is important that the teacher does not remain just as facilitator but may be open to expressing how their own views have been shaped by reflective dialogue with the pupils.

Link resource

The resource arises from the four key findings and from a survey of elective students about the kind of INSET they would value in this area. The need would seem to be very much in the area of developing staff skills in reflective dialogue as part of the kind of self-evaluation exercise which LEAs and OFSTED will be expecting schools to undertake. The exercise may take more than one session and questions need to be explored in pairs, groups and in plenary.

Conclusions

The introduction of citizenship into the curriculum may be an opportunity to firm up pedagogic skills which have been required in the areas of religious and personal and social education but which have not received sufficient attention. The identification of a common skills base across religious education and citizenship should not be seen as a threat to the former but rather as an opportunity to enhance the quality of teaching in both areas without detracting from their distinctive contributions. What we might hope for is that the introduction of citizenship does begin to address the unfulfilled expectation of a broad and balanced curriculum which does promote the spiritual and moral, social and cultural.

Useful further reading

Education for Human Values, J. Auton (ed.) (1995). Ilminster: The Human Values Foundation.

This provides curriculum materials for implementing a whole school values education programme.

Quality Circle Time in The Primary Classroom, J. Mosley (1996). Wisbech: LDA.

This book offers one of the leading approaches to conducting circle time, and links it to developing dialogue between pupils.

Discerning the Spirit: Teaching Spirituality in the Religious Education Classroom, A. Wright (1999). Abingdon: Culham College Institute.

This is a practical user-friendly version of a more academic book that applies the theory of spiritual education to classroom practice.

References

Advisory Group on Citizenship (AGC) (1998) *Education for Citizenship and the Teaching of Democracy in School* (the Crick Report). London: QCA.

Bottery, M. (1990) *The Morality of the School.* London: Cassell.

Hay, D. and Nye, R.(1998) *The Spirit of the Child.* London: HarperCollins.

Hobson, P. and Edwards, J. (1999) *Religious Education in a Pluralist Society.* London: Woburn Press.

Home Office/Citizenship Foundation (1994)*You, Me, Us.* London: Home Office.

Hughes, M. (1975) Egocentrism in Pre-school Children. Unpublished Ph.D. dissertation, University of Edinburgh.

Lawrence, D. (1988) *Enhancing Self-esteem in the Classroom.* London: Paul Chapman.

Lipman, M. (1991) *Thinking in Education.* Cambridge: Cambridge University Press.

School Curriculum and Assessment Authority (SCAA) (1994) *Religious Education Model Syllabuses.* London: SCAA.

School Curriculum and Assessment Authority (SCAA) (1996) *Education for Adult Life: The Spiritual and Moral Development of Young People.* London: SCAA.

Religious education link resource: Staff self-assessment exercise and skills audit for the teaching of religious education and citizenship

1. To what extent do we as a staff share the values of the school as stated in the school prospectus and in our mission statement?

2. Can we identify skills common to religious education and citizenship which might strengthen the values of the school?

3. How often do we give children time to reflect on a belief or value and how often do we invite them to give reasoned points of view?

4. Can you think of an occasion when children developed their moral outlook as a result of having dialogues with one another?

5. What does being a citizen mean to me?

6. Do I feel that I am developing morally and spiritually as a citizen?

7. How often are my own moral and spiritual views developed or modified as a result of having dialogues with children?

Identifying Pedagogic Skills Common to Primary Religious Education and PSHE/Citizenship and the Implications For Continuing Professional Development.

Nick Mead

Introduction

In the light of the introduction of the Personal, Social and Health Education and Citizenship Framework (PSHE/Ct.1999), this paper seeks to identify pedagogic skills which are common to Religious Education and PSHE/Citizenship. The research findings highlight the processes which teachers should be encouraged to engage with if such skills are to be developed in the classroom. The conclusion reached is that attention paid to the development of such skills may begin to address the notion of a, as yet, unfulfilled broad and balanced curriculum which contributes to children's moral and spiritual growth.

Pedagogic Skills Common to Religious Education and PSHE/Citizenship

Hobson and Edwards (1999) have shown how Religious Education is being challenged to go beyond an understanding of religions to providing skills of critical reflection and evaluation which will enable children to interpret and make sense of our pluralistic world. This challenge to Religious Education has coincided with the emergence of a global concern for the moral nature of citizenship. SCAA's (The Schools Curriculum and Assessment Authority) Mori Poll (1996) which informed the Crick Report (1998) showed that young people are interested in moral questions but are cynical about political leadership.

The challenge to Religious Education to become more reflective and evaluative in its approach to beliefs and values and the coincident concern for the moral nature of citizenship bring in to sharp relief the nature of the relationship between Religious Education and citizenship within the primary curriculum. This is not only a philosophical issue but also a practical one, bearing in mind that the Crick Report recommends 5% of curriculum time for Citizenship in an already crowded curriculum.

Concern about teacher and pupil skills within citizenship pedagogy came to the fore in the Crick Report consultation process, following the first draft of the report. Those consulted expressed a need for teachers to have 'The confidence, knowledge and skills to be able to deliver effective Citizenship education' (p.75). In relation to pupils' skills, the point was made that in some cases the culture of a school might need to change to enable pupils to be given opportunities to reflect and critically evaluate. Participants in the consultation exercise wanted further clarification about the relationship between Citizenship Education, other subject areas and The Spiritual, Moral, Social and Cultural. In

43

the light of the development of skills in reflection, application and evaluation in Religious Education, it would seem logical to look to existing good practice in that subject within a school for exemplification of pupil and teacher skills in Citizenship.

The Crick Report has three strands, the first of which may be described as moral development:

'Children learning from the beginning self-confidence and socially and morally responsible behaviour both in and beyond the classroom, both towards those in authority and towards each other'. (para. 2.II p.11)

The report makes the important point that the whole of primary education is not pre-citizenship:

Children are already forming through learning and discussion, concepts of fairness, and attitudes to the law, to rules, to decision-making, to authority, to their local environment and social responsibility. (ibid).

The research of Hughes (1975) cited in Bottery (1990 pp.63-65) has demonstrated that children could make sense of what they were asked to do in his 'hiding from the policeman' moral task because they know what it is to hide from somebody - it is part of their experience and they can become involved in it. Piagetian moral tests by contrast can be artificial, abstract and outside the children's experience. Such research benefits the development of skills in Religious Education and Citizenship because it suggests that moral development is a product of social communication and that one of the crucial roles of the teacher is to provide guidance for the child in the structuring and facilitating of communication situations.

Here we can begin to see the mutual benefits to be gained from pursuing a relationship between Religious Education and Citizenship. The concept of the primary

classroom as the 'community of inquiry' developed by Matthew Lipman (1991) provides a good model for both curriculum areas. There is a need in Religious Education to use moral and religious narrative out of which pupils identify key issues they wish to discuss in order to achieve learning *from* religions (QCA, Qualifications and Curriculum Authority RE Model Syllabuses, Attainment Target 2). The skills of empathy, reflection, application and evaluation associated with Attainment Target 2 in RE correspond to skills identified in the Crick Report (and now evident in the PSHE/Ct.framework, 1999) from Key Stage One onwards:

- 'The ability to make a reasoned argument both verbally and in writing
- Ability to consider and appreciate the experience and perspective of others
- Ability to tolerate other viewpoint
- Ability to develop a problem-solving approach
- A critical approach to evidence put before one and ability to look for fresh evidence
- Ability to identify, respond to and influence moral challenges and situations' (p.44)

The social communication facilitated by the model of the 'community of inquiry' not only develops skills common to Religious Education and Citizenship but also key attitudes crucial to positive moral development. The QCA Model Syllabuses and probable most recently revised Local Agreed Syllabuses refer to the attitudes of commitment to a set of values by which to live one's life; fairness in terms of giving careful consideration to other views; respect for those who hold different beliefs and avoiding ridicule; self-understanding, including a sense of self-worth and value and finally, a positive attitude of enquiry which includes a readiness to change one's point of view. There is much here that is common with the values and disposition identified in the Crick Report and which subsequently underpinned the PSHE/Ct. Framework (1999):

44

- 'Belief in human dignity and equality
- Judging and acting by a moral code
- Courage to defend a point of view
- The practice of tolerance
- Willingness to be open to challenging one's opinion and attitudes in the light of discussion and evidence' (p.44)

To conclude our examination of the first strand of the Crick Report, we can say that exemplification of good practice in moral development may be already in place within a school's Religious Education programme; if an audit of skills in moral development show this not to be the case, then let the implementation of Citizenship be the catalyst to improve the quality of Religious Education!

The second strand of the Crick Report is community involvement:

'Children learning about and becoming helpfully involved in the life and concerns of their communities, including learning through community involvement and service to the community'. (para 2.11b)

Within the PSHE/Ct.Framework (1999), evidence of this strand is found in statements such as:

'Pupils should be taught that they belong to various groups' (p.137)
'Pupils take part in discussions about topics of local interest' (p.139)
'Pupils meet and talk with people who work in the neighbourhood, such as religious leaders'. (p.141)

One of the key points emerging from the Crick Report consultation process was that teachers need to take into account the local context in which schools would be teaching about citizenship and democracy. The local context is also crucial in the formation of the Religious Education scheme of work and it is a legal requirement that the policy document clearly relates the aims of the subject to the local needs. What can be learnt from the distinctively local organisation of Religious Education which will complement this second strand of Citizenship?

The close relationship between Religious Education and the local community encourages teachers to use visits and visitors which, if done well, help to develop many of the moral and social skills common to Religious Education and PSHE/Ct. The emphasis on learning *from* religions corresponds very much to the Crick use of learning *through* community involvement. The most effective use of RE visits and visitors involves dialogue between the children and members of the faith communities which encourages empathy, reflection and evaluation and in turn develops positive attitudes of respect, fairness and enquiry. Again, are the pedagogic skills to facilitate open dialogue with community members in place already in Religious Education? If not then let Citizenship be the inspiration to make this happen.

The third strand of The Crick Report is political literacy:

'Children learning how to make themselves effective in public life through knowledge, skills and values. Political literacy is wider than political knowledge alone. It encompasses preparation for conflict resolution and decision-making in relation to the economic and social problems of the day'. (para. 21 p.13)

Within the PSHE/Ct. Framework (1999) this finds expression in statements such as:

'Pupils are to realise that people and other living things have needs and that they have responsibilities to meet them' (p.137)

'That there are different kinds of responsibilities that can sometimes conflict with each other' (p.139).

45

Political literacy in democratic education promotes spiritual, moral and intellectual autonomy; this means that spiritual education is about engaging in dialogue with others who hold different values, as part of the process of achieving spiritual autonomy. It involves self-understanding in terms of the value of the individual in relation to the community. For Religious Education, spiritual autonomy and the value of the individual is at the heart of political literacy. It follows that pedagogic skills in facilitating children's spiritual development is at the heart of Religious Education and Citizenship.

Hay and Nye (1998) have been able to identify for teachers the conditions, processes, and strategies which facilitate spiritual development. Conditions such as religious language, the language of beliefs and the language of fiction, the processes of interiorising, self-identification and the strategies of philosophising, reasoning and moralising. Clearly, creating such conditions, involves the skills of learning *from* religions in particular, and the skills of Citizenship, such as the ability to respond to and influence social, moral and political challenges which impinge on the spiritual dignity and autonomy of the individual citizen.

The international trend towards inter-cultural discourse in Religious Education and concern about the moral dimensions of Citizenship have led to an examination of the three strands of the Crick Report in terms of skills common to both curriculum areas. Having identified common skills we now turn to research evidence which assesses teachers' current understanding of the relationship between the two curriculum areas and the implications arising from this for professional development.

Evidence of Current Understanding of Common Pedagogic Skills in Religious Education and PSHE/Citizenship Amongst Primary School Teachers.

The following findings are based on questionnaires sent to the RE and PSHE/Ct. co-ordinators in six primary schools and transcribed interviews with both co-ordinators in two of the schools. Four questions were asked in the questionnaire:

1. To what extent are RE and PSHE/Ct. related in your school?
2. Do you discuss the relationship between the two curriculum areas with colleagues?
3. Have you felt that RE and PSHE/Ct. complement each other, particularly in developing reflective and reasoning skills?
4. Do you think that your teaching skills in RE and PSHE/Ct. complement and enhance each other?

In addition to exploring these questions in more depth in the transcribed interviews, some of the responses to the questions in the self-assessment exercise below were also used.

Finding 1. The significance of the teacher's **understanding** of a) the relationship between RE and PSHE/Citizenship and b) the relationship of both to whole school effectiveness.

a) The relationship between RE and PSHE/Citizenship in terms of *planning and skills:*

Planning - teachers were able to identify the following planning issues:

1) Preoccupations with separating out the two curriculum areas - e.g. 'We discuss to avoid merging'.
2) Blurring the two areas, especially at Key stage One - e.g. topics like Friends and Caring which confuse implicit RE and PSHE/Ct.
3) Achieving the right understanding of learning *from* religion - how is learning *from* different from PSHE/Ct? There cannot be learning *from* without explicit RE.
4) The teacher's skill in enabling children to gain in their personal development from

46

the complementary and distinctive aspects of RE and PSHE/Ct. In answer to question three of the questionnaire, a PSHE/Ct. co-ordinator described something of this skill:

'Before half-term we did some work on Pentecost which was interesting, very difficult. I find that very difficult to put over to the children. We talked about power and how that was given to the disciples, keeping the basic idea that the disciples were there spreading the word and they had the power to do that. Then we talked about power and the uses and misuses of power. So, although they wrote about the meaning of Pentecost they reflected on different kinds of power, spiritual and worldly, particularly political and commercial power, and their uses and misuses.'

Skills -   teachers were able to identify the following skills common to RE and PSHE/Ct:

1) Evidence of the complementarity of key skills in empathy, application, reflection, evaluation and expression.
2) Key speaking and listening skills - found in all curriculum areas and part of the National Literacy strategy, but RE and PSHE/Ct. offer particularly rich opportunities.
3) Persuasive writing - empathise, apply, reflect, express - found in all curriculum areas and part of the National Literacy Strategy, but RE and PSHE/Ct. offer particularly rich opportunities.
4) Shared methods of developing common skills e.g. circle time, such as developed by Jenny Mosley (1996) and the use of story as a stimulus for moral reasoning, such as found in The Citizenship Foundation's *You, Me and Us* (1994).

b) *The relationship of both RE and PSHE to whole school effectiveness*

Teachers understand the complementarity of RE and PSHE/Ct. skills because they perceive how *both* curriculum areas can contribute to whole school effectiveness:

Egs.
1) Staff, pupils and parents in *dialogue* - e.g. family nurture programmes.
2) Reasoning and bullying - staff/pupil *dialogue* in a formal meeting.
3) Reasoned *dialogue* in the School Council - staff/pupil dialogue.
4) Addressing attitudes across PSHE/Ct. & RE through staff/pupil *dialogue*:

e.g. Q. 'You mean they may display blatant prejudice?'
PSHE co-ordinator: 'Yes we would bear that in mind in PSHE.'
RE co-ordinator: 'And in RE as well. In RE you are careful about the positive images you convey'.
PSHE co-ordinator: 'We have tackled any racist incidents through circle time and *talked* about it in every class.'
RE co-ordinator: 'But in RE there are not incidents, but children who have been brought up to hold a racial point of view and for those children one wants to be very positive and proactive'.

(5) Staff dialogue on ethos and teaching: reflecting, applying, evaluating, e.g. staff in a church school decided on reflection that they wanted to reinstate grace before lunch. 'I think they wanted permission again that they could finish numeracy in time to do it'. (RE co-ordinator).

Finding 2 - teachers, although not always explicitly, recognised the significance of the relationship between their ***self-understanding*** and their exemplification of skills in RE and PSHE/Citizenship:

a) *The teacher's self-understanding:*

The following examples reflect answers to questions 6 and 7 in the self-assessment

47

exercise below which ask teachers about how they are developing morally and spiritually as citizens and whether dialogue with pupils contributes to this development. These examples show how teachers are making the links between their own spiritual and moral development and that of the pupils:

e.g. 1)

A teacher was challenged by one of the fundamentalist Christian sect who attend her school, 'Asking me if I thought it was morally right for me as a woman to wear trousers and have short hair. I am accepting this as perfectly all right *but I need to think it through*'.

e.g. 2)

A teacher recalls being challenged by the attitude of a Muslim boy who was incensed by the Satanic Verses and said that Rushdie should be killed: 'I was horrified by this and *for a while was at a loss to know how to deal with it*'.

e.g. 3)

A teacher gained an insight into the personal relevance of the spiritual and religious through children talking about death in the context of Easter. The RE co-ordinator described how the teacher was, *Spiritually affected by pupil responses and was taken aback by this*'.

e.g. 4)

One teacher reflected on her PSHE/Ct. work in relation to the new performance management system and the process of 'crossing the threshold':

'All of us who have gone for it have had to think long and hard about our way of teaching. When I was reflecting on the professional characteristics standard *it made me think about how I do get these reception children to socialise and respect each other*'.

b) *Teachers provided examples of evidence of the relationship between self-*

understanding and exemplification of skills common to RE and PSHE/Citizenship through:

1) The teacher's example - as they model skills such as empathy, reflection.
2) The teacher's self-respect and self-esteem frees them to respect and build up the self-esteem of their pupils.
3) The teacher's fairness in handling the moral maze reflects the skills in 1 & 2 above.
4) The teacher's desire to enquire - 'how can the teacher say that discussion is of value if they stick to their point. You/You've got to be able to say, thank you, that's really important, I'll think about that one'. (PSHE co-ordinator)
5) The teacher's listening skills - children can take time to get an idea out and they need to be heard seriously and perceptively.
6) The teacher's skills in sensitive questioning so that pupils reflect rather than simply react.

Finding 3

Responses to the question, 'What does being a citizen mean to me?" in the self-assessment exercise below, highlighted the way in which many teachers defined being a citizen as essentially *belonging* to a community. The following statements were fairly common:

'Contributing in some way to society'.
'Being part of a community and respecting others'.
'People within the community respecting and accepting each other'.
'Giving back - contributing to society'.
'Belonging, respecting others, understanding how our actions affect others'.
'Caring for others, recognising and accepting differences, tolerance, helping others valuing others'.
'Discuss and exchange opinions and make allowances'.

48

These statements certainly reflect an aspect of the community strand in the Crick Report which is extremely important and something that schools, and primary schools in particular have been good at. However, what it also reflects is a more protective model of citizenship associated with preserving freedoms within the local community, rather than the challenge of active citizenship which is represented by the new strand of Political Literacy in the Crick Report and evident in the new section called 'Preparing to Play an Active Role as Citizens' in the PSHE/Citizenship Framework (1999).

This finding brings us back in particular to teacher self-understanding and the whole issue of confidence about handling and modelling values in the classroom. Tolerance and acceptance can be passive qualities and both RE and Citizenship can be accused of wishy-washy liberalism that encourage teachers and pupils not to get involved as long as I am not affected.

Clearly, the requirements of the new framework require more than this, and, as has been argued, RE also requires more than the Cook's tour of world religions or, at the other extreme, simply implicit RE, but something much more dynamic that engages pupils in inter-cultural dialogue and leads to views being challenged and perhaps revised.

A glance through the active citizenship sections of the PSHE/Ct. Framework (1999) gives us a more energetic use of language than the words accept, understand and tolerate suggest: The language is the language of active doing, involving the development of skills and abilities:

'Pupils should take part in discussions' Key stage 1 (p.137).
'Pupils should be taught to research, discuss, and debate topical issues'. KS 2 (p.139).
'To reflect on spiritual, moral, social and cultural issues'. KS 2 (ibid.)
'To resolve differences by looking at alternatives, making decisions and choices'. KS2 (ibid.)
'Developing skills of enquiry and communication, participation and responsible action'. KS3 (p.14)
'Pupils should be taught to use their imagination to consider other people's experiences and be able to think about and explain views that are not their own'. KS3 (ibid.)
'Negotiate, decide and take part responsibly'. KS3
'Reflect on the process of participating'. KS3 (p.14)

What is significant about this active language is that it highlights a dynamic link between rights and responsibilities, something that a protective model of citizenship doesn't fully convey. A recent training exercise for trainee teachers based on the development of citizenship saw most presentations focusing on teaching pupils about their rights. How often teachers point out to pupils that they are responsible as well as entitled to rights but this link isn't really made because, one suspects, the teachers themselves have not fully related active citizenship to their own self-understanding. The self-assessment exercise below highlights the need to introduce professional development, such as this, which harnesses the skills base of both RE and PSHE/Citizenship and can begin to address the relationship between teacher self-understanding and the exemplification of those skills.

Implications of The Findings For Continuing Professional Development

The very small group of RE and PSHE/Ct. co-ordinators in this study, when either filling in the questionnaire or being interviewed together, were aware of the potential for pedagogic skills to be transferred across both curriculum areas, and how this could benefit the teaching of both and whole school effectiveness. This could become more explicit and consistent with professional development focused on pedagogic methods such as circle time and Lipman's 'community of enquiry' and in the

49

development of pedagogic skills such as empathy, reflection and evaluation, associated with learning *from* religion. What does need developing is the teacher's awareness of how their own personal development as citizens interacts with their exemplification of these common skills. The implications of this would seem to point to the area of developing staff skills in *reflective dialogue* and this could be part of the kind of self-evaluation exercise which Local Education Authorities and OFSTED (Office for Standards in Education) will be expecting schools to undertake. The self-assessment exercise below, which has contributed to some of the findings in this study, could be introduced to schools with RE and PSHE Co-ordinators planning joint staff development sessions. The exercise may take more than one session and questions need to be explored in pairs, groups and in plenary:

Staff Self-Assessment Exercise and Skills Audit for The Teaching of Religious Education & PSHE/Citizenship

1. To what extent do we as a staff share the values of the school as stated in the school prospectus and in our mission statement?
2. Can we identify skills common to Religious Education and Citizenship which might strengthen the values of the school?
3. How often do we give children time to reflect on a belief or value and how often do we invite them to give reasoned points of view?
4. Can you think of an occasion when children developed their moral outlook as a result of dialoguing with one another?
5. What does being a citizen mean to me?
6. Do I feel that I am developing morally and spiritually as a citizen?
7. How often are my own moral and spiritual views developed or modified as a result of dialoguing with children.
    (Reprinted from Mead, N. (2000 p.175)

Conclusion

The inclusion of the PSHE/Citizenship Framework in the revised National Curriculum may give schools an opportunity to firm up pedagogic skills which have been required in the areas of Religious and Personal and Social Education but which have not received sufficient attention. The identification of a common skills base across Religious Education and PSHE Citizenship should not be seen as a threat to the former but rather as an opportunity to enhance the quality of teaching in both areas without detracting from their distinctive contributions. What we might hope for is that the introduction of PSHE/Citizenship does begin to address the unfulfilled expectation of a broad and balanced curriculum which does promote the spiritual and moral, social and cultural.

Reference

Advisory Group on Citizenship (1998) *Education for Citizenship and the teaching of Democracy in School*, The Crick Report QCA 1998.

Bottery, M. (1990) *The morality of The School*, Cassell, London.

Department of Education & Employment/QCA (1999) *Citizenship Key Stages 3-4*, London, DfEE/QCA

Department of Education & Employment/QCA (1999) *The National Curriculum, handbook for primary teachers*, London, DfEE/QCA

Hay, D. & Nye, R. (1998) *The Spirit of the Child*, Fount.

Hobson, P. & Edwards, J. (1999) *Religious Education in a Pluralist Society*, Woburn Press, London.

Home Office/Citizenship Foundation (1994) *'You, Me, Us'*, London, Home Office.

Lipman, M. (1991) *Thinking in Education*, Cambridge U.P.

Mead, N. (2000) *Researching Skills Common to Religious Education and Citizenship* in Clipson-Boyles, S. (Ed.) Putting Research into Practice in Primary Teaching and Learning, London, Fulton, chap. 15.

50

Mosley, J. (1996) *Quality Circle Time in The Primary Classroom*, LDA, Wisbech.

Qualifications and Curriculum Authority, (1994) *Religious Education Model Syllabuses,* QCA, previously published by SCAA.

School Curriculum and Assessment Authority. *Education for Adult Life, The Spiritual & Moral Development of Young People,* SCAA, 1997.

School Curriculum and Assessment Authority (1996) Mori Poll on Values, SCAA.

Useful Further Reading

Auton, J. (Ed) (1995) *Education for Human Values,* The (Moral reasoning using narrative and based on Lipman's 'Community of enquiry') Human values Foundation, Ilminster, Somerset.

Mead, N. (1999) *The Challenge of Citizenship to Religious Education,* in RE source, Vol. 22 pp.12-15.

Wright, A. (1999) *Discerning the Spirit: Teaching Spirituality in the Religious Education Classroom* (Abingdon: Culham College Institute).

51

Section Four

Values in secondary teacher education through Citizenship Education and Every Child Matters

The Management and Impact of a Student Led Iraq War Protest in a Fresh Start School

NICK MEAD, *Oxford Brookes University, Oxford, UK*

A student led Iraq war protest in a Fresh Start school provides a case study for examining the relationship between political literacy and institutional change. Pragmatic and creative management of the protest encourages a democratic problem-solving process, which contributes to mutual respect and sustained trust between pupils, and staff and pupils. There is evidence to suggest that this democratic experience within the school has the potential to bring a democratic problem solving ethos into the classroom, where learning may increasingly become characterized by individuals achieving autonomy with and for each other.

Keywords: political literacy; school protest; citizenship; democracy.

Introduction

I visit School H on a regular basis as a PGCE tutor and happened to be in on Friday 21 March 2003. This date is significant as it was five days after the Government had decided to send troops to Iraq and it was the day before the largest anti-war demonstration in London. At morning break, a group of students, including a number of Muslims, decided that they were going to protest against the war. They had planned to get as many students together as possible and remain on the school playground at the end of break. The rumour was that they intended to take their protest to the school gates, with every potential for a riot with pro-war protestors and hangers-on at lunch time.

In consultation with senior staff the Head decided that this was the opportunity to capitalize on all the work that had gone into establishing the school council as the pupil voice. She convened a meeting of the school council and those involved in organizing the demonstration. They talked about the effect of such a demonstration on the whole school. The key question discussed was; 'Who are we trying to influence?' The discussion developed along the lines that a protest at the gate would come to the attention of the local residents but a more appropriate audience would be the local member of parliament (MP) and the Prime Minister.

It was agreed that a much more effective way of protesting would be for those for and those against the war to write and sign a letter to go to the local MP and to the Prime Minister. Instead of a protest at the school gate there would be a two minute vigil when the bell rang two minutes early at the end of the school day. Those not wishing to participate could leave school, everyone else would return to their form room, followed by a signing of whichever letter students felt they wanted to sign. The Head had told the organizers of the protest and the school council that these were *their* letters and she gave them time off lessons, following the school council meeting, to draft the letters. The Head explained the school council decisions to year assemblies and Year Managers ensured that all groups were clear about what was going to happen at the end of school and why. In turn, the Head, on behalf of the school, made it clear to all that she was going to write to the Prime Minister asking him to respond to the way in which pupils had conducted themselves as democratic citizens. This letter was to be published in the school newsletter, along with the reply and the two protest letters sent, plus a reply from the local MP. The Head was anxious to affirm the students' approach publicly.

At the end of the school day fewer than ten pupils left the school building. About four fifths of pupils signed the letter against the war, the rest signed the letter for. Two pupils involved in organizing the protest at the school gate were not ready to accept the agreed plan of action at the end of the school council meeting in the morning. The Head excluded these pupils for the day.

This scenario provides us with an example of what Crick and Porter (1978) describe as the 'unpredictable inconveniences of action and participation' which we 'have to tolerate if we want citizens' cited in Maitles and Deuchar (2003, p. 11). It also provides us with evidence of the considerable interest in single issue politics amongst school students. Maitles and Deuchar's study of Scottish primary 7 pupils identified strongly held views for and against the Iraq war, and strong views about the right to, and effectiveness of protesting.

The scenario undoubtedly highlighted the challenge to schools posed particularly by a war, which divided public opinion and still does a year later. Within twenty miles of School H pupils had left school and joined a major city centre anti-war protest. Head teachers stated publicly that these pupils would be marked down as truanting. The contentious single issue of the war posed a moment of truth for political literacy: could the need for pupils to express views be accommodated within the democratic structures of a school, thereby providing a natural development of their understanding of society?

As a failing school which had been closed and reopened with a fresh start, the protest had wider implications for School H, which is an 11–16 non-selective upper school in a selective area with 35 per cent of pupils entitled to free school meals and about 38 per cent with special educational needs. The results are below average but are improving, with the proportion of students gaining five grade C's or better at GCSE rising from 20 per cent in 2002 to 30 per cent in 2003. More than half the pupils are from an ethnic minority with about 30 per cent British Asian.

Background

How School H handled the protest provides us with an ideal opportunity to look at the relationship between democratic structures, values, and teaching and learning. That there is such a relationship is premised on the fact that the leadership of a school would not take the risk of managing a student war protest unless it held a firm conviction that developing democratic structures impacted on school values and, in turn, the quality of teaching and learning. However, before looking at any empirical evidence, we need to underpin such a premise with some theoretical considerations of the process of developing democratic autonomy within the educational context.

Political literacy, as defined in the Crick Report, involves children:

> Learning how to make themselves effective in public life through knowledge, skills and values. Political literacy is wider than political knowledge alone. It encompasses preparation for conflict resolution and decision-making in relation to the economic and social problems of the day.
> (Advisory Group on Citizenship, 1998, p. 13, para. 211)

Such active citizenship takes us beyond the liberal autonomy of those such as R. S. Peters, which characterized the mid-twentieth century:

> It is therefore legitimate, and in each person's interest, to acquire the capacity to choose and sustain the most desirable way of life for themselves, subject only to the requirement to respect the rights of others to do likewise.
> (Wringe, 1997, p. 115)

Political literacy also takes us beyond the communitarian model of selfhood, such as that put forward by McIntyre (1981) and Sandel (1982). Both argue that our selfhood is constituted by our social context and the values of our community. However, Wringe (1997) argues that if individual values have no other source than the community, it is unlikely that school communities will look for alternative ways of viewing the world. School H did recognize a range of views about the Iraq war and took the risk of engaging in conflictual values, involving aspects of conflict resolution and decision-making, rather than imposing an authoritarian stance on such protests.

The element of risk-taking is borne out by previous research into the concept of citizenship prevalent in a sample of primary schools (Mead, 2001). When asked in situ what being a citizen meant to them, a sample of primary teachers emphasized *belonging to a community*. This may reflect a more protective model of citizenship, associated with preserving freedoms within the local community, rather than the challenge of active citizenship represented by political literacy.

Maitles and Deuchar (2003) have demonstrated that Scottish primary pupils, when given the opportunity, are ready to engage in conflictual views about the Iraq war, including different views about the best way to voice arguments for and against. Pupils in School H were given the formal opportunity to voice conflicting opinions. It would seem that active citizenship may require the community of the school to step outside the safe parameters of protective citizenship.

Fundamental to such a process taking place is the school leadership's understanding of the impact of democratic structures on the quality of education within their school. Roker, Player and Coleman (1999) have produced evidence of the widespread involvement of young people in protesting, petitioning and letter writing in relation to single issue politics. Perceptive leaders, who know their pupils well enough to trust them, may see considerable educational advantage in acknowledging the pupil voice:

> Many of the structures and processes which characterize effective schools, in meeting the learning needs of their students, align with democratic principles and practices.
> (Dimmock, 1995, p. 165)

School leadership of this kind is looking for a process of autonomy which is neither of the liberal nor communitarian kind, but, rather, as Smith (1997) expresses it, a process in which 'freedom is to be found in what we do with and for each other on the public stage in reasoning, arguing, supporting, challenging and confronting, as particular occasions require' (p. 128).

A second factor in the process of developing such autonomy will be values, and most significantly the relationship between pupil and teacher values. Previous research (Mead, 2004) has identified the inter-dependency of different sets of values held by individual teachers, which can be categorized as personal, institutional and subject values. The inter-dependency of these sets of values plays a significant part in the human development of the individual teacher, not least when sets of values may be in conflict. Do teachers feel confident and equipped to engage in the democratic process of achieving autonomy together with pupils? For pupils, there is a the potential for a significant shift in their relationship with staff, based on building trust in the school's democratic structures and the consistency of approach across the life of the school. The challenge of this situation is captured well by Tubelsky (1995) in his study of the democratizing of Russian schools when he states that, 'in the beginning children did not believe that conflicts among teachers and students could be resolved legally' (pp. 195–6).

Thirdly, the inter-dependency of pupils' and teachers' values in the process of achieving autonomy might lead to a qualitatively different experience of teaching and learning. There might be the potential for the curriculum to become the focus for problem-solving rather than the transmission of knowledge and understanding. Conflict resolution and decision-making about a student led Iraq war protest one Friday morning might, in fact, have a direct bearing on the truly educational process of achieving autonomy through questioning, doubting, judging and making up one's mind for oneself. Is this not at the heart of George Mead's and Lev Vygotsky's social constructivist theories of learning, and glimpsed in the learning and behaviour of the Scottish primary class, observed by Maitles and Deuchar (2003), who discussed controversial issues, including the Iraq war and forms of protest. The class teacher believed that:

Such discussion allows children to grow in confidence and to learn the skills of convincing other people about their opinions, while at the same time gaining a respect for other people's views. (p. 9)

This teacher also identified the development of transferable skills through pupils enhancing their skills in writing about controversial issues. Thirdly, they believed that discussing issues like the war and ways of protesting actually minimized indiscipline because pupils will be less frustrated at school:

A lot of your discipline problems are solved by allowing the children to voice their opinions because they at least feel they are important in the process. (ibid.)

So far I have tried to argue that a moment in time, like the Iraq war protest in School H, puts into sharp relief and tests the relationship between democratic school structures, pupils' and teachers' values, and teaching and learning. The process of political literacy, which enables individuals to achieve autonomy through conflict resolution and decision-making, is more likely to occur where democratic structures, values and teaching and learning are developing into an organic whole. The absence of this may be reflected in the fact that the majority of school councils surveyed by Taylor and Johnson (2002) gave pupils experience of procedural aspects of democracy but most councils did not contribute to institutional change. By contrast the relatively new school council (only in its second year) at School H played a strategic role in managing and developing the protest through that Friday.

We shall want to find out if the Iraq war protest at School H has made a contribution to a developing organic relationship between democratic structures, values and teaching and learning. As such, our task is nothing less than trying to establish whether or not political literacy can contribute to institutional change.

Methodology

The occurrence of a student Iraq war protest in a Fresh Start school provided an ideal case study for exploring the relationship between political literacy and institutional change.

An initial interview with the head teacher shortly after the protest enabled me to ascertain the sequence of events on the day of the protest, and gain a leadership overview of how the situation was handled. It was important to interview the assistant head responsible for pastoral care and staff development, as this teacher worked closely with the senior members of the school council on the day of the protest, but who also has had particular interest and oversight for developing the pupil voice. The interview took place some ten months after the event in order to gain insights into institutional development, particularly in relation to staff and pupil values and their impact on teaching and learning.

A group interview with six pupils representing the school council and form groups across years 8–11 took place eight months after the protest, and again was timed to set the protest in a context of a period when the pupil voice was being developed. Pupils were asked about how staff and pupils handled the protest, its influence on their understanding of citizenship and its impact on their learning. There was a 50 per cent return on a questionnaire sent to staff ten months after the protest who were teaching in the school at the time it occurred. Semi-structured questions invited staff to express how they felt the protest was handled, if and how it had influenced their values as teachers, and its impact on their teaching, if any.

Summary of the Findings

1. The data suggests that the protest, as an expression of political literacy, highlighted the balance between pragmatic and creative leadership, which may be a necessary feature of institutional change.
2. It would seem that the protest, as an authentic experience of political literacy may have the potential to challenge and develop the relationship between pupils' and teachers' values.
3. The protest as an authentic experience of political literacy may be a contributory factor in the development of collaborative and problem-solving learning.

Analysis and Discussion of Findings

1. The balance between pragmatic and creative leadership

For the head teacher the sequence of events was as much an exercise in containment and pragmatism as democracy. This is a Fresh Start school trying to build a new and positive reputation in the area. She admitted that the press would have swooped on any protest at the school gate as an opportunity to cast doubt on any fresh start. However, she also acknowledges that the rapid decision-making process she and the school went through on the morning of the protest actually exemplifies the reality of democracy: pragmatism, containment, compromise and conflict resolution.

The senior management at School H were able to talk confidently about the protest in the light of a much broader development of the pupil voice. The balance between the pragmatic and the creative is well expressed by the assistant head who saw that, 'the priority was to keep calm, but the main priority was to let the pupils have a voice':

> First of all we wanted to stop a full riot or protest, or stop a protest but we did feel that the students had a point, especially as we are trying to foster a pupil voice and allow the pupils to have a say in what they do at school. That had begun with the school council and so the most appropriate thing to do, we felt, was to get the school council together, and particularly the most senior members in year 11 with whom the protest had started and we moved forward through a discussion with them.

A crucial part of balancing pragmatic and creative leadership is giving pupils the benefit of the doubt, always listening to them, but wanting them to listen to staff as well. Here lies the potential shift in the relationship between pupils' and teachers' values. The outcome would seem to be more authentically democratic, as described by the assistant head:

> Certainly, the benefits of working it through properly were not only that we stopped a riot, but that the students actually believed that they had

come to the conclusion themselves, and I think they had. I don't think it was forced by us. They had the opportunity to give their voice and say what they felt, and on top, they had the opportunity to protest properly through a written letter, which is demonstrating good citizenship as well. That is the right and proper way to go about making a formal protest.

According to the assistant head, balancing the pragmatic and the creative may not be as risky as it seems, if you know your pupils well:

> I think we knew the majority of the pupils involved in the protest well and we knew that these weren't pupils who would do something like this just for fun. We knew which pupils we could reason with and talk to and we believed that those pupils could win round the others, because they were central to the year group.

It is for these reasons that the assistant head described the protest as 'one moment in time you couldn't afford to lose':

> If you want to improve a school you have got to have the pupils on board and once you have got that, then they will move things on themselves because they feel valued.

The pupil group interview did demonstrate an understanding of the pragmatic/creative balance and what they had learnt from it:

> We weren't being told off or anything, it was a talk like any other assembly, and they weren't saying you must do this and that. They explained to us what was happening because most didn't know, people were saying different things, some people didn't know the reasons for and against the war, and were just going along with it, they didn't read the news, they didn't have the background information. (Pupil L)

> The letter was probably a better idea than protesting because if you just went and protested outside in the playground no one is really going to take notice, but if you wrote a letter to the Prime Minister he would know and he did actually read them and replied to us. (Pupil D)

Pupil D went on to point out, pragmatically, that, had they protested at the school gates the locals may have thought that School H was, 'like the kind of school it was a few years ago, and they might think it was going back to its old self'.

The staff questionnaire confirms the balance between creative and pragmatic leadership. Some staff respondents, in the words of teacher A, tended to emphasize how the protest provided a 'meaningful and constructive medium in which students could express themselves', while others emphasized its pragmatic nature:

> I was relieved that a potentially dangerous and unpleasant situation was diffused. (Teacher D)

> It was a way of controlling a situation that could have easily got out of hand. (Teacher F)

Teacher H saw it purely as a chance occurrence, unrelated to aspects of the pupil voice:

> It all came about by chance. It was managed because students would have walked out of school and caused problems in the local area. The action taken pre-empted a walkout and therefore any bad publicity for the school.

In conclusion, the balance between creative and pragmatic leadership may express how pupils and teachers achieve democratic autonomy together.

2. The contribution of the protest to the relationship between pupils' and teachers' values

Pupils believed that mutual respect was a key value developed by the way in which the protest was handled. Contributing significantly to mutual respect across ethnic groups was the presentation in the assemblies of the two letters for and against the war as a *pupil* initiative. This generated respect for the leaders of the protest who got everyone thinking and respect for each person as they worked out their point of view. Finally, there was respect for the teachers because of 'the way they handled it, showing respect for everyone's views and without saying do it this or that way' (Pupil D).

When interviewed ten months after the protest, pupils were particularly aware of how fragile mutual respect can be and how necessary it is to build up trust which can sustain it. Senior managers' trust in the integrity of key leaders of the protest was wise because the debate about the validity of the war has continued and as one pupil said: 'teachers now have to understand that everyone is still going to have their own point of view, whether it's right or wrong'. The issue of the war has provided a unique focus for understanding how the values of mutual respect and trust underpin the democratic process of achieving autonomy together. One pupil is able to translate this aspect of political literacy into national terms:

> Yes but the Government have got to listen and they didn't over the war, and it seemed like there were more people against it and many more people signed the letter against in this school. Tony Blair went and won it without any real communication between the citizens of England and him. There

were so many people who protested and were against the war and that is why people may not vote. (Pupil L)

Some staff respondents agreed with the overall view of the pupils that the protest had contributed to the relationship between pupils' and teachers' values. Mutual respect and trust seem evident in Teacher C's response: 'I really only chaired the debate in the tutor group and offered my own views'.

Two teachers felt that the protest confirmed deeply held values:

> My values as a teacher have always been to see both sides of an argument and then make decision based on the facts I have at my disposal. My hope is that students recognise that this is the way of approaching decision-making. (Teacher B)

> No, my values as a teacher have not been changed. I am known for listening to both sides of a conflict, for working things out in a calm manner, for recognising good in even the most poorly behaved students. I don't hold grudges and I always believe tomorrow is another day. (Teacher E)

What both teachers express is the inter-dependence of pupils' and teachers' values, which, as I have discussed earlier, is fundamental to the process of achieving autonomy as citizens for and with each other. However, for the majority of staff and pupils, the protest was only one contributor to this process, which has to evolve in an organic way, permeating the life of the school. This was authenticated by those staff who either saw the protest as pragmatic, reflecting communitarian values, or who felt it conflicted with liberal values which would rather leave such issues at the school gate, because they might 'fuel tension between different sections of the school community' (Teacher H).

3. The contribution of the protest to teaching and learning

Can a protest, which seems to contribute to mutual respect and trust between pupils, and teachers and pupils, also contribute to the development of teaching and learning? For the pupils, the protest relates to teaching and learning through the experience of problem-solving:

> To be a good citizen of the school is not to go out and just explode and skip school, just to make a point, but instead to talk or write a letter. (Pupil F)

In the same vein Pupil L believes that:

> There will always be problems everywhere and there is always going to be an argument somewhere, but a good community will have all its citizens in it who

deal with problems so they perhaps won't happen again.

Pupil C, like Pupil L, is in Year 11 and perceives the changes in the school over the period of time including the protest, which have brought a problem-solving ethos into the classroom:

> There used to be a gap between students' and teachers' relationships because we used to work against them rather than with them, but now we work with them so they consider our point of view more and we consider their's and pull together.

When questioned in more depth about their learning experiences over the period including the protest, pupils are able to identify some key features of achieving autonomy as citizens together:

> I think the atmosphere now is not to sit in that classroom and listen to your teacher; we now have to actually speak in lessons, as long as it doesn't get too overpowering and we can actually hear the teacher. Obviously we are speaking about points in our lesson so now it's more like speaking and listening than just writing. The best way is to learn by actually doing something, because you do it and see it from your view, and through your eyes you learn more. People want to learn more now. (Pupil I)

Just as pupils credited staff with a great deal of respect for the way they handled the protest, so in class the teacher's role seems to be given new value because it is based on enhanced recognition of the independence, maturity and responsibility of pupils:

> We feel like a community, it doesn't feel like you're here just to be taught, you feel that many of the teachers don't just teach you, they like to help you to learn for yourself as well. (Pupil R)

There are strong echoes here of 'the freedom which is to be found in what we do with and for each other in reasoning, arguing and supporting' (Smith, 1997, p. 128), and which lies at the heart of the process of achieving autonomy together. That this is a two way process in the classroom, which enables teachers as well as pupils to develop, is clearly recognized by Pupil L:

> The teachers say that they are not here to do it for themselves, they've already got the stuff, they're here to help us and I think a lot of the teachers are now seeing this and come to school to see pupils grow and be involved.

Confirmation of these pupil perceptions is to be found amongst staff responses to the question concerning the impact of the protest on their teaching:

> Perhaps the protest reminded me to listen and respect pupils' opinions. At the end of the day they are trying to make sense out of things and they often need our help. I ignore first assumptions and take their views at face value. (Teacher A)

Teacher B identifies the pursuit of truth as an educational ideal, which we would argue, is at the heart of achieving autonomy together:

> The war and now the fallout from the war has provided a good deal of material for teaching – reference points for degrees of truth, for example.

Teacher E identifies that high expectations in learning are closely related to respecting pupils' social, cultural and religious background, factors which figured in the motivations of the protest leaders who did not want to be labelled 'bad Muslims':

> I do think I have changed because I have learned a lot about cultures. Eid just passed me by. Now I must consider it and plan work around it. I want to wish my students a happy Eid and ask them about it on their return.

Conclusion

> I think the school has improved, but I think that there is only so much that you can do to improve it as things get built on; for example, after the protest about the war we didn't just feel like children, we felt like responsible people who have their views heard and are not just silenced. (Pupil D)

No neat formulaic approach to school improvement from Pupil D, but instead a genuine expression of the problem-solving process whereby individuals working together achieve autonomy with and for each other. We have briefly glimpsed in this study that when senior management seize the opportunity for such a process to develop through a war protest, it has the potential to challenge and develop the relationship between pupils' and teachers' values; in turn the development of mutual respect and sustained trust can contribute to teaching and learning, characterized by collaborative problem-solving, involving listening and responding to a range of opinions. To sum up, Pupil D reminds us that institutional change is a gradual process, and one, which, if it is to be authentic and enduring, will reflect the democratic process of achieving autonomy together.

References

ADVISORY GROUP ON CITIZENSHIP (AGC) (1998) *Education for Citizenship and the Teaching of Democracy in Schools* (The Crick Report). London: QCA.

CRICK, B. and PORTER, A. (eds) (1978) *Political Education and Political Literacy*. London: Longman.

DIMMOCK, C. (1995) 'Building Democracy in the School Setting: The Principal's Role', in J. Chapman, I. Froumin and D. Aspin (eds), *Creating and Managing the Democratic School*. London: Falmer.

McINTYRE, A. (1981) *After Virtue*. London: Duckworth.

MAITLES, H. and DEUCHAR, R. (2003) '"Why are they bombing innocent Iraqi's?" Encouraging the expression of political literacy among primary pupils as a vehicle for promoting education for active citizenship'. Scottish Educational Research Association Annual Conference 29/11/03, unpublished paper.

MEAD, N. (2001) 'Identifying Pedagogic Skills Common to Primary Religious Education and PSHE/Citizenship, and the Implications for Continuing Professional Development', *Curriculum*, 22 (2), pp. 43–51.

MEAD, N. (2004) 'The Significance of Values in the Professional Development of Beginning Secondary Teachers', unpublished paper, Birmingham University.

ROKER, D., PLAYER, K. and COLEMAN, J. (1999) 'Young Peoples' Voluntary and Campaigning Activities as Sources of Political Education', *Oxford Review of Education*, 25 (1 & 2), pp. 185–198.

SANDEL, M. (1982) *Liberalism and the Limits of Justice*. Cambridge: Cambridge University Press.

SMITH, R. (1997) 'The Education of Autonomous Citizens', in D. Bridges (ed.), *Education, Autonomy and Democratic Citizenship*. London: Routledge.

TAYLOR, M. with JOHNSON, R. (2002) *School Councils, Their Roles in Citizenship and Personal and Social Education*. Slough: National Foundation for Educational Research.

TUBELSKY, A. (1995) 'The Acquisition of the Democratic Experience', in J. Chapman, I. Froumin and D. Aspin (eds), *Creating and Managing the Democratic School*. London: Falmer.

WRINGE, C. (1997) 'In Defence of Rational Autonomy as an Educational Goal', in D. Bridges (ed.), *Education, Autonomy and Democratic Citizenship*. London: Routledge.

Correspondence
Nick Mead
Oxford Brookes University
Westminster Institute of Education
Harcourt Hill
Oxford, OX2 9AT
Tel.: 01865 488294
E-mail· nmead@brookes.ac.uk

Pastoral Care in Education
Vol. 28, No. 1, March 2010, pp. 45–57

Routledge
Taylor & Francis Group

Conflicting concepts of participation in secondary school Citizenship

Nick Mead*

Oxford Brookes University, UK

(*Received 16 July 2009; final version received 28 October 2009*)

This paper examines a rare response by Ofsted to academics' concerns about a prevailing compliance model of Citizenship in secondary schools. Ofsted's defence of a non-compliance model is then tested against a small sample of Ofsted inspection data. The limited evidence suggests that Ofsted's defence is undermined by the adoption of an instrumentalist approach to participation, driven by the school improvement agenda, and, it is argued, reinforced by the Every Child Matters agenda. The outcome of this approach, which promotes an uncritical concept of participation, is an uncoupling of the political, moral and community that lay at the heart of the Crick Report. Parallels are drawn with the late-nineteenth-century compliance model of Citizenship, which Ofsted claim in their defence is very different from the twenty-first-century participatory model. There follows a review of political change since the Crick Report, which suggests that lack of participation by young people—which is the premise of both that report and Ofsted's depoliticized version of it—is no longer the issue; instead, the question is about whether there should be participation at any cost. To exemplify what this critical concept of participation might look like in a school context, the author draws on his case study of an Iraq war school protest in a fresh start school. It is argued that this example of critical participation maintains the link between the political and moral, and thereby actually makes a contribution to school improvement, by acknowledging staff and pupils' awareness of the complexities, emotions and contradictions of participation. The paper concludes that depoliticized dutiful citizenship will be encouraged if the prevailing concept of participation in schools is an instrumental and uncritical one. This in turn may lead to a widening gulf between the school's and the pupils' understanding of participation, which may eventually impact on sustained school improvement.

Keywords: *participation; citizenship education; secondary education; student-led protest*

*Oxford Brookes University, Department of Professional and Leadership Education, Westminster Institute of Education, Harcourt Hill, Oxford OX2 9AT, UK. Email: nmead@brookes.ac.uk

ISSN 0264–3944 (print)/ISSN 1468–0122 (online)/10/010045–13
DOI: 10.1080/02643940903535959

Definitions of participation

The focus of this study is on participation in the context of Citizenship education. The definition of such participation is grounded in an integral relationship between the moral and political: moral questions arising from young people's judgements about what kind of political participation is appropriate and just. In schools, such participation might be achieved in critical contexts inside and outside the classroom when young people encounter the relationship between critical inquiry and action (Advisory Group on Citizenship, 1998; Mead, 2004b; Banaji, 2008). This definition of participation is related to, but clearly distinguished in process and purpose from, participation through pupil voice, which has had a particular, although not exclusive, focus on school improvement (Ruddock & Flutter, 2004). It is also distinguished in process and purpose from the current use of the term in the Every Child Matters (ECM) framework, which in school contexts refers to social inclusion and participation in learning, particularly by those pupils hard to reach, through the outcomes of 'enjoy and achieve' and 'make a positive contribution' (Department for Education and Skills, 2004, p. 5). In political terms, the latter two definitions may be described as communitarian, whereas the first definition and focus of this paper refers to justice-orientated citizenship (Westheimer & Kahne, 2004). It is acknowledged that participation is a multi-layered term (Department for Education and Skills, 2003) but it is the particular concern of this paper that, in the context of Citizenship education, one definition that may convey the message that all should participate does not deny the opportunity for young people to consider whether or not all participation is a good thing.

Introduction: what does Ofsted mean by participation in the context of secondary Citizenship education?

Since the introduction of statutory Citizenship education into the secondary curriculum in 2002, following the Crick Report of 1998, there has been much discussion about the compliance model it offers young people. Faulks (2006), Leighton (2004), Moore (2002), and Cunningham and Lavalette (2004) argue in particular that a traditional top-down approach towards conceptions of politics lies at the heart of the Crick Report. As Leighton observes, the official line on citizenship education is that it is 'designed to encourage participation in the system, not to question or challenge it' (2004, p. 171). As a result, as Moore (2002) argues, participation is understood in the Crick report as individual acts, such as voting, rather than collective actions such as protest and struggle. This definition of participation corresponds to Westheimer and Kahne's communitarian, as distinct from participatory and justice-orientated citizenship:

> Fostering honesty, good neighbourliness and so on are not *inherently* about democracy. Indeed government leaders in a totalitarian regime would be as delighted as leaders in a democracy if their young citizens learned the lesson put forward by many of the proponents of personally responsible citizenship: don't do drugs; show up at school; show up at work; give blood; help others during a flood; recycle; pick up litter; clean up a park;

treat old people with respect. These are desirable traits for people living in a community. But they are not about democratic citizenship. To the extent that emphasis on these character traits detracts from other important democratic priorities, it may actually hinder rather than make possible democratic participation and change. For example, a focus on loyalty or obedience (common components of character education as well) works against the kind of critical reflection and action that many assume are essential in a democratic society. (2004, p. 244)

Ofsted (2006), in its review of the progress of Citizenship education, addresses the criticisms of compliance specifically in the context of the curriculum and teaching:

> In its focus on the intentions of the national Curriculum Ofsted disagrees with this view and sees much that takes forward the notion of 'critical democracy'. For example, Ofsted's reports have noted good practice in campaigning and challenging—including defending the status quo. When taught correctly the National Curriculum and post 16 citizenship education encourage these elements'. (Ofsted, 2006, para. 12, p. 8)

What Ofsted claims to be fundamentally different about the current concept of Citizenship in schools is the inter-relationship between knowledge and understanding and the active elements of enquiry and communication and participation and responsible action; these elements provide 'critical citizenship', unlike any previous compliance model, such as 'The Citizen Reader of 1885. Ofsted argues that:

> It is these active elements that make citizenship new and challenging and so moves the curriculum away from 'compliance' towards 'critical democracy' in a school context. The National Curriculum is explicit about this: in the enquiry and communication strand pupils should offer their own opinions, discuss and debate, think about and explain views that are not their own; in the participation and responsible strand they should become actively involved in school and community issues' (2006, para. 14, p. 8)

It would seem that, for Ofsted, participation is not separate from learning and is measured through effective teaching and learning, hence the secondary importance it attaches to participation *per se*:

> Exponents of citizenship education refer to citizenship as a subject but also more than a subject. The problem in some schools is that they only have the 'more than' with citizenship almost invisible in the curriculum itself. Particularly in the early days of citizenship as a new subject, many headteachers claimed that their ethos as a main plank of their citizenship provision—headteachers may well point to the demeanour of their pupils as good citizens in a general sense—but they have missed the point that NC citizenship is now a subject that is taught, learned and assessed and practised. (Ofsted, 2006, para. 20, pp. 10–11)

As a result, Ofsted state that, 'while subject inspections will give credit to this wider context, the focus, very much is on the subject itself' (2006, para. 25, p. 12).

Even where there is acknowledgement from Ofsted that community action ought to be typical but can cause severe logistical problems, pragmatic advice is offered suggesting that participation in class debate, written work taken to sensible conclusions and containing responsible suggestions, and drama and other presentations would all suffice as evidence of participation (Ofsted, 2006, para. 39, p. 18).

We increasingly get the impression that participation is circumscribed by the Citizenship curriculum and teaching and learning frameworks in order to ensure that all participate and, at the same time, learning outcomes can be measured. Pupil-led participation cannot be a significant indicator because it is too random and does not involve the entire school community. Ofsted are adamant that the short GCSE is the most effective form of achieving consistency and evidence-based outcomes in Citizenship for inspection purposes.

Not surprisingly, action in the new secondary curriculum of 2007 is aligned with Citizenship subject skills:

> Action should be informed by research and investigation into a political, social or ethical issue or problem. This includes developing and using skills, while applying citizenship knowledge and understanding. (Qualifications and Curriculum Authority, 2007, p. 31)

It is debatable whether Bernard Crick intended there to be such constraints, even though it is argued that a top-down political model dominates his report. The Crick Report speaks of aiming at 'no less than a change in the political culture of this country' (Advisory Group on Citizenship, 1998, p. 7) and 'making young people individually confident in finding new forms of involvement and action among themselves' (p. 8). McLaughlin (2000) considers the Crick Report to contain evidence of 'maximal' or 'active' elements compared with the minimalist interpretations of citizenship in an earlier attempt to introduce Citizenship into schools in 1991.

This leads us to speculate on the extent to which apolitical analyses of the benefits of Citizenship education to school improvement have influenced the judgements of Ofsted, bearing in mind that they are held accountable for the persistence of a significant minority of failing secondary schools. By contrast with those who have grounded their citizenship research in a theory of democracy based on young peoples' rights (Alderson, 2000), there are those, such as Flutter and Rudduck (2004), whose justification of student participation is entirely pragmatic in terms of a better learning climate and reduced exclusions.

How is participation in the context of Citizenship education exemplified in secondary Ofsted reports?

It would be reasonable at this stage to ask whether or not Ofsted reports show any indications of an instrumental approach to Citizenship education. In order to address this question, a small-scale online study of Ofsted reports written in the 2007/08 academic year was undertaken (Ofsted, 2007/08). A sample of 30 reports was selected, which consisted of 10 reports from each of the Ofsted categories described as outstanding, satisfactory and inadequate. Schools were selected from the southeast region in which the author's university is located. The 10 schools selected in each category represented a range of type of school—for example, selective, secondary modern and comprehensive—as well as a range of socio-economic areas. The outstanding schools were selected from Ofsted's outstanding providers list for 2007/08 and the inadequate schools were selected from Ofsted's notice to improve/special measures lists for 2007 and 2008. The method of documentary analysis involved identifying and categorizing how participation in the context of Citizenship education is exemplified in the content and language of those report paragraphs referring to the overall effectiveness of the school, personal development and well-being, teaching and learning and curriculum and other activities.

To summarize the tentative findings from a small sample, there are indications that where positive attitudes to participation in learning and in the life of the school generally exist there are few references to the knowledge and understanding required in Citizenship and the quality of the teaching and assessment of the subject. Where attitudes to learning, behaviour and attendance are satisfactory, inspectors may make positive comments about aspects of some pupils' participation in the life of the school, but links are not made between this wider participation and the need to improve the quality of teaching and learning through greater pupil participation in lessons, the lack of which is often the cause of a satisfactory grading. Usually in these reports the content and quality of teaching in Citizenship is commented on in terms of how well all pupils are achieving and therefore participating in Citizenship, rather than just an active minority. Finally, in reports where the school's overall effectiveness is judged inadequate, and there are negative attitudes to participation in learning and school life, references to the quality and content of Citizenship education are always explicit. A closer examination of each of the three categories of report now follows.

In the following two examples, and in the majority of reports like them in the sample of outstanding schools, the style of language used in the reporting is holistic or organic: inspectors presumably see no need to mention the quality of Citizenship because the reported attitudes to teaching and learning speak for themselves:

Example 1
High academic standards have not been achieved at the expense of the students' personal development and well-being, including their spiritual, moral, social and cultural development, which is also outstanding. Students show high levels of confidence and maturity. They have a genuine zest for learning and display excellent attitudes in all aspects of school life. Students develop into articulate and thoughtful young people well prepared for their future lives. (Ofsted, 2007/08, p. 2)

Example 2
Another key factor in students' excellent academic achievement is the great strength in their personal development and well-being. Their mature and responsible attitudes also prepare them very well for the next stage in their lives. The overwhelming majority of students behave exceptionally well, are courteous and are proud of their school. They contribute strongly to its positive atmosphere, evident in the excellent relationships with each other and with their teachers. Students engage well with difficult cultural and moral issues and this continues effectively in the sixth form. (Ofsted, 2007/08, p. 6)

One hundred per cent of the outstanding reports sampled use these blanket statements found in the overall effectiveness section of the reports without any reporting on content, assessment and quality of Citizenship curriculum work. The words 'citizen' or 'citizenship' are likely to occur in generalized statements such as: 'students show a very good awareness of what it means to be a citizen in the UK in the 21st century' (Ofsted, 2007/08, p. 1). There are no examples in the sample of inspectors demonstrating how the teaching of Citizenship might provide these 'confident and articulate students' with a critical citizenship education that goes beyond a communitarian model.

It is worth noting at this point that in selecting the 10 outstanding schools for the sample, one cannot ignore the fact that a significant proportion of all of these schools are in middle-class catchment areas, a minority with small pockets of deprivation. It also needs to be said that in doing justice to the range of types of school in the Ofsted outstanding providers list for the southeast, there is a significant representation of selective schools that has also been taken into account.

In the sample of reports graded as satisfactory, inspectors, in 80% of cases, report on any positive participatory ethos and opportunities for pupils to act independently, albeit usually in a communitarian mode and the style of language reflects this. For example, one head teacher is quoted as saying that the school is developing people who you would want to live next door to. The inspector reports that in this school diversity is highly valued and celebrated so that students from a wide variety of backgrounds learn to appreciate and value their own and others' cultures, and, as a result, 'tensions between different cultures in the outside world do not affect the excellent relationships in the school' (Ofsted, 2007/08, p. 1).

However, no links are made between these qualities and the more than frequent reference to the same pupils in classrooms as passive learners who underachieve. Ofsted action points in these reports for Citizenship and other subjects refer to the technical specifics of teaching and learning, pace and challenge and assessment for learning, but could also, for example, encourage more critical, authentic and possible controversial participation that might galvanize pupils in the classroom to express their opinions and drive their own issue-based inquiries.

In another example, an inspector reports briefly on the influence of a small group of dynamic students who are participating in the wider school life. No links are made between this example and the over-riding view expressed under teaching and learning and curriculum that in the majority of subjects, including Citizenship, pupil behaviour is 'characterized by passivity rather than purposeful independence' (Ofsted, 2007/08, p. 1).

In stark contrast to the outstanding reports, all of the reports in the inadequate sample reported on the content and quality of Citizenship teaching, making explicit and prescriptive links between content lacking in the Citizenship curriculum and pupils' attitudes and behaviour, which, by implication, have a bearing on their attitude and receptivity to learning:

Example 3
Attendance is below the national average, although the range of strategies employed by the school is having a satisfactory impact on improvement. The strategies for reducing fixed-term exclusions at KS3 are having an impact, although this is not the case at KS4. Students' spiritual, moral, social and cultural development is satisfactory. However, students have a limited understanding of Britain as a diverse society, and the promotion of cultural diversity is currently underdeveloped. (Ofsted, 2007/08, p. 5)

Example 4
The advances in spiritual, moral and social development are greater, however, than those in their cultural development. Although comfortable with their own community, in conversation with inspectors, some displayed a limited understanding of our multicultural society. (Ofsted, 2007/08, p. 2)

These explicit references to Citizenship subject content, which is believed to support compliance, are matched by a frequent reporting on the close monitoring of the statutory provision for the subject and the requirement to report to parents on pupils' assessed achievement in the subject. The quality of the teaching and learning is systematically reported on; for example, fine judgements are made about the degree to which 'some students already appreciate the importance of Citizenship Education and its relationship to their own lives' (Ofsted, 2007/08, p. 1).

By contrast, there is no explicit evidence in the outstanding school reports of any systematic reporting on Citizenship statutory provision, or on the quality of the teaching and learning, and assessment and reporting to parents.

It needs to be noted here that, in making the selection for the sample, one cannot ignore the fact that 90% of these schools in the inadequate sample are in challenging circumstances and in socio-economic contexts where attitudes to learning in diverse contexts may be negative. There is some recorded evidence in these reports that pupils do participate in resolving localized challenging situations, and these may reflect their understanding of the moral choices open to them; however, this is given little recognition in an inspection process that describes the curriculum and much teaching and learning as inadequate, behaviour as only just satisfactory and persistent absenteeism as needing serious attention.

What we see happening in these examples across all three report categories is Ofsted both uncoupling and exploiting the integral links between knowledge, critical inquiry and participation, and for pragmatic reasons, thereby undermining their own defence for why Citizenship education does not foster compliance. We get the feeling that pupils in socio-economically disadvantaged communities only need more Citizenship knowledge in order to improve their behaviour and attitudes in lessons; that is, to become more compliant. It will be argued in the next section that a similar reductive narrowing down of moral education for all took place in the late nineteenth century for the same reasons. The spiritual, social, moral and cultural are frequently mentioned in these reports, but not the political. The fundamental link between political participation and moral development that lay at the heart of the Crick report appears to be severed.

Late nineteenth-century parallels: participation moulding the urban poor

A similar uncoupling of the moral and political took place within the moral instruction found in a number of late-nineteenth-century elementary schools. This is worth noting as Ofsted argue in their 2006 report that critical citizenship of the twenty-first century is very different from the compliance model of the late nineteenth century, such as found in the Citizenship Reader of 1885. Wright's (2009) research into late-nineteenth-century moral instruction makes clear comparisons between the way in which in both periods universal goals for citizenship are narrowed down to instrumental strategies directly related to the needs of the urban poor.

Wright observes that the late-nineteenth-century expansion of the state, for example through extensions to suffrage and increasing intervention of state agencies into different aspects of individual's lives, required new educational means to ensure that citizens were able to fulfil their new functions. The relationship between the political and moral was initially intrinsic to the thinking of movements such as the Moral Instruction League, who claimed that 'the future of a nation depends on how those invaluable opportunities [in school] are utilized for moral ends' (Dixon, 1879, pp. 16–23, cited by Wright, 2009, p. 11). However, Wright demonstrates the way in which claims to universality regarding moral instruction and citizenship were frequently interpreted as something specifically for the urban poor. In effect, Citizenship became merely moral instruction 'to remedy perceived deficiencies in the families and communities of poor pupils' (Wright, 2009, p. 15). Of particular concern were the bad examples that children living in poor areas of towns and cities were exposed to at home and in their local communities. For example, Henry Major, inspector for the Leicester school board, argued for 'teaching the child in the first years of school life to understand better some of the duties and relations of family life, its genesis and evolution, leading to the subject of the state, loyalty and patriotism' (Major, 1902, source unknown, cited by Wright, 2009, p. 17). To achieve this end, the pedagogy of moral instruction was designed primarily to mould the child and in the thinking of educationists such as Frank Hayward, inspector for the London County Council 1935: 'morality was central to pedagogical theory' (cited by Wright, 2009, p. 17). For others, like Henry Major in Leicester, such pedagogy was found to be 'an auxiliary to maintenance of school discipline' (Major, 1905, cited by Wright, 2009, p. 22).

Wright concludes her study with a comment from the former Prime Minister, Tony Blair, shortly before the introduction of Citizenship into the National Curriculum:

> A significant minority of children, often in sink estates, grows up amid instability, poor education, endemic crime, drug abuse and few decent job opportunities ... It is simply not acceptable for young children to be left without supervision, parental or otherwise, free to truant, vandalise and roam the streets at all hours ... Education is our number one priority because nothing does more to reduce exclusion than confidence and achievement at school. But schools are not value-free zones. They are an integral part of society and shape its character. That is why the curriculum reforms to be announced tomorrow emphasize personal, social and health education, including the importance of marriage; and why citizenship education is to be given a firm place in the curriculum. (Blair, 1999)

Wright sees the parallels with a century before, and her work lends weight to the central argument of this paper. Of particular significance is the way in which a universal citizenship education to enable all to participate more fully within the new functions of the state is reduced to an instrumental pedagogy in a handful of urban schools: political participation that involves moral choices is reduced to participation in learning (i.e. not being excluded).

To return to the twenty-first century, inclusion remains a major theme, providing the driver for key national strategies. Much of the good or outstanding participatory citizenship described in Ofsted terms is communitarian, which may sit well with improving teaching and learning in secondary schools. This is reinforced by the concept of participation within the ECM framework, considered by Ofsted to be closely aligned with, and measurable through, Citizenship (Ofsted, 2006, para. 139, p. 5). The fifth outcome of ECM is 'making a positive contribution', which has led to certain groups of students such as 'hard to reach' being helped to participate. May (2005) views this as disenfranchising of pupils and begs the question 'whose participation is it anyway?' She observes that:

> There is an onus on putting pupil participation on the professionals' agenda, yet there is not an equivalent regard (or acknowledgement) of how pupils potentially influence, and contribute to, their own participation. It is interesting, and perhaps a cause for concern, that pupil participation is portrayed as a contrived matter, requiring professional intervention. (May, 2005, p. 29)

Williams takes up the point that ECM is strong on protection and recognition of needs, especially for educational achievement, 'but far less forthcoming in how to create a culture of respect for children' (2004, p. 411). In the same vein, Jans (2004) argues that participation becomes an instrument to deal with the insecurities and unpredictability of a risk society. He believes a 'systems perspective' on participation is used by authorities 'as a strategy to broaden their policy basis or a strategy to keep growing conflicts of interest under control' (Jans, 2004, p. 31). Jans concludes that such systems-controlled participation models do not relate meaningfully to those matters which are of direct interest to young people.

Is all participation a certain good?

It is not then surprising that the instrumental model of participation dominating both the Ofsted standards and ECM agendas does not reflect the significant changes in citizenship participation in Britain since the Crick Report, as identified by Pattie *et al.*:

> We believe that the Citizen Audit reveals that citizens have not contracted out, but are engaged in a multiplicity of political activities beyond the traditional; three in every four people are engaged in political activity, defined as attempting to influence rules, laws or policies. Political engagement does not lie upon one single continuum. Rather there are distinct individualistic, contact and collectively organized forms of political engagement. (2004, p. 107)

Significantly, it is those aged 24 and under, and those remaining in full-time education to 19 years of age who are much more likely to be involved in the collectively organized actions. In the light of the Citizen Audit, what concerns researchers such as Banaji (2008) is not the question about whether young people are participating, or participating less than other age groups, but how they are navigating the complexity of active democracy:

> There are plenty of examples of political or civic outcomes that have conflicting and potentially undemocratic overtones for some people while being unquestionably democratic to others. (Banaji, 2008, p. 550)

Hence Banaji poses a much more dynamic question to young people: civic engagement at any cost? In other words, does Citizenship education make a simplistic assumption that all participation is a 'certain good' (Banaji, 2008, p. 553). This is essentially a moral question that arises from the challenges presented by political participation and exemplifies the integral relationship between the political and moral, between action and critical inquiry. However, pupils will not engage in such moral questions if the message is simply that all must participate, and if not, then they must be helped to participate.

The example Banaji develops concerns what Cunningham and Lavalette describe as 'the overwhelming response of the educational establishment to castigate and "punish" those who took part in the school "strikes" against the 2003 Iraq war' (2004, p. 551). Banaji cites this author's case study of a student-led protest against the Iraq war in a fresh start school with a 30% British Asian make-up (Mead, 2004b). On the day before the major anti-war march in London, a group of mature and respected Year 11 Muslim pupils staged a protest against the Iraq war at morning break. As a result, the head teacher mobilized the school council, who, with the protest leaders, discussed the question 'who are we trying to influence?' It was agreed that assemblies and tutorial time that day would be devoted to discussing the war and at the end of the day there would be a short vigil in tutor groups, followed by the signing of petitions for and against the war that would be sent to the Prime Minister and the local MP. What is important about this example of participation is the complexity of the actions involved for all parties involved: senior management, staff and pupils. For example, does the head teacher address the concerns of a strong Muslim lobby for creative or pragmatic reasons, or both? Some staff viewed the way the situation was handled as 'a meaningful and constructive medium in which students could express themselves' (Mead, 2004b, pp. 9–10), while others saw it as a way out of crisis for the school's delicate reputation:

> It all came about by chance. It was managed because students would have walked out of school and caused problems in the local area. The action taken pre-empted a walkout and therefore any bad publicity for the school. (Mead, 2004b, p. 10)

Not all staff have their attitudes changed or confirmed positively by the protest and some see it as a dangerous precedent as viewed from a communitarian perspective; these staff would 'rather leave such issues at the school gate, because they might fuel tension between different sections of the school community'. (Mead, 2004b, p. 10)

A minority of protest organizers were not willing to accept the agreed plan of action at the end of the school council meeting, and the head teacher excluded these pupils for the day. Some pupils chose not to stay for the vigil at the end of the school day and did not sign either of the petitions. Key leaders of the protest and school council representative believed that they had achieved a sense of agency in the public sphere. Interviewed 10 months after the protest, and with the public debate about the war still raging, they were confident about how teachers now 'have to understand that everyone is still going to have their own point of view, whether its right or wrong' and they believed that this had impacted on the way their views were treated in the classroom: 'after the protest about the war we didn't just feel like children, we felt like responsible people who have their views heard and are not just silenced' (Mead, 2004b, p. 11). One pupil was able to translate this sense of agency into national terms:

> Yes but the Government have got to listen and they didn't over the war, and it seemed like there were more people against it and many more people signed the letter against in this school. Tony Blair went and won it without any real communication between the citizens of England and him. There were so many people who protested and were against the war and that is why people may not vote. (Mead, 2004b, p. 10)

Students' sense of agency is matched by the authoritarian and disapproving stance of some staff coming from a communitarian perspective and who believe such conflictual issues raise tensions in the community and should be left at the school gate (for further discussion about such challenges to teachers' values, see Mead, 2000, 2003, 2004a). For Banaji, these contradictory views of the civic lie at the heart of any discussion about young people's civic participation. This school took the risk of engaging in these contradictions, but the majority of students (10,000 in London alone) in the same week in March 2003 found themselves facing exceptionally serious and authoritarian consequences the following day (Al-Ghabban, 2004; Cushion, 2007). As one sixth former said, 'Suddenly the politicisation of youth looks unattractive to those who have called us apathetic for too long' (*Guardian*, 22 March 2003, quoted in Smith, 2003).

Conclusion

To conclude, the case study enables us to glimpse a much more complex and dynamic picture of participation that cuts right across the simplistic model that participation *per se* is desirable, and which can be modelled through teaching and learning in secondary school classrooms. The case study suggests that a failing school which had been reopened for two years was improving (and described as such in its 2003 Ofsted report) in part because it was acknowledging young people's awareness of the complexities, emotions and contradictions of participation. It did this through the engagement of senior managers, staff and pupils in those complexities, emotions and contradictions.

This is very different from instrumental participation that uncouples the political challenge from moral decision-making, and is 'done' by staff to pupils. Of course we want pupils to participate in their learning, but if that alone is the prevailing and uncritical concept of participation, it will surely lead to a depoliticized dutiful citizenship, a far cry from the interwoven political, moral and social dimensions of Citizenship found in the Crick Report. In turn, this may lead to a widening gulf between school and pupil understanding of participation, bearing in mind the degree and variety of young peoples' activism outside school and the complexity of moral decision-making this must involve (Banaji, 2008). It is not unreasonable to suppose that such a gulf might ultimately begin to impact on any one school's sustained improvement through a degree of pupil disaffection; however, this would require further independent research, particularly as Ofsted school reports and its recent report on 12 outstanding schools (Ofsted, 2009) are so instrumental in their approach.

References

Advisory Group on Citizenship (1998) *Education for citizenship and the teaching of democracy in schools.* The Crick Report (London, QCA).

Alderson, P. (2000) *Young children's rights: exploring beliefs, principles and practice* (London, Jessica Kingsley).

Al-Ghabban, A. (2004) Unpublished interview data, student protesters 2003–4. Cited in Banaji (2008).

Banaji, S. (2008) The trouble with civic: a snapshot of young people's civic and political engagements in twenty-first century democracies, *Journal of Youth Studies,* 11(5), 543–560.

Blair, T. (1999) *The Times,* 8 September.

Cunningham, S. & Lavalette, M. (2004) 'Active citizens' or 'irresponsible truants'? School student strikes against the war, *Critical Social Policy,* 24(2), 255–269.

Cushion, S. (2007) Protesting their apathy? An analysis of British press coverage of young anti-Iraq war protestors, *Journal of Youth Studies,* 10(4), 419–437.

Department for Education and Skills (2003) *Building a culture of participation* (London, DFES).

Department for Education and Skills (2004) *Every child matters: change for children in schools* (London, DFES).

Dixon, G. (1879) Lecture on elementary education in the Birmingham board schools, presented to the Birmingham Teachers' Association. Cited by Wright (2009).

Faulks, K. (2006) Education for citizenship in England's secondary schools: a critique of current principle and practice, *Journal of Education Policy,* 21(1), 59–74.

Flutter, J. & Rudduck, J. (2004) *Consulting pupils: what's in it for schools?* (London, Routledge).

Jans, M. (2004) Children as citizens: towards a contemporary notion of child participation, *Childhood,* 11(1), 27–44.

Leighton, R. (2004) The nature of citizenship education provision: an initial study, *Curriculum Journal,* 15(2), 167–181.

Major, H. (1905) *Ethical world,* 2 December. Cited by Wright (2009).

May, H. (2005) Whose participation is it anyway? Examining the context of pupil participation in the UK, *British Journal of Special Education,* 32(1), 29–34.

McLaughlin, T. (2000) Citizenship education in England: the Crick report and beyond, *Journal of Philosophy of Education,* 34(4), 541–570.

Mead, N. C. (2000) Researching skills common to religious education and citizenship, in: S. Clipson-Boyles (Ed.) *Putting research into practice in primary teaching and learning* (London, Fulton), 165–175.

Mead, N. C. (2003) Will the introduction of teaching standards in professional values and practice put the heart back into primary teacher education, *International Journal of Pastoral Care in Education,* 21(1), 37–42.

Mead, N. C. (2004a) The provision for personal, social, health education and citizenship in school-based elements of primary initial teacher education, *International Journal of Pastoral Care in Education,* 22(2), 19–26.

Mead, N. C. (2004b) The management and impact of a student led Iraq war protest in a fresh start school, *International Journal of Pastoral Care in Education,* 22(4), 6–12.

Moore, A. (2002) Citizenship education in the UK: for liberation or control, paper presented to the *Knowledge and Discourse: Speculating on Disciplinary Futures Conference,* Hong Kong, June. Cited in Faulks (2006).

Ofsted (2006) *Towards consensus? Citizenship in secondary schools* (London, Ofsted).

Ofsted (2007/08) A selection of school inspection reports. Available online at: http:// www. ofsted.gov.uk/oxedu_reports/display (accessed 25 February 2009).

Ofsted (2009) *Twelve outstanding secondary schools, excelling against the odds* (London, Ofsted).

Pattie, C., Seyd, P. & Whitely, P. (2004) *Citizenship in Britain: values, participation and democracy* (Cambridge, Cambridge University Press).

Qualifications and Curriculum Authority (2007) *Citizenship: programme of study for Key Stage 3* (London, QCA).

Ruddock, J. & Flutter J. (2004) *How to improve your school; giving pupils voice* (London, Continuum).

Smith, M. K. (2003) *School protests and the war in Iraq.* Available online at: www.infed.org/ talkingpoint/war_school_protests.htm (accessed February 2009).

Westheimer, J. & Kahne, J. (2004) What kind of citizen? The politics of educating for democracy, *American education Research journal,* 41(2), 237–269.

Williams, F. (2004) What matters is who works: why Every Child Matters to New Labour. Commentary on the DFES Green paper Every Child Matters, *Critical Social Policy,* 24(3), 406–425.

Wright, S. (2009) Moral instruction, urban poverty and English elementary schools in the late nineteenth century, unpublished paper.

Students', parents' and teachers' understanding of civil learning outside school and its relationship with formal learning inside school

Nick Mead, Oxford Brookes University, UK, 2011

Introduction

The impetus to write this paper stemmed from an observation noted during a small-scale online study of how Ofsted reports on pupil participation in Citizenship Education:

> There is some recorded evidence in Ofsted reports on inadequate schools in challenging circumstances that pupils do participate in resolving localized challenging situations and these may reflect their understanding of the moral choices open to them; however, this is given little recognition in an inspection process that describes the curriculum and much teaching and learning as inadequate, behavior as only just satisfactory and persistent absenteeism as needing serious attention (Mead 2010, p.51).

Only occasionally did inspectors give glimpses of young people having agency to broker disputes and work with staff on restoring peer relationships, drawing on family, friendship and associational networks. Although it was not assumed that such examples would automatically appear in a small-scale study such as the one reported on here, it was felt that these civil learning experiences, different from the formal curriculum definition of 'active citizenship' (Jerome 2011), deserve attention, not least because of the pedagogical challenges they bring if they are to shape formal learning.

Background

1. The Legacy of Crick

The moral, community and political literacy strands of the Crick Report (1998) made it clear that there is an important interrelationship between the civil and the civic in the development of citizens. The Report (1998, 2.8) makes it clear that freedom and full citizenship in the political arena itself depends on a society with a rich variety of non-political associations and voluntary groups – what some have called civil society. The Report also states that 'voluntary and community activity cannot be the full meaning of active citizenship' (1998, 2.8). As Peterson states:

> Statements such as this have provided citizenship education in England with an essentially *political* concept of active citizenship as a supplement to, but not as a replacement for, voluntary and community engagement (Peterson 2011, p.125).

This interrelationship between the civil and the civic has strong roots in political theory. The Marxist political philosopher Gramsci (1971) defined civil society as the space in which political engagement with the state (civic society) is learnt, and political dispositions developed organically through family, friendships and community associations. For Gramsci this was no passive affair, as Edwards states: 'civil society was the site of rebellion against the orthodox as well as the construction of cultural and ideological hegemony' (2009, p.8).

It is unfortunate, but perhaps inevitable, in the process of Citizenship Education becoming a credible statutory subject from 2002, that some commentators and policy-makers have, in the words of Peterson, 'sought, in both theoretical and practical terms, to separate voluntary and community activity from political engagement in a way which downgrades the former in favour of the latter' (2011, p.125). This separation of the civil and the civic has been reinforced by the focus of Ofsted inspections since 2006, which, 'while giving credit to the wider context, will focus on the subject itself' (Ofsted 2006,, para 25, p.12). The concern here is that these factors, along with a strong Key Stage 4 emphasis on subject knowledge through GCSE short courses and assessed outcomes for all, have led to what Bentley (2005) has described as a disconnect between students' personal choices and collective consequences and between political decisions and personal experience. This disconnect reinforces the schools' view that students are citizens-in-waiting who need to be given the knowledge and skills to become citizens (Leighton 2004). It also conveys the message that student participation is primarily about compliance in the classroom, rather than a challenging and dynamic process of moral decision-making about action or inaction within a variety of community contexts (Mead 2010).

2. Reconnecting political literacy and students' experience of being citizens

Finding ways to reconnect political literacy and the moral and community within students' experience, as envisaged by the Crick Report (1998), has led to some debate about the uses of the terms 'civil' and 'civic'. Biesta, for example, talks about civic learning as:

> Something that, in principle, goes on all of the time, and that in principle can happen anywhere. Young people learn continuously from the situations, practices, relationships and experiences that make up their lives. It is in situations that they learn the values of democratic and non-democratic ways of action and interaction and it is through such experiences that they also learn about their own position as a citizen (Biesta 2007, p.4).

For those who have sought to define the rigour of Citizenship Education as a credible curriculum subject, Biesta's more social than political understanding of Citizenship poses a challenge to the conceptual base of the subject. Audigier talks about the need for a definition to 'have a vital "hard-core" without which the very idea of citizenship will consist of mere woolly affirmations' (1998, p.15). Davies is mindful of this point in his introduction to citizenship for new teachers: 'Citizenship education involves direct connection with action that relates to key concepts about social justice in public contexts' (2007, p.8). However, a number of writers discuss such concepts being learnt within the 'politics of everyday life', notably in those three areas identified by Gramsci: family, friendships and associations (Boyte 2004; Bentley 2005; Crick 2005; Ginsbourg 2005; Stoker 2006; Annette 2009). Bentley, for example, notes how, within the democratic family:

> In practising dialogue, negotiation and distributive fairness family members are training for the allocation of roles and resources in wider life, as well as adapting spontaneously and flexibly to changes in family circumstances, household technology and so on (Bentley 2005, pp.37-38).

Key understandings and values about consumption, saving and emotional resilience are learnt, which Bentley argues will shape family members' actions related to social justice in their public lives. The key action for schools is first to recognise the existence of this kind of experiential civil learning rather than simply 'do more to help young people engage with their local communities' (Davies et al 2013 p.3). All young people do develop, to varying degrees, some conceptual understanding about social justice in public places through family, friendships and associations: what they would value is the recognition of that learning within the classroom (Davies *et al* 2013, p.3). This means that the second key action for schools must be to make the links between civil learning experiences and aspects of civic education explicit both within PSHEe and Citizenship Education and across the curriculum. Peterson (2011) is right to argue that this is a pedagogical responsibility and it is one which, as Davies *et al* recommend, will empower young people to be able 'to use their existing knowledge and experience in the development of education to explore and support citizenship communities' (Davies *et al* 2013 p.3). It is this pedagogical responsibility and its implications for teacher education which is a particular focus of this study.

Research context

The above debate is an important backdrop to the aim and methodology of this paper. The aim of the paper is to address the two school actions discussed above: how to develop recognition of students' civil learning experiences in the community and how to build links between pupil civil learning experience outside school and formal learning in school. This was to be done in the context of a review of the structure of Personal, Social Health and Economic Education (PSHEe) and Citizenship curriculum delivery in the case study school. Five conference, or drop-down, days a year had been devoted to these subject areas. Some days had worked better than others but the overall judgement of senior management was that they lacked personalisation and engagement. The case study school is an 11 18 community college with 1295 students set in a market town in the east of England. The area is largely rural with agriculture as the main activity but recently housing has expanded to accommodate those who commute to a nearby city and to London, using the good rail links. Most students in the school are from white British backgrounds. An increasing proportion of students are from minority ethnic backgrounds. There are also some students from Traveller backgrounds. The proportion of students eligible for free school meals is below the national average. There are similar proportions of students with special educational needs and/or disabilities to the average school. The school is a specialist college in business and enterprise.

Methodology

The data collection tool used was the focus group. There were five focus groups in total: year 7 pupils; year 9 pupils; combined years 10 and 11 pupils; one teacher group, consisting of the Head of History, Head of Music and Head of ICT; and one parent group, made up of five parents representing years 7, 9, 10 & 11. Traditionally, focus groups have been used in consumer research to gain an understanding of local opportunities and constraints. Essentially, the participants rather than the researcher's agenda predominates and it is from the interactions of the group that the data emerge (Cohen, Manion & Morrison 2007, p.376). Values, attitudes and opinions are key features of the data and for these to emerge the researcher needs to empower participants to speak out. Size of focus groups, selection of participants, the setting and the management of the process are all key conditions influencing successful outcomes (Newby 2010, pp.350-353). More recently, the theory underpinning focus groups has been deepened in the context of Participatory Action Research. This is defined as 'a participatory democratic process concerned with developing practical knowing in the pursuit of worthwhile human purposes' (Reason & Bradbury 2001, p.1). This definition is particularly appropriate for the problem-solving approach taken to addressing the needs of the case study school, which offered to engage with the research because of concerns about the quality of personalisation and progression within its PSHEe and

Citizenship programme. The choice of the focus groups representing students, parents, and teachers reflects this democratic process of finding solutions 'which lie in the local' (Ger 1997, p.116) and, as such, was a civil learning experience.

In the conducting of the focus groups it was important to convey the assumption that the participants were collaborators because they had committed themselves to the process (Bige Saatcioglu & Ozanne,J ,2008 p.3). The researcher heeded the advice of Robson in getting the balance right between an active and passive role in order to 'generate interest in a topic close to their academic/professional interest without at the same time leading the groups to reinforce existing expectations or confirm prior hypotheses' (2002, p.287). To achieve the best outcomes, participants were selected by the school with groups of no more than seven, which ensured that all had good opportunities to contribute. Parents of participating pupils in years 7, 9 and 10 and 11 and participating teachers and parents received letters from the school outlining the project and guaranteeing confidentiality and anonymity.

The focus group schedule was based on the following questions:

1. What are the things which really matter to you (or young people) and in which you (they) have some say and can make a difference outside of school? eg family, friends, leisure, clubs, hobbies, part-time work.

2. What do you think you (they) have learnt from these situations?

3. Do any of these situations connect with school or are they completely separate?

4. Could your (their) learning outside school be used in any aspect of school life?

5. If your (their) learning outside school could be used in school, would that make a difference to how you (they) learn and how much influence you (they) feel you (they) have?

6. What would make it possible for you (them) to use things you've (they've) learnt outside of school both in lessons and in the general life of the school?

An audio recording was taken of each focus group with permission from members. Each recording was transcribed using the question schedule and then key points were extrapolated across the groups converging on the three broad areas identified below.

Analysis and discussion of the findings

Three key areas were identified based on the focus group transcriptions:

1. What do students, parents and teachers understand by student civil learning outside school?

2. Do students, parents and teachers believe that student civil learning can connect with and be used in any aspect of school life?

3. Do students, parents and teachers believe that the integration of student civil learning and formal learning would make a difference to how pupils learn?

Students' understanding of civil learning outside school

The overall responses of the students reflected the findings of the English regional study of Biesta *et al* (2009), as well as Hoskins *et al*'s(2011) study of European countries: that civil understanding, skills and dispositions are learnt primarily through the family and friendship groups, and through a variety of individual and associational activities. Students talked about how decisions were made in their families:

> Everyone is very open in my family and everyone has an equal say. My parents will listen to me and this has made me mature. My parents don't mind if my views differ (Year 10 girl).

Friendship groups involve decisions about where and who to meet and negotiating to make friendships work:

> Family and friendships are important and negotiating with friends. We sort it out then and there or by texting. Deciding to go to town shopping, buying birthday presents by putting our money together. We organise and plan together for all members of the friendship group. I got asked to go and see Justin Beiber in Never Say Never but it's not my thing – I decided to opt out but the group is easy- going like that. I have learnt how to treat other people and not to leave people out. I negotiate, talk it through and see what they want to do (Year 9 girl).

The way in which longstanding friendship groups can shape different civil identities is well articulated by Year 11 students who feel that they have learnt to negotiate difference:

> In our friendship groups we are all good friends in and outside school. There has been some falling out recently. We've learnt how to be open to our differences. We don't all have the same interests – similarities and differences have to be recognised equally and the fact that we have changed as we have got older. This is the same as when we met – it teaches you to be more open and prepares you for when you leave school and the move to the sixth form – it will help us with new friends (Year 11 boy).

Following family and friendship groups students identify individual and associational activities which matter to them, in which they have a say and which can make a difference outside school. One example of an individual activity which stood out was reading. A Year 9 girl felt strongly that because she read a lot 'that helps me express views. I can get my point across because I have a good vocabulary'.

Associational activities involve negotiating with different kinds of people who are not all members of the school friendship group. As well as negotiating, associational activities offer good opportunities for autonomous and collective decision-making. This is well demonstrated through sport leadership:

> I am a team captain in a Sunday football league. This involves responsibilities such as communication with the team and always turning up. I have to make sure that people come to training. I am learning how to make decisions; for example, some people aren't dedicated to training, they just want to play the games, but they can't

play if they haven't trained and I have to make that decision and tell them (Year 10 boy).

Hoskins *et al* (2011) identify how music and drama groups figure largely in the lives of their European sample of young people. In the locality of the case study school these groups provide opportunities both to interact with a wider age range and variety of people and make decisions with them:

> I am in a theatre group for different ages up to 21. The over 16s go to the Edinburgh Fringe. We put on mini shows. In these we can put forward ideas about which movements to put in the show and which costumes. Choreographers, directors and under-studies from professional shows come to work with us. If you are in the chorus you work independently in groups to plan your actions (Year 7 girl).

Similarly, engaging with different and older young people in a youth choir has developed the civil skills and dispositions of a Year 11 girl:

> I am in a youth choir and this boosts my confidence because I meet new people – some younger, some older in the 13-18 age range. I have learnt a lot about myself through the choir – I feel accepted – I don't have to be perfect and can make mistakes (Year 11 girl).

Older students are able to articulate civil skills developed form part-time work:

> I do a paper round. There are a lot of them to deliver and it is tedious and boring. Most of the time the individual resident will call in to my boss if I fail to deliver. I sometimes can forget but the odd one is OK. They ring up a number of residents to find out if I have delivered. When I do the paper round I do it whatever the weather – it is a commitment (Year 11 pupil).

Finally, it is possible to find within the range of associational activities an example of a formal civil contribution. One student was a member of the town youth council convened by the mayor and he was involved in decision-making about facilities for young people in the town.

Parents' understanding of civil learning outside school

The focus group with parents demonstrated how parents attach a good deal of significance to student civil learning outside school because it is an expression of their high expectations of the person they want their child to become. One parent has a Year 11 daughter working in a tea shop 'where she is obviously communicating with the general public, politely, hopefully'. The mother of a Year 7 pupil describes her daughter as feeling very passionate about environmental and animal welfare issues and these are issues which they discuss together a lot. Another parent is very proud of the way her shy son has gained confidence as a result of being put in charge of the stores on army cadet camps. A Year 9 mother describes the negotiating that went on with her daughter to encourage her not to drop out of her dance group at the same time as her close friend: 'M has decided that this is not a good thing to do because she has spent a lot of time on it and mum has spent a lot of money on it and from that point of view it is not good for her to go into things lightheartedly but she must show her commitment'. Parents put great store by their children behaving appropriately in public and texting parents to say that they are safe.

Parents' understanding of civil learning is closely related to their high expectations for their child and as a result appears to be both a positive and a constraint. This tension becomes clearer when parents are asked about the connections between civil learning and school. Parents understand and value civil learning but there is a strong view that school should moderate and modify learning outside school. This is focused particularly around taking other people's opinions into account: 'maybe they are not always right and that's a thing they should take into account'. Parents want their children to listen more in school rather than be too opinionated:

> Focus group chair: do you think they give their opinions in lessons?

> Year 11 parent: Oh yes.

> Year 9 parent: Too much sometimes.

> Year 10 parent: I think one thing they don't do is listen. I think that listening is a skill that has become…. Because they have become so opinionated. I don't know if society has made them more opinionated?

> Year 7 parent: So maybe we have gone too far so listening is a real issue.

This modification of civil learning would seem to be more of a priority to parents than the integration of the latter with school, and this will become more evident when we look at parental expectations about learning.

Teachers' understanding of civil learning outside school

The teachers began their discussion with setting out what they thought should matter to their students. This included civic matters, dealing with different agencies, the law and road safety. In particular they emphasised the need for their pupils to be equipped to deal with the social and ethnic setting in which they live:

> It's very different living here from living in central Birmingham or wherever, in that the ethnic mix of people, the expectations are very different, so being sensitive, that students need to know that the right thing does vary in terms in terms of dealing with other people in the community (Head of ICT).

When the discussion moved on to what they thought did matter to the pupils outside school, the teachers identified friendship groups which span inside and outside school, with Facebook and mobile phones figuring highly in their responses:

> They need to communicate with each other and show open affection towards each other, even having been parted for an hour by a lesson – they need to regroup and reaffirm the friendship group (Head of Music).

The teachers recognise the importance of the learning that goes on in friendship groups and understand it as fundamental to self-esteem; however, they feel that they have to control its impact in school – 'a time and a place', 'so again, it's about appropriate behaviour in the context they are in' (Head of History).

Students' thoughts about how civil learning can connect with and be used in any aspect of school life

Students make connections in terms of links with teachers who are involved in clubs and organisations they attend, like scouts and drama club. These links actually affect the way pupils learn with these teachers in school which we will discuss later. They gave examples of knowledge and skills acquired in outside activities which they can use in class, such as demonstrating a drama technique or using team captaincy experience in a sports leadership course. Social skills and dispositions learnt at home are considered useful in school, for example in 'discussing ways to let other people have a say' and 'you learn to negotiate with your mum and take this experience across to negotiating with your teacher'. These same skills are referred to by those involved in the student chamber, the enterprise group, the prom committee and charity groups. A Year 9 girl believed that the way she had learnt to treat others as she wanted to be treated had a direct bearing on her learning in RE/Citizenship. A Year 9 boy felt that his part-time job has influenced his ideas about employability and this had found particular expression in his commitment to collaborative work in school. Factors to bear in mind are that students may choose to withhold civil learning in school and, secondly, they in turn may feel that the school is restricting opportunities for this kind of learning. Students, for example, believed that it was less stressful to negotiate differences of opinion in friendship groups without the involvement of teachers. A Year 11 student who had gained a great deal of self-confidence from joining a youth choir did not bring this confidence into school because 'people don't like you to be too confident'. Year 11 students all agreed that 'school life (GCSE work) impacted on life outside school but not vice versa'.

Parents' thoughts about how civil learning can connect with and be used in any aspect of school life

Parents question whether students are entitled to have any influence on the content and process of their formal learning through the integration of civil learning 'because they are here to learn and to listen. It's actually not their fault if the curriculum doesn't warrant them having an opinion and it depends what's in the curriculum and what they are learning' (Year 7 parent). As a result of this perception parents may have low expectations that their child would, for example, say anything in class about an activity which they might be involved in outside school and which really matters to them. Where pedagogy creates opportunities for this to happen, parents are surprised, as was the case with one mother who learnt from another parent in the focus group, who was also a teaching assistant in her son's class, that her son had actually given a talk on the army cadets in English and had inspired some of his friends to think about joining.

Teachers' thoughts about how civil learning can connect with and be used in any aspect of school life

Teachers' responses to any connection between civil learning and aspects of school life were inclined to separate out the two kinds of learning:

> In one of my previous roles I ran Duke of Edinburgh and I noticed the difference...
> I noticed there in that learning was that I actively encouraged students to learn by
> making mistakes whereas actually in my classroom I actively encourage students to
> learn by modelling the positive behaviours or outcomes or completed product which

I wish to see. I think that they do learn by making mistakes in their civil learning, like you fall into the wrong friendship group, something happens and you learn from that experience to tread more carefully (Head of ICT).

In section one it was stated that teachers have a good understanding of the importance of friendship groups for civil learning but this has to be managed in school. Similarly, here pedagogical reasons are given for putting down a marker between experiential and planned learning. Pedagogical issues will be returned to in the next teachers' section. In addition to pedagogy, teachers give management and organisational reasons for not integrating experiential civil learning:

I think this is great but I think quite often in the classroom you can't afford to do that because you haven't got the time and you have the specifications to cover or that kind of thing. I wouldn't have a problem doing it but then the consequences I feel quite uncomfortable about. I feel quite nervous about going there (Head of History).

Students' thoughts about what impact the integration of student civil learning with formal learning would have on how they learn in school

Student responses in the focus groups identify three key factors, the first of which is relationships with teachers. It was noted earlier that students feel it makes a difference if the teacher knows something about your life outside school:

In our Maths lesson the teacher knows one of my friend's mum who is having a baby – this is nice. It makes a difference to how you work if the teacher knows about you. We had a primary teacher who was in an outside school drama club with us and she gave us a Oscar ceremony when we left the school (Year 7 pupil).

Teachers' awareness of student civil learning can determine the opportunities for students to influence their learning. This may be through explicit lesson content so, for example, the Year 10 student who captains a football team is asked to draw on his experience of this in his sports leadership BTEC. A year 7 student recounts how 'a friend of mine had learnt a puppet dance in her out of school drama club and she had quite a lot of influence because she suggested to the teacher that we use it in our drama lesson'. More implicit is the ethos of a lesson created by the teacher:

How I use my outside school experience in school will depend on the group of people I am with and my relationship with my teacher. Whether I can influence the learning and the lesson will depend on the teacher. I can say what I think about how to treat others in RE because this is an open lesson. We are free to express our opinions and most people feel they can do that. My views have developed outside school but I am shy and the teacher encourages you (Year 9 pupil).

The second key factor identified by the students is the way in which the PSHEe and Citizenship curriculum design influences how they learn by determining the extent to which they can integrate their civil learning within the formal curriculum area. The school had moved from weekly tutorials to five conference days throughout the year which provided more flexible contexts in which to explore key themes, largely delivered by visiting experts. The range and expertise brought in for these days is impressive. Students enjoy the more active of these days, such as putting together a school newspaper in Year 7, and they do believe that there is a place for fewer days which are led by teachers and supported by visiting experts. However, there is often a disconnect between the imparting of information and the civil learning of pupils. For example, year 10 students on their employability day were invited to come in dressed as for a job interview: 'work experience was a good theme and you were taken through a job interview but we didn't actually get interviewed. You could use the experience I have got from being a team captain' (Year 10 student). This disconnect is exaggerated for Year 11 students for whom GCSE pressures restrict civil learning anyway. Instead of providing an opportunity for making civil learning valued and explicit, these students describe conference days as 'days when you don't do lessons and they take you away from your GCSE work. Our values and views are not included in the days – we are just receiving information.' (Year 11 student). Lack of progression in some topics means that content does not necessarily match the civil learning experiences of pupils as they mature:

> Some people mess about because they don't want to learn and we already know it. We want to discuss the interesting side in an active way using music and role play so that we can bring in our own experience. We had done the sorts of topics on conference days in primary school. We now want to look at the actual issues (Year 7 pupil).

As well as highlighting the need for progression, students identify the need for personalisation which only teachers, rather than visiting speakers can provide:

> We have never done a role play about conflict but that would be better than copying. Talking about our values depends on who's leading. If they are not teachers then they are not helping you to engage. You need the teachers to actually engage with you: know your personality, know what you have to offer based on outside as well as inside school. Outside speakers know about the topic but it also needs to be motivating (Year 9 pupil).

The third factor identified by students is that of groupings. The integration of civil learning into Citizenship Education would put more of a focus on how students learn in groups. They feel strongly that the size, unity and security of the grouping as well as the range of views expressed all matter. Citizenship in RE is more characterised by these qualities: 'people will be told off if they contradict' and 'you don't need to stick your neck out in RE because there will be a range of views in the class, not all are against you. There are people with similar views and that gives you confidence' (Year 10 student). By contrast, conference days have more of a feeling of coercion: 'you are put in groups for team building but people muck about and working in our form group is difficult because they mix sensible and difficult people together and this is awkward' (Year 11 pupil).

Parents' thoughts about what impact the integration of student civil learning with formal learning would have on how students learn in school

Where parents do see civil learning influencing how their children learn is through effort, commitment and 'whether to go with the crowd' or not. They see their child's self-discipline learnt through family, friendship and associational groups as permeating all lessons. As a result of this there are concerns about getting carried away:

> My daughter's a very keen little girl and has her hand up all the time to the point where she needs to give other people a chance, so she might say something and go off on bit of a tangent, wouldn't surprise me, start off on one thing and go to another (Year 7 parent).

Teachers' thoughts about what impact the integration of student civil learning with formal learning would have on how students learn in school

As discussed in the previous teachers' section, the teachers had separated out the differences between civil and planned formal learning. A key distinguishing feature of civil learning was described as learning by accident. There was a strong view that:

> While we are talking about learning from mistakes or learning through experience, I think we have got to make reference to the fact that if someone is coming to observe what takes place in our classroom, nowhere in the definitions of outstanding learning does learning by accident or default occur (Head of ICT).

In response to this the Head of Music introduced the Musical Futures pedagogy (2010):

> The last three years we have been modelling musical futures, which is informal learning, and you have got to have a lot of bottle as a teacher to stand back. At the heart of it we try to re-create youngsters working together in their dad's garage with their mates, but in this case with musical instruments. Learning does come almost by accident and you are there to resource that. One of the big obstacles to success is social interaction – they have to stay committed to their group (Head of Music).

This analysis of a particular pedagogy actually deepened the focus group discussion and took it beyond some of the constraints in teachers' perception and attitude which we have identified in previous sections. In initially suggesting that civil learning in History randomly influenced lesson content and pedagogical process, the Musical Futures discussion led the Head of History to identify that students are more readily engaged in expressing opinions informed by civil learning when they feel passionate about an issue. The resources have to elicit some anger and outrage, such as with slavery or the Holocaust. This echoes what the students have defined as the nature of teacher engagement with them as people who they understand and know something about. The Head of ICT returns more positively to the pedagogical discussion:

> The Holocaust or slavery are quite remote concepts to them until you find something to which they can relate and then they are prepared to bring in all the other learning they have done in their own time. In IT, for example, we teach copyright, and actually they don't see it at all as a concept that has anything to do with them because we talk in very general terms about the penalties etc, but when we start to look at the plagiarism perspective, from someone nicking a copy of their work from out of a bin, they will then get fired up about it and they will start bringing in their civil learning about how they feel that this is unfair. I have had groups take the copyright law to bits but only when you find the trigger to get them to share the the fruits of their civil experience (Head of ICT).

The conclusion to the teachers' focus group discussion was a strong view that Citizenship Education has become citizenship knowledge with content which quite often obscures the things which really matter to young people in their civil experience. Being a knowledgeable citizen rather than a questioning one has influenced pedagogy across the curriculum but particularly in the format of the conference days, which were designed 'to bring in the experts for topics which we found difficult' (Head of Music). There was an acknowledgement that more 'talk-time' was needed with students and this supports the students' view that the relationship with staff is a key factor in integrating civil and formal learning.

Conclusion – with implications for teacher education

What recommendations can be made to the case study school, in the light of the influences and constraints affecting the integration of civil learning into formal learning that have been analysed and discussed in the focus group findings? In the initial setting up of the case study with the senior leadership team in the school, the terms of reference adopted by this study were readily understood. The immediate concern of the school to improve progression and personalisation in PSHEe and Citizenship learning matched well with a readiness to move into those features of civil learning discussed earlier in this paper. In particular, there was an acknowledgement of the significance and nature of civil learning outside school and the relationship between the myriad of experiences it represents and the personalisation of learning in school. Very much in the transactional mode of learning which Woods (2006) advocates for democratic leadership in school, the discussion went beyond the PSHEe and Citizenship curriculum to pedagogy. This meant that, as a result of framing the initial discussion around a re-definition of learning embodied in civil learning, the senior leadership team concluded that the focus groups would be 'timely' and 'challenging' for the whole school.

In taking forward the terms of reference into the focus groups with students, it is clear from the discussion of findings that teachers need to recognise and give value to the myriad of experiences which constitute civil learning. What emerges is ownership of new knowledge and spaces where it has been learnt. However, teachers cannot assume that students will always use their civil learning in school. The findings identify personal reasons, peer pressure and group/school ethos as key determinants. What needs to be flagged as an important action point for pre-service and in-service teacher education is that students' use of civil learning is significantly determined by how well teachers know students and provide them with learning opportunities which engage them in what matters to them. Critical here are the findings of Hoskin *et al* (2010) which identify less formal, more contextualised and student-led learning as facilitating the integration of civil and formal learning. Here lies the answer to much of the school's concern about progression and personalisation and should be borne in mind in future planning of discrete and cross-curricular PSHEe and Citizenship learning. It is also recommended that maximising student engagement through knowledge of and harnessing of their civil learning is a focus for staff development. These findings confirmed the school's decision to move away from the knowledge-driven and expert-led conference days and to reintegrate PSHEe and Citizenship learning back into discrete and cross-curricular time, including tutor time, with a particular emphasis on teachers' knowledge of students informing a student led pedagogy.

The most significant findings from the case study relate to the mix of positive and constraining factors evident in parent and teacher responses to the concept of civil learning. The researcher's initial meeting with the senior leadership team moved very quickly to pedagogy and it is essentially in that area where the solutions lie. As has already been stated, the teachers' focus group generated transactional learning which went beyond the constraints of discussing an outcomes-driven pedagogy to consider a variety of student-led learning opportunities. Staff discussion groups of this kind are powerful and allow an understanding of the wider factors constraining or influencing professional practice. It is recommended that such groups are used in pre-service and in-service teacher education to contribute to the development of a much more student–led pedagogy which assumes and expects students to be confident and express opinions. It is likely over time that parents will become less concerned about their child's compliance in school, once opportunities to speak out and express opinions, informed not just by knowledge but also by experience, becomes more of a consistent expectation. At the same time it would be valuable for parents and teachers to have joint discussions about how the latter engage individual students and how together they can promote the value of civil learning opportunities. Ultimately this will be part of what Hannon, Patton, and Temperley describe as the creation of 'an interconnected learning ecosystem' (2011, p.2) within which students become 'agents of their own learning, apply their own insights and become co-producers of learning' (p.2).

References

Advisory Group on Citizenship (1998) *Education for Citizenship and the Teaching of Democracy in Schools,* The Crick Report (London QCA).

Annette, J (2009) ' 'Active learning for active citizenship': democratic citizenship and lifelong learning', *Education, Citizenship and Social Justice,* 4 (2) pp.149-160.

Audigier, F (2000) *Education for Democratic Citizenship, Basic Concepts and Core Competencies for Education for Democratic Ditizenship* (Strasbourg, Council of Europe).

Biesta, G (2007) *A school for citizens: civic learning and democratic action in the learning democracy* (University of Stirling).

Biesta, G, Lawy, R & Kelly N (2009) 'Understanding young people's citizenship learning in everyday life: the role of contexts, relationships and dispositions', *Education, Citizenship and Social Justice,* 4(1) pp.5-24.

Bentley, T (2005) *Everyday Democracy* (London, Demos).

Bige Saatcioglu J & Ozanne, j (2008) 'Participatory action research', *Journal of Consumer Research,* 35.(3) 423-439.

Boyte, H (2004) *Everyday Politics, Reconnecting Citizens and Public Life* (University of Philadelphia, Pennsylvania Press).

Cohen L, Manion L & Morrison K (2007) *Research Methods in Education* (Abingdon, Routledge).

Crick, B (2005) *In Defence of Politics* (London, Continuum).

Davies, I (2007) 'What is Citizenship Education?' in Gearon, L (Ed) *A Practical Guide to Teaching Citizenship in the Secondary School* (Abingdon, Routledge), chap. 1, pp.1-8.

Davies, I, Hampdon-Thompson, G, Jeffs, J, Lord, P, Sundaram, V, & Souroufli, M (2013) *Creating Citizenship Communities Project,* University of York, NFER & Esme Fairburn Foundation (York, University of York).

Edwards, M (2009) *Civil Society* (Cambridge, Polity).

Ger, G (1997) 'Human development and humane consumption: well-being beyond the good life', *Journal of Public Policy and Marketing,* 16 (1) pp.110-125.

Ginsbourg, P (2005) *The Politics of Everyday Life* (USA, Yale).

Gramsci, A (1971) *Selections from the Prison Notebooks* (London, Lawrence & Wishart).

Hannon V, Patton, A & Temperley, J (2011) *Developing an Innovation Ecosystem for Education,* White paper, Innovation Unit & GELP (Cisco, San Jose, USA).

Hoskins B, German Janmaat, J Villalba, E (2011) 'Learning citizenship through social participation outside and inside school: an international, multilevel study of young people's learning of citizenship', *British Educational Research Journal,* iFirst Article, pp.1-28

Jerome, L (2011) 'Service learning and active citizenship in England', *Education, Citizenship & Social Justice,* 7(1) pp.59-70.

Leighton, R (2004) 'The nature of citizenship education provision: an initial study', *Curriculum Journal,* 15(2) pp.167-181.

Mead, N (2010) 'Conflicting concepts of participation in secondary school citizenship', *Journal of Pastoral Care in Education,* 28(1).45-57

Murphy, T (2004) 'Deliberative civic education and civil society: a consideration of ideals and actualities in democracy and communication education', *Communication Education,* 53(1) pp.74-91.

Musical Futures, http://www.musicalfutures.org.uk, accessed 1.39am 13.4.11.

Newby, P (2010) *Research Methods for Education* (Harlow, Pearson).

Peterson, A (2011) *Civic Republicanism and Civic Education, the Education of Citizens* (London, Palgrave Macmillan).

Reason, P, & Bradbury, H (2001) 'Introduction: inquiry and participation in search of a world worthy of human aspiration', in Reason, P & Bradbury, H (eds) *Handbook of action research* (Thousand Oaks, CA, Sage) pp.1-14.

Robson, C (2002) *Real World Research* (Oxford, Blackwell).

Stoker, G (2006) *Why Politics Matter? Making Democracy Work* (London, Palgrave).

Woods, P (2006) 'A democracy of all learners: ethical rationality and the affective roots of democratic leadership', *School Leadership and Management,* 26(4), pp..321-337.

Review

Civic Republicanism and Civic Education
Andrew Peterson (2011)
Basingstoke: Palgrave Macmillan 200 pp.,
ISBN 978-0-230-25194-6 hardback, £50

Peterson's aim is to introduce the work and ideas of contemporary civic republicans to civic educators in an accessible way and to point to some of the issues within the field which may impact on citizenship education in schools.

The author begins by contextualising the civic republican revival within the liberal and communitarian debate. Essentially, he argues that civic republicans are united in their call for a reawakening of the civic mind through dedication to the practice of citizenship as a result of a recognition that liberal models of freedom as non-interference are passive and limited. In developing this argument, Peterson's intention is to reveal the complexity of civic republicanism in order to flag its own strengths, challenges and pitfalls when applied to education. An important part of the fulfilment of this intention is his identification early on of two versions of civic republicanism: intrinsic and instrumental. The former, represented by civic republicans such as Sandel and Oldfield, defines freedom as self-government, while the latter, represented by Maynor, Pettit and colleagues, defines freedom as non-domination. These two versions can be complementary and overlap with other political theories and can also cause imbalances if too rigorously applied within education. Recognizing the risk of over-simplification, the author sustains the application of these two versions of civic republicanism throughout the text, citing consistently their attendant theorists, in such a way as to make the educational implication of civic republicanism that much more accessible to the practitioner.

After a review of the origins and evolution of civic republicanism from Aristotle to Madison, Peterson reaches the central section of his text which identifies the key tenets of civic republicanism. These tenets are fundamental to any well-informed consideration of the contribution that civic republicanism might make to citizenship education. Reacting against individualism and atomization of the liberal project, Peterson argues that civic republicanism reminds us that there is an important and necessary public life beyond our private interests and that engagement in that public life carries with it a number of benefits. The prerequisites for engagement in the public life are obligations to and responsibilities for the common good, the possession of civic virtues and skills in deliberation, involving empathy and reflection. Each of these tenets is systematically examined in relation to liberalism and from the intrinsic and instrumental perspective but without the author losing the sense that civic republicanism is an evolving, complex and challenging project. For example, there is considerable difficulty about the use of the term 'virtue' which intrinsic republicans prefer as it suggests the internalization of dispositions, whereas instrumental republicans prefer to use 'principles' instead to describe a cognitive willingness to act and behave in a certain way. It is within this systematic structure that Peterson provides the complex critical insights needed for his final section which applies civic republicanism to education.

Those complex critical insights acquired in the central section of the text prepare us well for the author's statement at the beginning of the final section of his text that no full and complete civic republican theory of civic education exists. The author offers his analysis and suggestions in the spirit of republicanism to be deliberated over. At the same time, he does this, as he has throughout the text, in a systematic way for the sake of accessibility. Peterson takes each tenet and explores its implications for education from the intrinsic and instrumental perspectives. What arise with striking clarity are some of the key issues which citizenship educators have had to wrestle with. For example, since statutory provision has been in place in England, a narrower, instrumental version of obligations and the common good has tended to develop within citizenship education. This in turn has encouraged educators to separate civic activity from civic engagement.

Peterson's final chapter strikes a sophisticated balance between the challenges which civic republicanism presents to liberal influences in current citizenship education and its unresolved weaknesses in its educational application. The challenges are drawn directly form the tenets of the civic republicanism project and its intrinsic and instrumental expressions. Peterson argues that civic republicanism challenges current citizenship education to examine freedom – at present an under-analysed concept. Obligations and the common good challenge liberal influences of individualism and require educators to look at responsibilities which arise independently from rights. Civic virtue challenges educators to examine the moral purpose of citizenship education and deliberation challenges educators to assess the quality of empathetic and reflective dialogue across the life of the whole school.

Key weaknesses in the application of civic republicanism to education are only briefly considered. However, those concerned about the way in which republicanism might be undermined by an uncritical view of the state have some reassurance from the author's recognition that the reconciliation of plural interests within the common good may lead to a neutral public sphere. This, as well as the issues of globalisation and patriotism are highlighted by the author as key issues in citizenship education which, as yet, civic republicanism has not resolved.

Pastoral Care in Education
Vol. 29, No. 1, March 2011, pp. 7–24

Routledge
Taylor & Francis Group

The impact of *Every Child Matters* on trainee secondary teachers' understanding of professional knowledge

Nick Mead*

Oxford Brookes University, UK

(*Received 20 October 2010; final version received 23 November 2010*)

This study is concerned with the way in which the introduction in England of *Every Child Matters* (ECM), a mandatory framework for the well-being of all pupils, has created new intraprofessional and interprofessional expectations about the development of professional knowledge for pre-service secondary school teachers. In the light of current literature, the paper seeks to establish whether ECM for secondary teachers provides a simple reconciliation between subject expertise and the facilitation of human learning or a much more profound challenge to the development of values-based autonomous professional knowledge. The research undertaken using questionnaires and interviews with cohorts of trainee secondary teachers between 2005 and 2008 aims to identify the impact of ECM on the development of their pre-service professional knowledge. The data demonstrate a degree of movement in emphasis from an organic, values-based understanding to a propositional, skills-based understanding of professional knowledge. It is argued that this movement in emphasis is, to some degree, related to the instrumental implementation of a social justice policy that may have contributed to the weakening of the intrinsic relationship between teachers' values, ownership of professional knowledge and pupil well-being. The study concludes that the challenge for teacher educators is to find the critical questions and pedagogies to counter the view that professional knowledge is simply the acquisition of strategies, skills and safeguarding knowledge that ensures accountability and legality in the classroom.

Keywords: *initial teacher education; Every Child Matters; professional knowledge*

Introduction

The introduction in England of *Every Child Matters* (ECM) (DFES, 2004) was a landmark policy shift to address the fragmentation of children's services that seemed

*Oxford Brookes University, Department of Professional & Leadership Education, Westminster Institute of Education, Harcourt Hill, Oxford OX2 9AT, UK. Email: nmead@brookes.ac.uk

ISSN 0264–3944 (print)/ISSN 1468–0122 (online)/11/010007–18
© 2011 NAPCE
DOI: 10.1080/02643944.2010.548396

to undermine the effectiveness of interventions to address truancy, child poverty and health, and under-achievement. As part of the integration of children's services we are now witnessing the establishment of directorates of children's services in local authorities and the setting up of multi-agency children's centres across each authority. Teachers are now part of the Integrated Children's Services and should be introduced, as part of their training, to *The Common Core of Skills and Knowledge for the Children's Workforce* (DFES, 2005). The strong emphasis within the Common Core on effective communication, safeguarding, multi-agency working and sharing information should equip teachers to fulfil their legal obligations within the interprofessional Common Assessment Framework for pupils at risk, which could involve them becoming the Lead Practitioner in a pupil referral. This means that, in order to be prepared for their specific role within the children's workforce, teachers need to have an initial training that introduces them to interprofessional work, as well as developing their pedagogical knowledge, understanding and skills, which enables them to personalise learning. As a result, the five outcomes of ECM (be healthy, be safe, enjoy and achieve, make a positive contribution and achieve economic well-being) and the Common Core of Skills and Knowledge have been embedded in a revised framework of *Professional Standards for Teachers* (Training and Development Agency for Schools [TDA], 2007). This embedding has created some tension for trainee teachers between the mastering of the processes of teaching and learning and the high-profile attention that needs to be given to safeguarding. TDA policy has provided little guidance here except to pose the question 'how can knowledge and skills defined in the Common Core be developed alongside those defined in the new standards' (Rowe, 2006, p. 3). The impact on teacher education has been two-fold: trainee teachers are confronted by the challenges of accountability and legality surrounding safeguarding and well-being, and they are confronted by a plethora of national inclusion strategies (DCSF, 2010). The result is that there is a danger of a transmission pedagogy coming to dominate Professional Studies as the growing amount of required information is imparted to trainees. Evidence for this is found in the 2009/10 trainee evaluations of Professional Studies from the focus university in this study. These indicate that 27% of trainees strongly agree that Professional Studies is well taught and challenging, compared with 73% who think the same about Subject Studies.

Background

Although less directly focused on well-being and more on standards, the US Government's No Child left Behind (NCLB) (US Department of Education, 2002) was intended to provide a mandate for fundamental reforms comparable to the later ECM (DFES, 2004). Significant to both is the link between raising achievement for all and the initial preparation of newly qualified teachers. Smith and Gorard (2007), in their study of the implementation of NCLB in the states of Wisconsin and California, found that a Federal Government strategy for social justice could be at odds with a State's definition of a 'highly qualified' teacher. The authors conclude that The Federal Government's mandatory requirement that states should be NCLB compliant has led to 'a mandate for change which emphasizes teachers' content knowledge over pedagogic skills' (Smith & Gorard, 2007, p. 191):

> The definition of 'highly qualified' is linked only to an individual's knowledge of the subjects that they teach as defined by teachers' content tests that can be overly complicated and confusing. (Smith & Gorard, 2007, p. 202)

Smith and Gorard identify how a national mandatory education reform rooted in the relationship between social justice, pupil achievement and a disputed definition of 'high quality' teachers can lead to a shift in emphasis in teacher professional knowledge. Such a shift may constitute an increased emphasis on the professionalisation of acquired content knowledge and, because of their need to be compliant, teachers' loss of opportunities to build confidence in their analytical and critical pedagogical thinking. Darling-Hammond and Younge (2002, p. 13) have argued that the policy objectives of NCLB essentially mean the 'dismantling of teacher education systems and the re-definition of teacher qualifications to include little preparation for teaching'.

George and Clay (2008) take up the same relationship between social justice, pupil achievement and a disputed definition of 'high quality' teachers that is assumed within the Standards agenda of the TDA in England. The authors acknowledge that the revised framework of *Professional Standards for Teachers* (TDA, 2007) has addressed concerns raised by many educationists about the neglect of issues around social justice. They note that the professional standards for Qualified Teacher Status are now populated with references to inclusion and well-being in relation to learning. For example, Standard Q18 requires trainees to:

> Understand how children and young people develop and that the progress and well-being of learners are affected by a range of developmental, social, religious, ethnic, cultural and linguistic influences. (TDA, 2007, p. 8)

However, George and Clay argue that:

> The continued preoccupation with a narrow set of 'standards' that negatively impacts on both teacher recruitment and representation alongside teacher pedagogy will fail to contribute to the development of an equitable and socially just society. It is vital therefore that we educate future teachers to see the connections between schooling, education and the wider society. (2008, p. 110)

The degree to which such teacher education is achievable is profoundly affected by the centralised structures for teacher education in England. Stephens *et al.*, in their comparative study of teacher education and teacher training in England and Norway, demonstrate how English Initial Teacher Training (ITT) provides training in the practical skills of teaching, whereas Norwegian Initial Teacher Education is concerned with the 'cultivation of public duty, construed as moral and pedagogical stewardship' (2004, p. 110). The authors contrast the 'commonsense' approach of the Standards movement in England with the more moral flavour of the Norwegian approach:

> Intending teachers are expected to base their professional work on core Christian and humanistic values, such as equality, compassion and solidarity. They are also reminded

that teaching is a caring profession, care being understood as creating an enabling environment for all children. (Stephens *et al.*, 2004, p. 113)

The pedagogical implications of such an understanding of the teaching profession contrast significantly with those of NCLB and ECM. For example, the teacher is leader and not manager, which places more emphasis on democratic decision-making rather than control; in turn this enables the teaching process to 'connect with young and adult learners on their own terms' (Kirke, Utdannings- og Forskningsdepartementet, 1999, p. 18). Essentially, this is a child-centred pedagogy that 'both identifies and builds upon the cognitive (and cultural) ecology of the individual child' (Stephen's *et al.*, 2004, p. 125).

It is not surprising that the most striking contrast between English and Norwegian teacher preparation is in the area of duty of care. English ITT presents the teacher as a legal carer, whereas in Norway teaching is considered a caring profession. The English Qualified Teacher Status Standards emphasise that trainees should 'be aware of the professional duties of teachers and the statutory framework within which they work' (TDA, 2007, p. 5) and 'be aware of the current legal requirements, national policies and guidance on the safeguarding and promotion of the well-being of children and young people' (2007, p. 7). By contrast, Stephens *et al.* highlight how, in Norway:

> Caring for pupils is seen more in moral than in legal terms. Teachers must be known by their pupils as people they can turn to for help and support. What this implies, in Nordic terms, is attending to the emotional, as well as the learning aspects of child development. (2004, p. 124)

In the light of their findings, the authors recommend that the English ITT model might attach more importance to the spiritual dimension of teaching, which Mayes (2002, p. 704) has termed the 'spirit in teacher'. Mayes defines this as an 'ultimate concern' (2002, p. 704) for the development of the individual being of the child.

George and Clay argue that centrally prescribed standards in England, which relate to skills of practice and school-based performance, marginalise professional knowledge in the way the monitoring of the quality of training in these Standards is undertaken by Ofsted (The Office for Standards in Education). Wright and Bottery (1997) in their study of mentors' priorities have demonstrated the narrowing down of professional knowledge to 'reflective practice' based on the work of Schön (1983), which may prevent reflection on the 'wider ecological issues' (Wright & Bottery, 1997, p. 250). For example, the authors found that mentors gave little priority to engaging trainees in issues such as the relationship between schools and society, ethical dilemmas posed by legislation and the autonomy of the teaching profession.

International perspectives help us to see how mandatory social justice policies can contribute to a narrowing of teacher professional knowledge. What is required, then, to ensure that greater priority is given to what Mayes (2002) calls 'the spirit in teacher'? In this respect, Kirk and Broadhead have argued very positively that the perceived tensions between secondary subject specialists and the generic learning coordinator role of the teacher in ECM can be reconciled through a 'reaffirmation and reinterpretation of subject teaching' (2007, p. 14). They argue that:

> Under ECM the educational progress of learners will depend on how resourcefully teachers will be able to draw on their subject knowledge base, and how readily they will jettison the monocular professional vision that is associated with the blinkered pursuit of the subject, in favour of an approach that fully exploits all the opportunities for cognitive and affective development, and for the nurturing of skills, insight and judgement that subject teaching at its best involves. (Kirk & Broadhead, 2007, p. 14)

The definition of professional knowledge being developed here is one in which subject knowledge expertise and proficiency in the facilitation of human learning will be 'mutually reinforcing features, rather than being so antithetical that possession of the one rules out possession of the other' (Kirk & Broadhead, 2007, p. 14). What Kirk and Broadhead do not fully address is the complexity of achieving this mutual reinforcement when teachers' personal and professional values inevitably figure so largely in the process.

This study wishes to consider whether Kirk and Broadhead are too simplistic in their evaluation of the impact of ECM, especially in the light of the impact of NCLB on teachers' professional knowledge and Stephens *et al.*'s identification of a less values-based and more instrumental underpinning of well-being characterising English, compared with Norwegian, teacher education. Therefore, the main task of the study is to begin to identify the extent to which the development of autonomous professional knowledge in initial teacher education is compromised by a mandatory framework for social justice. The conviction driving the inquiry is that at the heart of professional knowledge there need to be personal and professional values that have been autonomously shaped to inform subject teaching (see also Mead 2003, 2007). This conviction owes much to the work of Carr (2000, 2007), who in applying the Aristotelian distinction between *phronesis* (practical wisdom) and *techne* (skills) to teachers' professional knowledge has been able to demonstrate, philosophically, the significance of non-instrumental qualities of a teacher's character that have a bearing on dispositions towards social justice. For example, he argues that difficulties in creating a positive and inclusive classroom climate may be a 'defect of *phronesis* rather than *techne*' reflecting the teachers 'lack of authentic engagement with or ownership of what they are teaching' (Carr, 2007, p. 381). By ownership Carr means that the teacher does not model qualities of social justice merely as a strategy to improve classroom climate, but because they believe these qualities 'have value in and of themselves' (2007, p. 382); lack of ownership in this sense denies 'their own reflection on the point and purposes of education' (Carr, 2007, p. 381), which is essential if they are to convey to pupils the educational significance of what they teach.

The relevance and timeliness of this study is clearly evidenced in the recent research survey of the professional development needs of teacher educators in higher education institutions (ESCalate/TDA, 2009). The survey identifies ECM as one of nine key areas where teacher educators would like more guidance, not least in what they describe as 'an unconvincing policy base'. Uncertainty here is mirrored in the Newly Qualified Teacher Survey (TDA, 2009), which identifies ECM as an area of initial training that could be improved. This is also reflected in a sweep of Grade 1 Ofsted reports for 2008, which all acknowledge that ECM is to the fore, but only one report refers to 'the highly impressive understanding that trainees have of the full implications of ECM for all aspects of their work' (Ofsted, 2008).

Methodology

Semi-structured questionnaires were administered to 125 postgraduate secondary trainee teachers in 2005, the year of the introduction of ECM into their programme, and to 85 trainees in 2007. Both cohorts were in the same university in the South East of England. The samples consisted of a 63%/37% female/male composition with 58% over the age of 25 in 2005 and a 60%/40% split with 53% over age 25 in 2007. The questionnaires were administered half-way through a one-year PGCE programme. Both questionnaires consisted of the same three questions:

1. As a trainee subject specialist, what do you understand professional knowledge to be?
2. To what extent is the university primarily responsible for providing and developing your professional knowledge?
3. How do you understand the relationship between professional knowledge and subject knowledge?

A limited number of semi-structured questions were selected in order to generate multi-layered responses in which personal and professional knowledge, understanding and values would emerge. After an initial explanation of the task, respondents had 40 minutes of silent writing in a controlled environment. The three questions were spaced out on two sides of A4 paper and so respondents had the page space to be able to develop thoughtful responses to complex issues.

In addition, four semi-structured interviews with trainees representing the Arts, Sciences and Humanities curriculum areas in the same university were conducted in phase three of the 2006/07 year. The timing of these interviews was intended to provide a bridge between the two sets of questionnaires. The interviews asked the same three questions as the questionnaires and through rich qualitative data highlighted any changes from the 2005 data and informed the analysis of the 2007/08 data. As well as giving deeper insights into trends across cohorts, the interviews were intended to confirm whether or not these trends were consistent within the Arts, Sciences and Humanities.

Two categories were used to sort the definitions of professional knowledge given in question one. An organic category was used to capture the relationship between the trainee's self-development and the well-being of learners; it is characterised by a blend of commonsense, intuitive, tacit and narrative language (Whitehead, 1989; Eraut, 1994; Von Manen, 1995; Page, 2001) A second propositional category was used, characterised by factual language (Shulman, 1986). Responses to question two were sorted in two ways: how trainees saw their responsibility for developing their professional knowledge; and any overall shift in balance between how they saw their responsibility and that of the school and university. Responses to question three were sorted into two categories: evidence of the embedding of the professional knowledge of ECM in subject planning, teaching, resourcing and assessing; and evidence of the degree to which this embedding is strategic rather than values-based.

Summary of findings

There is evidence for ECM principles becoming embedded in trainee planning, teaching, resourcing and assessment, and this could have the potential to contribute to a re-affirmation and reinterpretation of the values base of secondary subject teaching. However, there is evidence to suggest that this embedding may be perceived by trainees as strategic rather than values-based in the training process. This is tentatively demonstrated in the data by a possible declining clear relationship between the development of the values of trainee teachers and the well-being of pupils, which might be overshadowed by the professionalisation of the technical processes of learning. These findings echo Carr's (2007, p. 379) assertion that the teacher's character as well as their skills are fundamental to inclusive education.

Analysis and discussion of the findings

Definitions of professional knowledge

Although 66% of the 2007/08 respondents make explicit reference to ECM in their definitions, compared with 33% in 2005/06, there is a reduction in the number of definitions that might be categorised as 'organic'. What is noticeable is the percentage increase in components within definitions of professional knowledge that stand out strikingly as pure statement of fact or proposition. The definitions tend to fall into two categories that reflect trainees' increased knowledge about ECM (see Table 1).

First, there are those definitions that have a particular focus on teachers' legal duties:

- The knowledge of duties and responsibilities of being a teacher.
- An understanding of legislation, government initiatives and appropriate behaviour.
- Knowledge of the statutory requirements of teachers in relation to ECM, SEN, EAL etc.
- To understand the components of professional conduct, regulations, policy.

Table 1.   Categories of propositional definition 2005–2008

Category	2005/06	2007/08
Teachers' legal duties (%)	2.4	40
Working with parents, carers and other professionals (%)	4.8	24

The second category of definitions has a particular focus on working with other professionals, reflecting trainees' increasing awareness of interprofessional working:

- Ways in which students, parents/carers and colleagues should be handled.
- The knowledge required to allow a teacher to effectively work within a school and communicate with other members of staff within the environment and with associated professionals.
- Knowing about how to deal with sensitive issues regarding the pupils, like physical and sexual abuse. The trainee teacher needs to know about which channels to go through when coming face to face with any of these issues and the involvement of outside agencies.

By contrast, a higher proportion of the 2005/06 definitions of professional knowledge are more organic in terms of the relationship between the personal and professional development of the trainee teacher and the pastoral care of pupils in the context of the ethos and values of the whole school. Table 2 indicates some movement away by 2007/08 from this organic relationship to skills and competencies that are not matched by a particular emphasis on the development of personal values and attributes nor the appropriating of a fluid and ongoing professional knowledge that contributes to the development of self.

What needs to be drawn out from the data in Table 2 is the way in which trainees in 2005/06 refer to the development of their personal attributes and values that are enhanced by their appropriating of a fluid and ongoing professional learning and how this development of self is closely linked to the life, values and ethos of the school and classroom. There is a strong link made between the interplay of developing/discovering personal strengths and attributes and the life of the school:

> Professional knowledge is about growing insights into how our own personal strengths will contribute to the teaching contexts.

> An awareness of the characteristics and qualities necessary for all teachers in their dual role as imparters of understanding and as adults forming and developing children as human beings.

Table 2.   Organic definitions of professional knowledge 2005–2008

Category	2005/06	2007/08
Reference to trainees' personal development (%)	28	5.8
Reference to ongoing and fluid professional learning (%)	18	0
Reference to experience (%)	10	1.1
Reference to ethics (%)	7.4	0
Reference to pastoral care/ethos/values of school and classroom (%)	24	5.8
Reference to research informing practice (%)	2.7	5.8
Reference to knowledge for successful teaching competencies (%)	5.5	43.5
Reference to skills (%)	0.9	23.5
Reference to knowledge relating to the development of the whole child (%)	2.7	7.05
Reference to everything you need to know beyond your subject (%)	0.8	7

The knowledge acquired through understanding of what creates a good learning experience and your part in that experience.

Awareness of factors that contribute to the teaching and learning process. It includes not only an understanding of the necessary subject knowledge but also how best to be able to engage pupils in school and in their personal life. I also include how I need to personally develop as a teacher.

The collective life experiences used together with subject knowledge and an open mind with fair judgement, that enables a teacher to communicate in a logical way with pupils. It allows education to include life skills, moral values and a vast array of topics which pupils may not receive elsewhere.

This development of self in relation to the pastoral life of the school figures less in the 2007/08 data. Only 5.8% refer to professional knowledge as related to personal development, and ongoing professional learning is not referred to at all. The pastoral aspects of the school are only mentioned by 2.3% compared with 24% in 2005/06. Other categories related to self-development and the ethos of the school such as the place of experience and ethical understandings (not legal duties) are either less frequently referred to or not at all in the case of the latter in the 2007/08 data. By contrast we note an increase in professional knowledge defined as a set of skills (from 0.9% to 23.5%) and the significant increase in professional knowledge defined as 'knowledge for *successful* teaching *competencies*' (from 5.5% to 43.5%). These categories may reflect increasing awareness of ECM but it is interesting how the latter is not reflected in a significant increase in professional knowledge defined as knowledge relating to the development of the whole child (from 2.7% to 7.05%). Meanwhile, then, we note a declining relationship between teachers' self-development, fluid professional learning and pastoral values countered by a rising profile of skills and competencies.

There is also evidence from the definitions of professional knowledge in the 2006/07 interviews that the organic relationship between the development of the values of the trainee teacher and the well-being of pupils is gradually being replaced by the professionalisation of the technical processes of learning. The four trainee interviewees who are in the final phase of their training all talk about professional knowledge in terms of skills and priorities, which clearly reflects achieving competence in embedding ECM into subject planning and teaching:

Professional knowledge is complex. It requires skills such as AfL, seeking out information in a focused way, relating different aspects of learning, knowing how to use a behaviour policy, being clear in your mind about setting boundaries. It is also about forming your own opinion. Every school is different and you have to assess situations and make decisions about using a behaviour policy and evaluating a child's behaviour. Professional knowledge is also about framing opinions about priorities in Education. For example, balancing exam techniques with individual needs, and deciding what is important in your subject. (Science trainee)

One cannot help but contrast this with the sense of the expectations of the 2005/06 trainees who believe that their personal development will inform professional knowledge.

The movement detected in the data would suggest that increased trainee knowledge about the nature and structures of ECM is creating a more skills and competency-based professional knowledge relating to the well-being of pupils; however, at the same time, there might be a diminishing sense of trainee ownership of a more fluid professional knowledge rooted in the interrelationship between the ongoing development of self as teacher and the pastoral life of the school. These trends now need to be measured against trainees' perceptions of the role of the university in the development of the professional knowledge.

The role of the university in developing professional knowledge

Responses can be categorised in three ways that suggest 87.7% of 2005/06 trainees compared with 47.4% in 2007/08 consider themselves to be primarily responsible for their professional knowledge (see Table 3).

There are those in 2005/06 who see professional knowledge as 'something inherent in one's life experiences and jobs and, of course education'. As such, its development is a 'lifelong task which will draw in different sources in different ways throughout a teaching career'.

Secondly, there are those who understand the role of the university in professional knowledge development in terms of effective learning; for example, as a 'symbiotic relationship' based on interactions between the trainee, tutor and mentor, which 'inspires' rather than 'forces' professional knowledge and thereby facilitates learning which the trainee then applies and develops:

> The university gives me the direction and initial content of professional knowledge. What follows is in my hands and how I interact with the schools involved in my placements.

Thirdly, there are those whose definition of the role of the university in relation to professional knowledge is directly influenced by their understanding of the latter as fluid and constantly changing, reflecting personal responses to new and evolving national initiatives like ECM. These responses describe the university as providing a yardstick for current good practice, and also as the sounding board for trainees' opinions: 'I would hope that the university will challenge some of my pre-conceptions and ask questions which I have not previously considered'.

The fluidity of professional knowledge in the 2006/07 interviews is less about personal responses to change and more about the skills and strategies needed to manage change. In terms of the values underpinning ECM, the emphasis is on

Table 3.   Trainee perceptions of self-responsibility for professional knowledge

Category	2005/06	2007/08
Professional knowledge as inherent in life experience (%)	24.5	6
Symbiotic relationship between tutor, mentor and trainee (%)	50	39
Professional knowledge as ongoing and fluid but tested in the academy (%)	13.2	2.4

understanding and implementing and less on testing them in relation to self. For example, the Religious Education trainee highlights the need to understand, but not necessarily critique in relation to self, the values underpinning an ever changing national agenda like ECM:

> You are talking about a process which is changing all the time, as a trainee it is very difficult to grasp that, you need to understand what this means and the concepts underlying it, what is this thing which is changing all the time, why is it changing all the time. So rather than just getting caught up in the moving process, because that is something that you will develop as a teacher, I think you need to know what are the values which are contained within this (Religious Education trainee).

The emphasis here is on what do I need to understand in order to implement. Likewise, the Science trainee sees responsibility as self-evaluation of what I have *done* and what more do I need to *do*:

> you have introduced us to ECM and positive practices have been modelled, but you are talking about postgraduates here who should be able to go out and find their own information. It's on their own backs what they get out of this and the library is just round the corner. This is about how to become self-critical—the university gives you markers for self-evaluation. I've seen positive practice and know what I am aiming at—know how to change it. I have had the opportunity to think like this in Professional Studies. I find talking to other subjects useful in developing the language of ECM in my own subject. Discussion in other subjects helps you to realize what you have done and what more you need to do. (Science trainee)

These trainees view the role of the university as making research 'relevant and understandable' in order that it will 'show me the basic values which underpin ECM so that I can bring about change'.

There is an emerging contrast here between the generic, transferable skills model that enables you to manage constant policy change and the more holistic approach evident in the 2005 responses, which is about bringing life experience and existing values to a symbiotic relationship with teacher educators. Ownership of professional knowledge development seems to be shifting from a focus on 'who am I and what do I bring?' to 'what do I need to do?' The implication of this shift is significant for the personal development of trainee teachers, for knowing that I need to understand the values underpinning ECM is not the same as critiquing or choosing whether or not to own those values.

The full impact of ECM on ownership of professional knowledge becomes apparent from the questionnaire data, which suggest that 52.6% of trainees in 2007 compared with 12.4% in 2005/06 emphasise that, although the school and the trainee play their part, the university is *primarily* responsible for providing professional knowledge (see Table 4).

The data suggest first that there is movement towards emphasising an almost quasi-legal obligation on the part of the university to ensure that trainees have the required professional knowledge to undertake their work:

> The university is responsible for teaching us the statutory requirements of a professional teacher, in order for us to function within the safeguards of the Law.

Table 4.   Trainees' categories of university responsibility for professional knowledge, 2007/08

Category	2005/06	2007/08
University primarily responsible for required professional knowledge (%)	10	31
University entirely responsible for ensuring schools provide correct training (%)	0.8	4
University solely responsible for providing propositional knowledge (%)	1.6	17.6

Secondly, although slight at this stage, there is movement towards emphasising an almost quasi-legal obligation on the part of the university to ensure that schools are providing the 'correct training':

> The university definitely has a responsibility for professional knowledge and the university also needs to correspond with the schools to ensure that they are providing the correct training on placements.

To refer to teacher education in school as 'correct training' is out of keeping with its developmental nature and hints at the surveillance mentality that has emerged around ECM and safeguarding in particular.

Thirdly, the movement towards viewing the university as having sole responsibility for propositional knowledge could potentially lead to large parts of professional knowledge being viewed as a completely new layer of knowledge, unrelated to the trainees' previous experience or existing values:

> The university has a responsibility to a large extent, much more than subject studies. My professional knowledge has started from near scratch this year. My subject knowledge is largely already known. That's what the course is for.

These responses hint of an insecurity arising from an inherent contradiction between the trainees' instrumental, skills-based approach to getting to grips with the fluidity and flux of new policies like ECM and their pressure on the university to guarantee the professional knowledge that they believe this particular policy requires. Such a contradiction raises questions about whether or not we are giving trainees the opportunities for a personal testing of values underpinning what they recognise will be an ever-changing ECM agenda, and whether or not we are giving them the language to do this through intersubject and interprofessional dialogue, as well as through critical analysis of values-based research in the field.

Trainees' understanding of the relationship between subject knowledge and professional knowledge

Fifty-four per cent of the 2005/06 cohort see a non-strategic relationship between subject and professional knowledge under the headings shown in Table 5.

Of the remaining 46% of the cohort, 44% tend to see the relationship between professional and subject knowledge in terms of methodologies, a less instrumental terminology than strategies. The use of the term skills tends to be confined to classroom management. 31.5% (13% of the cohort) allude to other factors that will

Table 5. Non-strategic relationship between subject and professional knowledge, 2005/06

Relationship between subject knowledge and professional knowledge	Percentage of the 54%
Professional knowledge provides ethics, commitment, honesty, integrity, role model, attributes underpinning subject knowledge	63
Professional knowledge provides research and developing ideas about national and international issues in education underpinning subject teaching	28
Professional knowledge is about developing self as a professional subject specialist	9

become increasingly strategic (see Table 6). Interestingly, legal duties are only mentioned once within the 'other factors' category.

The relationship between subject and professional knowledge as understood by the 2005/06 cohort is quite well summed up by one respondent: 'professional knowledge is knowledge of teaching methods combined with a holistic approach to teaching which we apply to our subject knowledge. It encompasses values and cultural issues appropriate to the school'. The 2005/06 trainees wish to emphasise the relationship between their own values, ideas and self-development and the role of subject teacher:

> The relationship between professional and subject knowledge is that professional knowledge offers the ethics relating to the classroom.

> Professional knowledge is about the commitment of the subject teacher to the school and pupils.

In analysing extracts from the 2006/07 interviews it is possible to detect implicit ethical issues, such as the purpose of education and the relationship between subject values and inclusion; however, these are not explicitly informing subject knowledge teaching because they are obscured by technical and strategic actions to meet needs and therefore go unquestioned. The first example is an extract from the interview with the Science trainee:

> Interviewer: In terms of successful Science teaching do you need professional knowledge?
>
> Trainee: Without a doubt. You have to form opinions about the strengths and needs of your own pupils. This is something you have to do in order to get to know them.

Table 6. Relationship between subject and professional knowledge as methodology, 2005/06

Relationship between subject knowledge and professional knowledge	Percentage of the 46%
Professional knowledge provides teaching methods which underpin subject teaching	44
Professional knowledge provides classroom management skills underpinning subject teaching	24.5
Professional knowledge provides other factors; for example, inclusion, differentiation underpinning subject teaching	31.5

Interviewer: In relation to that do you see ECM, which is becoming the umbrella for
                professional knowledge as directly related to Science teaching?
Trainee: Yes, this is the whole reason for education. You cannot just teach one kid
                and not 29 others. You are teaching all 30 – most important point of teach-
                ing. If they need help, they need help and that is why you are in the job. It
                involves subject knowledge and ECM, whether you draw boundaries
                between them or not.

Further discussion followed about the tension between higher-order thinking, particularly in Physics and Chemistry, and the challenge of making concepts accessible to
all pupils. The trainee acknowledged the difficulties of retaining the integrity of a
traditional subject and that this was a challenge to the Science teaching profession.
However, he spoke confidently and with enthusiasm about differentiation, knowing
how pupils' learn, the roles of teaching assistants and laboratory technicians, and how
information and communications technology (ICT) is helping, for example with
imagining the concept of light years: 'it needs to be modelled and this is not compro-
mising the integrity of the subject'.

The relationship between professional and subject knowledge is exemplified
through need: the need to form opinions about pupils in order to get to know them,
the need to make the learning accessible to all through deploying teaching assistants,
laboratory technicians and the use of ICT. All of these things are important to ensure
pupils enjoy and achieve and make a positive contribution, but a fundamental part of
the process ought to be to engage this trainee in an examination of the values that
underpin his statement about 'the whole reason for education' and the ethical challenges that inclusion poses to the integrity of his subject.

The second example is an extract from the interview with the Art trainee:

you cannot meet every child's needs if your subject knowledge is poor because you are not
giving them the opportunity. My background is in ceramics, jewellery and textiles and
metal—I knew less about fine art, sculpture and painting, installation, digital media—and
I would not be able to provide opportunities to all pupils with those gaps in my subject
knowledge. So the Art course covers those gaps—I cannot provide different mediums for
different pupils' needs without these gaps filled. The overarching need is to help all pupils
achieve in the context of Art. In my own experience some pupils are very good at drawing
but then get to 3D and do not cope, and the converse is true, so there is the need to give
all pupils the opportunity to shine which is a key part of ECM. As they progress up the
school they know their strengths and can build on them and you know where their weaknesses are and where you need to lift them up. The fact that you are assessing your pupils
means you are thinking about what their needs are, that is ECM, but their needs are within
your subject.

Again the relationship between subject and professional knowledge is characterised
by need. Professional knowledge includes strategies to acquire gaps in subject
knowledge but this overlooks the trainees' value-laden statement that implies
inclusion is affected by teachers' subject knowledge. Her preoccupation with
providing different mediums for different pupils contains implicit ethical questions
about how the principles of her subject lend themselves to inclusive practices that
need explicit consideration. Her references to progression and assessment in Art

seem to point to a much more holistic understanding of how the subject can build self-esteem, but again this is hinted at in the language of needs and requires much more critical analysis.

The degree of movement between the 2005/06 and 2007/08 trainees' understanding of the relationship between subject and professional knowledge is evident in Table 7.

The percentage of those in 2005/06 who consider that professional knowledge provides an ethical underpinning of subject knowledge is virtually replaced in 2007/08 by those who consider it to provide a strategic underpinning. This movement is reflected in 2007/08 responses, such as:

> Professional knowledge allows you to deliver subject knowledge in a manner that is identifiable and accountable to professional bodies.

> Our professional knowledge helps us to deliver our subject knowledge. It allows us to get a job, stay within the legal requirements of the job and control classes so we can teach using our subject specific knowledge.

Over 50% of these responses reduce the relationship between professional knowledge and subject knowledge to 'how we teach and what we teach', thereby diminishing what should be values-laden to something like a means to an end:

> Professional knowledge is the method of delivery of subject knowledge.

> Subject knowledge is the content and professional knowledge is how to teach the content.

To conclude, this analysis of trainees' understanding of the relationship between professional and subject knowledge confirms to some degree a growing relationship between subject specialism and pupil well-being; however, the processes of learning are becoming increasingly instrumental and the relationship between professional and subject knowledge is perceived by a significant proportion of trainees as strategic rather than ethical or values based. It is clear that trainee teachers need to discuss the values base for their actions in their subject teaching if they are not simply to be driven by professional knowledge which merely serves to guarantee accountability and legality in subject teaching.

Table 7.   Relationship between professional and subject knowledge 2005/06 and 2007/08 comparison

Relationship between professional knowledge and subject knowledge	2005/06	2007/08
Professional knowledge provides ethics, commitment, honesty, integrity, role-model, researching ideas about education and self-development underpinning subject teaching (%)	54	3
Professional knowledge provides teaching methods, pedagogy and classroom management skills underpinning subject teaching (%)	46	45
Professional knowledge provides strategies—ECM, National Strategies, Assessment for Learning, English as an Additional Language — underpinning subject teaching (%)		52

Conclusion

There is evidence of ECM beginning to inform trainees' planning, resourcing, teaching and assessing. However, this does not entirely support Kirk and Broadhead's view that the perceived tensions between secondary subject specialists and the generic learning coordinator role of the teacher in ECM can be reconciled through a mere 'jettisoning of the monocular professional vision that is associated with the blinkered pursuit of the subject' (2007, p. 14). There are other less positive features emerging in the data, which might characterise an instrumentalist approach to social justice that impacts on categories of value and which go deeper than simply 'reconciling subject knowledge expertise and proficiency in the facilitation of human learning' (Kirk & Broadhead, 2007, p. 14). Most notable is the paradoxical way in which the instrumentalist implementation of what undoubtedly is a value-laden social justice policy can potentially weaken the intrinsic relationship between teachers' values, ownership of professional knowledge and pupil well-being, replacing it with the professionalisation of the technical processes of learning that are driven by accountability and legality.

The significance of this for teacher educators is considerable. Not least, how are they to give trainee teachers the opportunities to critically evaluate ECM in relation to their knowledge, experience and values? We have already stated that understanding the values underpinning ECM is not the same as critiquing or choosing to own those values. An example of universities beginning to address this issue can be found in the Scottish Teachers Education Committee's (2009) National Framework for Inclusion. This framework 'places a clear emphasis on the essential role played by the beliefs and values of each teacher in their commitment to the development of inclusive practice' (Scottish Teachers Education Committee, 2009, p. 3). It is question-based to encourage teachers to accept a shared responsibility for researching answers; the questions posed are both values-based and critical—for example, 'what does it mean to be human?' and 'what are the limitations of legislation?' It is only by exploring such questions through critical pedagogies in teacher education that the view will be countered that professional knowledge is simply the acquisition of strategies, skills and safeguarding knowledge that ensures accountability and legality in the classroom.

Finally, clarity of purpose of inter-professional education is also essential if it is going to contribute to this process. However, Taylor *et al.* (2008) have identified three key concerns relating to interprofessional education and learning for integrated children's services. First, that they are not conceptualised, resulting in an 'at best muddled and at worst over-rhetorical discussion' (Taylor *et al.*, 2008, p. 20). Secondly, learning and teaching about Integrated Children's Services is not informed by higher education research; and thirdly, the absence of research means a 'dearth of robust evidence about outcomes of teaching and learning for students' (Taylor *et al.*, 2008, p. 20). Anderson and Taylor (2008) in their ESCalate seminar suggested that university piloted interprofessional training opportunities highlight some tensions between uniprofessional ECM activities and the expectations of the Common Core. In spite of these weaknesses, Simco (2007) has argued for what we would support in teacher education, which is an ECM-driven reappraisal of the values base of professional practice in which trainee teachers' personal and professional values can be further tested and developed through their engagement in interprofessional dialogue.

References

Anderson, J. & Taylor, I. (2008) Building capacity for the children's workforce: findings from the knowledge review of the higher education response, paper presented at the *ESCalate Seminar*, UCET Annual Conference, Birmingham.

Carr, D. (2000) *Professionalism and ethics in teaching* (London, Routledge).

Carr, D. (2007) Character in teaching, *British Journal of Educational Studies*, 55(4), 369–389.

Darling-Hammond, L. & Younge, P. (2002) Defining 'highly qualified' teachers: what does 'scientifically-based research' actually tell us?, *Educational Research*, 31(9), 13–25.

DCSF (2010) *National secondary strategy*. Available online at: www.nationalstrategies.standards. dcsf.gov.uk/inclusion (accessed 18 July 2010).

DFES (2004) *Every Child Matters: change for children in schools* (London, DFES).

DFES (2005) *Common core of skills and knowledge for the children's workforce* (London, DCSF).

Eraut, M. (1994) *Developing professional knowledge and competence* (London, Falmer).

ESCalate/TDA (2009) *The professional development needs of teacher educators in higher education institutions (HEIs) and school-based mentors in schools* (London, University of Cumbria, ESCalate/TDA).

George, R. & Clay, J. (2008) Reforming teachers and uncompromising 'standards': implications for social justice in schools, *Forum (for Promoting 3–19 Comprehensive Education)*, 50(1), 103–111.

Kirk, G. & Broadhead, P. (2007) *Every Child Matters and teacher education: a UCET position paper* (London, UCET).

Kirke, Utdannings- og Forskningsdepartementet [Norwegian Ministry of Education] (1999) *Praktisk-pedagogisk utdanning* [Practical teacher education] (Oslo, Norgesnet-tradet).

Mayes, C. (2002) The teachers as an archetype of spirit, *Journal of Curriculum Studies*, 34(6), 699–718.

Mead, N. (2003) Will the introduction of professional values put the heart back into primary teacher education?, *Journal of Pastoral Care in Education*, 21(1), 37–42.

Mead, N. (2007) How effectively does the graduate teacher programme contribute to the development of trainee teachers' professional values?, *Journal of Education for Teaching*, 33(3), 309–322.

OFSTED (2008) *Grade one higher education provider inspection reports 2007–8*. Available online at: www.ofsted.gov.uk (accessed October 2008).

Page, R. (2001) Common sense: a form of teacher knowledge, *Journal of Curriculum Studies*, 33(5), 525–533.

Rowe, L. (2006) Every Child Matters: the role of the teacher in the changing context, TDA discussion paper presented at the *TDA/UCET Conference*, London, 4 July.

Schön, D. (1983) *The reflective practitioner* (New York, Basic Books).

Scottish Teacher Education Committee (2009) *National framework for inclusion* (Aberdeen, STEC Scotland).

Shulman, L. (1986) Those who understand: knowledge growth in teaching, *Educational Researcher*, 15(2), 4–14.

Simco, N. (2007) Collaboration in initial teacher training and education: a realisable vision for the future or a vision realised, Keynote Address 2/1 presented to the *Collaborative Approaches to Preparing and Developing Effective Teachers Joint UCET/HMI/STEC Symposium*, Glasgow, March.

Smith, E. & Gorard, S. (2007) Improving teacher quality: lessons from America's *No Child Left Behind*, *Cambridge Journal of Education*, 37(2), 191–206.

Stephens, P., Finn, E. & Kyriacou, C. (2004) Teacher training and teacher education in England and Norway: a comparative study of policy goals, *Comparative Education,* 40(1), 109–130.

Taylor, I., Whiting, R. & Sharland, E. (2008) *Integrated children's services in higher education project, knowledge review* (Southampton, The Higher Education Academy For Social Policy and Social Work, University of Southampton).

Training and Development Agency for Schools (2007) *Professional standards for teachers* (London, TDA).

Training and Development Agency for Schools (2009) *Newly qualified teacher survey* (London, TDA).

US Department of Education (2002) *No Child Left Behind, executive summary.* Available online at: www.ed.gov/nclb/overview/intro/presidentplan/page _pg3.html (accessed October 2008).

Von Manen M. (1995) On the epistemology of reflective practice, *Teachers and Teaching: Theory and Practice,* 1(1), 33–50.

Whitehead, J. (1989) Creating a living educational theory from questions of the kind, 'how do I improve my practice?', *Cambridge Journal of Education,* 19(1), 41–52.

Wright, N. & Bottery M. (1997) Perceptions of professionalism by the mentors of student teachers, *Journal of Education for Teaching,* 23(3), 235–252.